# Not Less
### than
# Everything

OMF International works in most East Asian countries, and among East Asian peoples around the world. It was founded by James Hudson Taylor in 1865 as the China Inland Mission. Our purpose is to glorify God through the urgent evangelisation of East Asia's billions.

In line with this, OMF Publishing seeks to motivate and equip Christians to make disciples of all peoples. Publications include:

- stories and biographies showing God at work in East Asia
- the biblical basis of mission and mission issues
- the growth and development of the church in Asia
- studies of Asian culture and religion

Books, booklets, articles and free downloads can be found on our website at *www.omf.org*

Addresses for OMF English-speaking centres can be found at the back of this book.

# Not Less than Everything

## Valerie Griffiths

MONARCH
BOOKS

Oxford, UK and Grand Rapids, Michigan

Overseas Missionary Fellowship

First published in the UK in 2004 by Monarch Books
(a publishing imprint of Lion Hudson plc),
Mayfield House, 256 Banbury Road, Oxford OX2 7DH
Tel: +44 (0) 1865 302750  Fax: +44 (0) 1865 302757
Email: monarch@lionhudson.com
www.lionhudson.com

UK ISBN: 1 85424 613 5
US ISBN: 0 8254 6056 5

Distributed by:
UK: Marston Book Services Ltd, PO Box 269,
Abingdon, Oxon OX14 4YN;
USA: Kregel Publications, PO Box 2607,
Grand Rapids, Michigan 49501.

**British Library Cataloguing Data**
A catalogue record for this book is available
from the British Library.

Book design and production for the publishers by
Gazelle Creative Productions Ltd,
Concorde House, Grenville Place, Mill Hill, London NW7 3SA.
Printed in Great Britain.

# Contents

# Acknowledgements

I owe a great debt to OMF directors who have given me generous access to materials, and members who have shared their lives with me and urged me on. I am grateful too to many friends who have waited patiently for the results. Julia Cameron, Sara Foster and Jan Greenough have contributed their editorial expertise and Tony Collins has been a most patient publisher.

A.J. Broomhall's seven volumes on *Hudson Taylor and China's Open Century* have been an indispensable treasure trove and we look forward to their reappearance in two volumes shortly. I wish we could have cross referenced this book with those.

Finally I am indebted to my family, and especially my husband, for the index, technical help, patience and support over quite a few years. I am deeply grateful to you all.

Valerie Griffiths

# Abbreviations

| CES | Chinese Evangelisation Society (1850–1860) |
| --- | --- |
| CIM | China Inland Mission (1866–1952) |
| CMS | Church Missionary Society (1799–present) |
| FMI | Female Missionary Intelligencer (1856–1899) |
| LMS | London Missionary Society (1795–1799) |
| SPFEE | Society for Promoting Female Education in the East (1834–1899) |

# Foreword

We have always known that women played a crucial part in the spread of the gospel through overseas mission. But this is one of the first books which shows us just how crucial that part was. There were so very many women whom God called into mission in China, from Maria Tarn Dyer and Maria Newell who set sail in the 1820s, to Phyllis Thompson who died in 2000, leaving behind a legacy in writing and in changed lives. And until the doors were shut to Western mission, women served in places that no Europeans had ever visited, making journeys so hazardous that these alone must have taxed their strength. Many faced extremes of heat, regularly crossing the Gobi desert and Tibetan foothills; others faced political tension, violence and civil war. Many of them faced loneliness and some had to make agonising decisions and choices that were sacrificial. And all of them were called to serve Christ in conditions and often acute hardships which few at home could ever begin to imagine.

Valerie Griffiths shows us that the women who served God in China during the period covered by this book fitted no stereotype. Both single and married, they came from different backgrounds with different gifts and abilities and a wide range of personalities. She tells their stories in wonderful detail. We read of the struggles of Maria Taylor whose commitment kept her going alongside her husband, Hudson Taylor, through miscarriage, the loss of children, and her own illness and frailty. We travel with three amazing single women, Mildred Cable, and sisters Eva and Francesca French, who shared a ministry for over 35 years before their deaths in the 1950s and 1960s. Their work and influence was breathtaking, spreading across the four northern provinces of China and beyond, training other women and spreading the gospel. In every chapter there are stories which are almost on the edge of credulity, painstakingly retold from records faithfully kept by the societies or the missionaries themselves.

Valerie Griffiths is a careful and accurate scholar. Yet the scope of this book has still taken me by surprise. Her patience in research and her attention to detail have produced a volume which serves us in so many different ways. It is an account of mission in China; it is a historical textbook; it is a case study of particular forms of ministry; it is a snapshot of early Christian education in China; it is an extended and illustrated argument for Christian women's leadership; it is a series of mini-biographies of amazing women spanning more than a century. Above all, it is a gripping, eloquent narrative, and a wonderful read.

It is important that the story of women's contribution to mission in China should be told in this way. In a climate where people find the very concept of "missionary" politically incorrect, we can very easily lose our history unless it is told accurately and with sympathetic insight. We can also forget what faithful obedience to Christ has cost so many of his disciples, and can shrug off their commitment and sacrifice. This book does not let us do that. Valerie Griffiths' work is one of faithfulness and compassion. More than most of us, she understands what overseas mission has been, and is, about, and can write with authenticity and love.

In drawing us into the lives of those who served God in China, Valerie tells a powerful story and offers a powerful challenge. And she does so in a way which is timely and thorough. We meet, in the pages of this book, ordinary women of extraordinary guts, faith and tenacity. And when we look at the Chinese church today, we can give thanks that there were those who gave "not less than everything" for the sake of the gospel.

Dr Elaine Storkey
Senior Research Fellow
Wycliffe Hall
Oxford
March 2004

# Preface

Two hundred years ago the women of China spent most of their lives in their homes. For over a thousand years the custom of foot-binding (to produce "lily" feet three or four inches long) had crippled millions of women, and made walking painful, if not impossible. The first missionaries to China soon realised that unless Christian women could visit them in their homes – a massive task – they would never hear the message of God's love.

In this book I have tried to trace some of the early women missionaries, married and single, who shouldered this task. The few here represent thousands more: the women of the China Inland Mission pioneered the Chinese interior alongside the men. By 1900 there were two missionary women in China for every man, and their work among Chinese women was crucial for the growth of the church.

In the process, these Western women were liberated from Victorian customs and expectations; they found themselves gifted for work in teaching and evangelism which would have been impossible in their churches at home. At the same time, the Christian message liberated their Chinese sisters too. For the first time in their lives the Chinese saw women living far away from their families, educated, unmarried, able to travel, and capable of more than they had ever dreamed. They were soon working together. The uneducated Bible women taught the missionaries how to communicate with the Chinese women, and the missionaries enabled the local women to take the message of God's love to their neighbours. Sadly, that lack of education has meant that the stories of the early Bible women can be accessed only through the missionaries; unable to write, they left no direct records of those early years.

I hope these stories give a glimpse of the extraordinary ministry of these women, who responded to God's call and found themselves freed to use their God-given gifts.

Valerie Griffiths
January 2004

*Chapter One*     # East of India

In the early nineteenth century there were no missions to China. That ancient and secretive country was closed to Westerners, and permanent residence there was impossible. The Far East was such an unknown quantity that the term "India" was often used for the entire area. A few men were permitted to live and work in Guangzhou (Canton) over the winter months in the foreign "factory" (business) area, but their wives and families had to remain 80 miles downriver in the port of Macao, a small Portuguese settlement in the south-east of the country. Members of the London Missionary Society, whose vision was to take the gospel to the Chinese people, found that the best they could do was to settle in Penang, Malacca, Singapore and Djakarta, Indonesia (Batavia) in the Malay Straits, hundreds of miles to the south: there at least there were immigrant Chinese populations.

The Chinese men who lived and worked in the towns of the Malay Straits were far from home – in Singapore there were four men for every woman in the port – and many of them took Malay wives. Malay was far easier to learn than Chinese, and consequently it usually became the language of the home for the next generation. The culture the missionaries encountered there was a mixture: while some Chinese daughters were welcomed at birth, loved and nurtured, others were seen as a financial burden because they had to be clothed and fed until they married. Education was considered a waste of money for girls, and most people assumed they were incapable of learning anyway, so both Chinese and

Malay women remained untaught and illiterate. The girls may not have had their feet bound, but their active life effectively came to an end when they were eleven: then they were confined to their homes until they married at fifteen to 18 years of age, after which they rarely left the house except on special occasions.

These girls and women could be reached only by other women, visiting them at home. Officially the LMS men were the "missionaries", and the wives' role was to support their husbands and mother their children. Indeed, family life, together with frequent childbearing and recurring illnesses, took up a great deal of the women's time and strength. Nevertheless the LMS wives in the Malay towns organised small schools for girls under twelve years of age, who were still allowed out of the house.[1] They learned reading, writing, basic arithmetic and domestic skills and, above all, they heard the message of the Bible. (There was a similar concern in British churches in this period that all children should be able to read the Bible, and in British cities Sunday schools were being set up to ensure children's literacy.) Contact with the children also enabled the missionary wives to make contact with the mothers. They sometimes had to pay the parents to allow their daughters to come to school, to compensate them for the little the girls might have contributed financially, and this attracted the poorer families. In return they asked for a legal undertaking that the girls would be left in the schools for a certain period. Because schools were few and widely scattered, and mothers were unable to walk their children to school, boarding houses were often necessary. Most of the schools began small with only a handful of pupils, though unwanted and abandoned children added to their numbers.

In 1824 Robert Morrison of the LMS was on leave in Britain, and he appealed for more men and women to go to the East. He suggested the founding of a society to help single women to go out and start schools, but at that time there was only a glimmer of response. He believed that all Christians, of whatever sex or occupation, "should subordinate all their

personal and domestic concerns to the cause of our Lord
Jesus Christ". To that end he had started classes in Chinese
for young men at a theological college in London, and even
had a class in his sitting room in Hackney three times a week
to teach Chinese to some young women. It was an act of considerable faith which was to have far-reaching consequences.
Three of those women would travel "east of India", while
China was still closed.

## Penang – Maria Tarn Dyer

Maria Tarn, whose father was a director of the London
Missionary Society (LMS), was one of that small group of
ladies who embarked on Chinese study in Morrison's home.
She married Samuel Dyer (another of Morrison's students)
and, with the LMS, they sailed for Penang in 1827, expecting
never to return to Britain again. (In fact Maria's health forced
them home once, from 1839 to 1841.) Morrison's Chinese
lessons had been effective: within a few weeks of their arrival
in Penang, Samuel was preaching in Chinese and they both
found they could make themselves understood.

Contrary to colonial custom, they settled in the Chinese
section of the town. Samuel gave himself to evangelism and
teaching, and also began working on a method for printing
the Chinese Bible more easily and cheaply. The first edition of
Robert Morrison's translation had been published in Malacca
in 1821, but it was bulky and expensive, as the individual
Chinese characters were carved from wood and used only
once. Dyer spent the next fourteen years perfecting metal
casts, a quarter the size of the wooden ones, which would be
moveable and reusable. Meanwhile Maria set up several
small, separate schools for boys and girls, first in Penang and
later in Malacca.

## The Malacca schools – Maria Newell, Mary Wallace and Mary Wanstall

Maria Newell, who almost certainly studied Chinese in Morrison's class, set sail with the newly married Dyers in 1827. Her acceptance as a missionary by the LMS was unusual, but her independent means may have made the decision easier – it often did where women were concerned! The plan was that she and a co-worker should set up girls' schools in Malacca, but her colleague became ill and unable to travel. (The stress of studying Chinese was blamed for her illness, and taken as another proof that girls should not study.) Maria Newell arrived in Malacca alone – the first Western single woman to go east of India as a missionary.[2]

It must have taken tremendous courage: there was only one other LMS couple there when she arrived, teaching at what had become the prestigious Anglo-Chinese College for boys.[3] Maria wrote for advice to Mary Cooke in Calcutta (one of the first single women to teach in India), and also corresponded with Morrison in Macao about his educational vision for the area. In Malacca there were several groups – Portuguese and other expatriate Europeans, as well as Malays and Chinese – who were interested in the provision of girls' education. During her two years in Malacca, Maria opened five schools, employing local men as teachers and using the Malay language which was spoken by both Malays and Chinese. She had plenty of scope for her activities, and within a year was writing to the LMS asking for more help. Friends raised the necessary funds, and Mary Wallace went out to join her in 1828.

In 1829 Maria Newell married the remarkable Karl Gutzlaff, a zealous trader who had made several journeys up the China coast, calling at ports where he slipped ashore and distributed Christian tracts and literature. At a time when foreigners were confined to Macao and Canton, he had a wide ministry in what were, in effect, forbidden places. After their marriage Karl and Maria moved to Bangkok, intending to reach the Chinese community there, and embarked on translating the Bible into Thai. However, the climate in Thailand made health far more precarious than in the Malay Straits, and Maria and her newly born twin babies died two years later in 1831.[4] The LMS did not accept another single woman as a missionary until 1863.

Fortunately Mary Wallace was already settled and able to take over when Maria Newell married, and by 1831 Malacca, with its population of 25,000, seems to have been a hive of activity. An LMS man was available to start day schools for boys in addition to the Anglo-Chinese College, and as a result there were 25 schools in the town for both boys and girls, with a total of 620 children. Mary Wallace was highly commended by her male colleagues for her diligence and perseverance, as well as for having "a fine school for girls", and when Samuel Dyer visited, he commented that "sister Wallace is a true missionary: she is a remarkably timid, modest, retiring character among English people, but bold, undaunted and active among the natives. We enjoyed her society very much when in Malacca."[5]

Mary's funding came mostly from friends, but this meagre income was erratic and inadequate. She could not afford the transport she needed (a horse and curtained palanquin) in order to visit her schools around the town, even though the college gave her a monthly gift and the Dyers also helped her personally. Her male colleagues commended her to the LMS, but although the society may have made her a grant, it never supported her financially as it had Maria Newell. The work kept her very busy, and the local teachers in the schools needed constant supervision. In two schools the teaching was so poor that she had to close them down, but she still had 70 girls under instruction. After Maria Newell Gutzlaff had left in 1829, Mary supervised the girls' work alone until 1832, when yet another Mary – Mary Wanstall – arrived to help. Their schools taught Malay, Chinese and Tamil girls, and another school for Portuguese girls was set up and run by a Miss Edwardes. It was an area of work with huge opportunities for expansion.

## The Society for Promoting Female Education in the East

In 1834 a young American clergyman found himself addressing a small group of ladies in a London drawing room, pleading with them to form a society to support women who were called to teach overseas. His name was David Abeel, and he had spent some years working in Macao and South-east Asia, before health problems forced him to leave. He had been impressed by the missionaries working in the Malay Straits and the free contact they had with the local Chinese, compared with the severe restrictions of life in Macao, where the study of Chinese was punishable by death! On a visit to the Malay Straits, Abeel had seen how the "supportive" wives worked alongside their husbands in evangelising and teaching women, and he knew how much the education work was needed. He also knew that in England there were women willing and eager to serve, but no one would send them abroad.

Most missionary societies were still strongly opposed to sending single women out alone. In 1834, most unmarried women in Britain had to live under the protection of their families until they married, and it was unthinkable that they should live alone overseas; the missions refused to take responsibility for them unless they could live with family or friends.[6] The LMS sent no more single women after Maria Newell Gutzlaff, and the Anglican Church Missionary Society (CMS) sent out only eleven single women – always to join relatives or friends – between 1820 and 1831.[7] If women felt called to go overseas, the only solution was to find a husband similarly called. (After Dorothy Carey's health broke down in India, the Baptist Missionary Society had decided that no wife should be expected to follow her husband overseas unless she too felt a sense of call.)

There was a further difficulty: at that time "missionaries" were by definition men, and mostly ordained men. Women could not be missionaries, even if, when their husbands died, they continued their work for several decades afterwards.

Women teachers were regarded simply as teachers, rather than as missionaries. It was all the more remarkable that, in his letter home in 1832, Samuel Dyer had referred to "Sister Wallace" as a "true missionary".

Abeel repeated Morrison's call for a society that would help single women to start schools for girls overseas. He stressed that in cities where there was foreign influence, single women could live safely, and a teacher could sometimes earn her financial support through the school. (This proved to be over-optimistic, since it was hard for the schools to attract the children of the wealthy.) Abeel appealed to the ladies to take action, and they did. At a meeting at St John's Church, Bow Street, in 1834, they founded a society with a good Victorian name which was abridged (leaving out "India, China and") to the Society for Promoting Female Education in the East (SPFEE) and simplified further, informally, as the Female Education Society (FES).

They aimed firstly at selecting "pious and well-educated persons to go out as superintendents" to facilitate "the training and encouragement of subordinate native teachers". Secondly, they undertook "to raise funds, by annual subscriptions, donations and all other advisable methods", and thirdly, they sought "to bring the pupils to an acquaintance with Scriptural truth, and to a belief in Christ as their Saviour". There was a president and a vice-president, a treasurer and two secretaries, and a committee of 24, two of whom would retire annually, and several of whom were titled ladies. The chairwoman (*sic*) would sign the minutes and have the casting vote when necessary.[8] The Victorians were well versed in good practice for committee work. It was one of the first "sending" societies of its kind, organised by women to support and help women who had been called to teach women and girls overseas.

David Abeel went on to make the same request in Boston, North America, and the ladies were as enthusiastic as those in London, but at the last minute a senior mission leader begged them not to send single women overseas, and reluctantly they complied. A society for sending out American single women would not be organised for another 26 years.[9] Abeel was left in tears, asking, "What is to become of the souls of those who are ignorant of the offers of mercy and of the Bible?"

From 1834 to 1875, the SPFEE committee forwarded 153 single women overseas and assisted a further 62. They tended to send mature women (including widows) with experience in teaching, and these women went to China, South-east Asia, India, South Africa and the Middle East, until they covered a wider geographical area than any other British mission. In all their schools, Bible teaching formed an essential part of the curriculum, in the hope that they might be able to lead their pupils to believe in Jesus Christ. To this end, the SPFEE certainly considered their "agents" to be "missionaries", and not just teachers. Other missions which refused to accept single women nevertheless relied on the SPFEE to supply them with staff for girls' schools.

The schools were generally small, since the children could not travel far from home, so one teacher might supervise several schools. Often it was a case of training local people to do the teaching and helping with discipline – this was very important, as the girls were usually under eleven years of age, and when they first arrived they had no understanding of the concepts of listening and studying. The monitor system was widely used, where the older pupils taught the younger ones.

In addition to their official "agents", by 1880 the society also supported 300 national teachers (mostly trained by them) in 370 schools, teaching some 20,000 children.[10] Many of the auxiliary groups in Britain raised money for the schools by sending out boxes of hand-crafted goods, and these Western "luxuries" were sold in the expatriate community. Later the girls responded with boxes of their own local crafts and embroidery, which could be sold in Britain. The SPFEE was not so much a "sending society" as a support group with flexibility to meet various needs in various ways. It expected high standards of its teachers, and woe betide any who were inadvertently involved in the social life of their dancing and card-playing compatriots!

## The Dutch East Indies – Mary Ann Aldersey

Mary Ann Aldersey was another student from Robert Morrison's Chinese class. Her interest in missionary work was excited by her childhood nurse, who married an early CMS missionary to Travancore, India, and ran a school there. Mary Ann was not physically robust, but she was not lacking in character and drive: she was active in Christian work at home, visiting the poorer parts of Hackney and persisting even when stones were thrown at her. In her twenties she was already on the Ladies' Committee of the Bible Society. At Morrison's Chinese class she met Maria Tarn Dyer and Maria Newell, and bought a copy of his six-volume Chinese dictionary, thinking she might be able to encourage others to go to the East.

At the time when the LMS were considering sending out Maria Newell and a colleague, Mary Ann was already 30 years old. She gave a donation to the LMS, sufficiently large that "the society might be induced" to send the two women out. A year later she canvassed her friends who supported the largely nonconformist British and Foreign Schools' Society, and raised money to send Mary Wallace out to join Maria. Finally a clergyman, impressed by Mary Ann's enthusiasm and drive, asked, "Why don't you go yourself, Miss Aldersey?" That thought had never occurred to her.

Initially, her widowed father was strongly opposed to the plan, but he unexpectedly changed his mind in 1832. She was on the point of leaving for Malacca with Mary Wanstall when her brother was widowed, and she had to take over the supervision of his household and eight children. When a guest commented, "How happy you must be here", she replied, "I would rather be in prison with Chinese children around me." She did not find it easy, dutifully shouldering her family responsibilities in this way, but the experience with children proved invaluable for her future work. Meanwhile, the SPFEE was launched in 1834, and she was one of the 24 women from different denominations who formed the first committee. When her brother remarried in 1837, she was at last free to leave for the Far East. She was now 40.

In 1837, foreigners were still forbidden to reside in China, so she sailed for Djakarta (Batavia) where there was a Chinese immigrant population. The voyage round the Cape took twelve weeks. It was spartan, uncomfortable and dangerous, with heavy seas, cold winds and occasional hurricanes, and passengers at that time often mentioned the unending boredom and difficulty of living in a cramped space with few amenities. She travelled with the Medhursts, veteran LMS missionaries; Miss Hulk, an SPFEE Dutch lady heading for Batavia to help in Mrs Medhurst's school; and the 18-year-old Theodosia Barker, who was going to help the second Mrs Gutzlaff with her school in Macao. She never returned to Britain.

On the advice of the Medhursts, and against the wishes of the Dutch government, who did not want foreigners causing trouble outside Djakarta, she settled by herself in the city of Surabaya, where she stayed with a Dutchman and his Javanese wife, and ate her meals "with the Malay dictionary propped up in front of her". She also resumed the Chinese language study she had begun with Robert Morrison thirteen years earlier, and it was said in later years that her girls could understand her even if others were mystified! Foreigners met a lot of opposition outside the capital, but she commented, "My weakness was my strength. It was not expected that a woman missionary's activities would do much good or harm."[11] There would be many times in the future when women missionaries could go where men could not, simply because of that assumption: they were women, inferior and insignificant, and "could not do much harm".

In Surabaya she started a Bible class using a recently produced translation in colloquial Malay, and curiosity drew various people to attend. She composed Christian verses in Malay because the children loved singing and there were no hymns. It was a lonely life with "neither scholars nor books nor help nor sympathy". She found a Chinese man willing to hold a meeting in his house, and persuaded a Chinese Christian to explain the Christian message once a week to the ten men and women who gathered. She then faced sneers and ridicule from the European population as they passed the open windows and saw her sitting with local people, and ultimately the anger of the Muslim leaders for holding Christian meetings. Her friends feared she might be poisoned, and she "commenced the night on one occasion not expecting to see the light of the next morning".[12]

Gradually her friends helped her to find girls for her school, and the number on the roll rose to 30. She made more contacts distributing tracts in the villages, and giving medical help. She found some influential friends, but the opposition continued, particularly when two girls became Christians and were persecuted by their families. In the spring of 1841, when Hong Kong was leased to the British, and political change was on the horizon, she decided to move to Macao, the Portuguese settlement on the Chinese coast.

## Singapore – Maria Tarn Dyer and Miss Grant

The boat for Macao called at Singapore, and there Mary Ann Aldersey must have met Maria Tarn Dyer again, 17 years after they had attended Morrison's Chinese classes together in Hackney. The Dyers had spent the intervening years with the London Missionary Society in Penang and Malacca, working in evangelism, education, and literature, and Samuel in particular had battled with the problems of printing the Chinese Bible. After fourteen years of work, success was in sight.[13] Samuel reluctantly took his family home in 1839 for the sake of Maria's health, but two years later they were back in the East, eagerly awaiting the moment when China would at last open her doors and allow them to live there. They brought a Miss Buckland back with them as governess for their children so that they would not have to send the children back to

Britain for their education. Miss Buckland gave a description of the children on that journey:

> ... the striking contrast between (the four-year-old) Maria and her gentle, thoughtful sister. Maria's volubility, lively repartee, her observation of what was passing around her, would not fail to attract my attention... I remarked to her mother that she would require careful and judicious training... [She was] a favourite on the voyage because of her lively disposition and warmth of affection. She had great discernment of character and frequently made precocious and striking remarks on the sayings and doings of our fellow passengers, not caring to conceal what she thought as regards right and wrong... She was noted for her affectionate nature, strong will, and quick temper.[14]

Writing after Maria's death in 1870, Miss Buckland made a revealing protest on her own account. Samuel Dyer's biographer had described her as accompanying the family to India (*sic*) as a governess in 1841.[15] She said the description had been very painful for her friends (and, by implication, for her). This was her "appointed work" for the time but she deeply regretted not being able to devote more time to direct missionary work. She kept this "in reserve" for the future. As early as 1841 she had a clear call overseas which went beyond teaching. Samuel Dyer recognised this when he and Maria offered to be brother and sister to her if she *shared with them* (his italics) by joining their family. "If you would, as far as time and strength would allow, unite with Mrs Dyer in labours among the heathen, oh, then we should find that we had a sister indeed."[16] Single women were sensing a clear call to serve God overseas at a time when few churches or mission boards recognised the possibility.

Like the other LMS wives, Maria Dyer had already started small schools in Penang and Malacca. When the Dyer family moved to Singapore in 1842, she launched the Chinese Girls' Boarding School (CGS). Her husband reported that Margaret Stronach, the wife of his LMS colleague, and Miss Buckland were helping her with the teaching. The Singapore school used Malay and English and focused on teaching skills appropriate for the children's daily lives in the future. There was an extraordinary dearth of Chinese women in Singapore, so the missionaries were concerned to provide indigenous Christian workers, as well as wives for Christian men. In addition to Bible teaching, they learned to read and write and master basic domestic skills, including cleaning, sewing, cooking and caring for children. Much of this was absorbed through the daily routine of their community as the older girls cared for the younger ones.

Then, in August 1842, the first Opium War in China came to a sudden end and everything changed – with the consequence that Chinese men and women on the mainland now had the opportunity to hear and embrace Christ's gospel. For the first half of the nineteenth century China had resisted attempts to open diplomatic relations with the West; it also tried to halt the opium trade, which was encouraged by foreign powers and draining the country's economy. China was decisively defeated in the resulting war, and was forced to cede Hong Kong to the British and to open five ports to foreign access. The Treaty of Nanking which established the five Treaty ports was signed in June 1843. At last foreigners could live and work on the mainland of China, and gain a foothold for missionary work in that country.

Some of the missionaries had been praying for this day for 25 years: when China opened, those who had been waiting to enter simply packed up and left. In the following years, Singapore and Malaysia were bereft of missionaries. The Malacca church, with 250 members, was left to fend for itself. In Singapore, Benjamin Keasberry and his wife alone were so committed to the local Chinese and Malays that he resigned from the LMS in order to stay. It was a courageous move.

The Dyers, busy with school and printing and befriending and visiting local people, would happily have stayed in Singapore in 1843, but the LMS directed them to China. It says much for Maria Dyer that she looked ahead to their expected move and had already written asking the SPFEE to send someone to take over her school in Singapore. The SPFEE had just received a letter from their ladies' auxiliary group in Huddersfield offering £100 per year for ten years to send a teacher overseas: Miss Grant was interviewed, appointed and her passage arranged: she reached Singapore in July 1843.[17]

She found a busy island, about the size of the Isle of Wight. The green slopes of Fort Canning rose behind the town of 40,000 people, and offshore hundreds of ships were anchored: British warships, tea clippers, Chinese junks and Malay *prahus*. Cargo was unloaded at sea and brought in on small boats. The Dyers' home, which also housed the school-children, was built on land near the shore (later to be occupied by the Raffles Hotel); St Andrew's Church stood nearby (later to be replaced by the cathedral). Miss Grant settled down quickly, won the children's allegiance, and took charge.

At the same time, missionaries from several different societies were travelling to Hong Kong to discuss how they should proceed. "All agreed that their plans and activities must be co-ordinated to complement and not duplicate or compete with each other's efforts, and a joint team and strategy for Bible translation must be drawn up."[18] It was an excellent start, although it soon foundered on translation problems, which would be unresolved for years to come.

Samuel Dyer was one of those who attended the Inter-Mission Conference to discuss the future, and it was agreed that he and his family would move to Fuzhou on the south China coast. However, it was not to be. A severe, unidentified epidemic was sweeping through Hong Kong island, leaving many dead, and it finally reached the conference. Samuel was struck down while up-river visiting Guangzhou (Canton); he appeared to recover and was on his way home to Singapore when he had a relapse and died in Macao at 39 years of age. He was buried next to Robert and Mary Morrison in the small Protestant cemetery originally acquired for Mary. In one of his last letters he told Maria that Mary Ann Aldersey had already "gone north" to Ningbo.

Within three months of Miss Grant's arrival, the news of Samuel Dyer's death reached them. Maria Dyer stayed on in Singapore with her four children, and was able to help Miss Grant for the first year. Close friends in Singapore took ten-year-old Samuel Dyer into their home to educate him with their own son, but further tragedy struck when the *amah* accidentally dropped Maria's infant son on stone steps, causing his death.

In 1844 Maria informed the LMS that she was returning to Penang with her two daughters to take over the Chinese Girls' School there, for which her husband had bequeathed money. LMS continued to provide £200 annually for Maria's personal support. There was no suggestion of the family returning to Britain. Maria, like her husband, had been called to serve the Chinese for life, and it had been their dearest wish from the beginning that their children should continue their parents' work. A year later Maria married Mr Bausum, an independent German missionary in Penang; she died the following year, in 1846. Her daughters, Burella, aged twelve, and Maria Jane, aged ten, embarked on the four-month journey back to Britain with their older brother Samuel to the care of William Tarn, their uncle, whom they would scarcely remember.[19]

In 1844 Miss Grant was left in Singapore with 20 girls, mostly under twelve years of age. Singapore was a rapidly expanding, multi-racial port and Miss Grant must have needed courage and commitment to stay on in the centre with her charges. Except for the Keasberrys, all the other missionaries had left for China. Most of the girls had Chinese fathers and Malay mothers and some had been handed over to Miss Grant because they were difficult or unwanted. The parents could be equally difficult! There were times when her Madras servant insisted on sleeping outside her door with a drawn sword at night. It was a demanding task, but she shouldered it for the next ten years, and established a connection with Mary Ann Aldersey's new school in China.

## Singapore – Sophia Cooke and the Chinese Girls' School

Sophia Cooke was 40 when the SPFEE interviewed her as a replacement for Miss Grant in 1853. Her education in Bury St Edmunds was good for the time – it included music, French and Latin. For 20 years she had worked as governess in various homes, including those of clergy families, and she had become increasingly interested in working overseas. Finally she was introduced to the SPFEE and discovered that it was possible for her to go abroad herself. In 1853, the society was sending prospective teachers to the Home and Colonial School Society for six months of teacher-training and assessment. Sophia's long teaching experience and good references stood her in good stead, and she stayed for only a short while before being accepted for Singapore. She lived there, with occasional visits to Britain, until her death in 1895.

Her biographer describes her as "thoroughly Saxon, with very fair hair, light blue eyes, and rather tall... a pleasant though not beautiful face, and an expression of mingled kindness, intelligence and decision. She was born to rule." Her first tasks were to learn Malay and to win the support of the girls who were devoted to Miss Grant. An English clergyman gives a picture of the town at that time:

> Singapore is a large convict state and a large number of the police are convicts, and very faithful they are: they are all natives of India and have been in heavy irons for two years after their arrival and knowing they cannot escape, and feeling that if they behave well they will be treated kindly, they soon become useful members of society and do all the government work. The new and handsome church [the present cathedral] about to be erected will be built altogether by these convicts.[20]

Indeed it was – that was one way to get public service! However, another visitor in 1856 reported that there were no missionaries in Singapore. Perhaps the Keasberrys were away and Sophia, as a woman, did not count. The word "mission-ary" was still used primarily of ordained men, and not of wives and teachers, to the indignation of some of the LMS wives who worked as hard as their husbands and shared the same privations. It is significant that by this stage the SPFEE did describe their teachers as missionaries, and in that same year the Bishop Daniel Wilson, in Calcutta, reported that the Singapore school was "training girls to be missionaries to their own people".

Soon after Sophia arrived, she obtained the help of Miss Ryan, a local lady, and they worked together for the rest of Sophia's life. Little is known of Miss Ryan except that she was born in Singapore. She started on a salary of £10 a month, but was later to become the only SPFEE agent to be accepted out-side Britain. When Sophia went on leave, Miss Ryan was left in charge of the school.

Over the years Sophia exercised a significant influence over the lives of several hundred girls. (When she had reason to check 150 of them in 1865, only four were not doing well.) When Singapore was founded by Sir Stamford Raffles, slavery was forbidden, but sometimes sailors would buy small girls from poor families in China, hoping to sell them as slaves or prostitutes in Singapore. The police rescued those they could and handed them over to Sophia. Others were found aban-doned in the street. Some of the older girls with such back-grounds proved too unruly to keep in the school, but others were transformed by Sophia's loving care. Four years after her arrival, the number of pupils had risen to 30. In 1861, they moved into new and larger premises on Sophia Road, possibly named after Sophia Cooke herself.

Sophia employed several teachers – including some of her graduates – and gave her own time mainly to administra-tion and Bible teaching. The girls learned to read the Bible in English and Malay, including the Arabic script. Arithmetic, geography, history and general knowledge were included, as well as Chinese gold-thread embroidery. The Christian con-cept of serving others was also stressed. At a later date they started a "ragged" day school in the city and the older girls would help there, and also visit the poor and sick. No one was idle. In 1875 one of their graduates returned to China as the first Chinese missionary to her own people. Some of the girls became "Bible women" (evangelists). Over 200 of them became wives of Christian pastors and preachers in China, and the Church Missionary Society sent one, with her Anglican husband, as a missionary to Korea for a while. The early LMS missionaries in Malacca who founded the Anglo-Chinese College for boys had always hoped to send its graduates out as missionaries, but it never happened. Sophia Cooke achieved it.

Her influence extended beyond the school to the city. When she arrived in Singapore, all the missionaries who had been working with the Chinese had left, and the existing churches ministered only to the expatriate population in English. The Malay chapel opened in 1843 and the girls from Sophia's school worshipped there, but there was nothing for the 50,000 Chinese. It was Sophia's concern for the husbands and fathers of her girls which facilitated the first Chinese language service in Singapore in 1857, although she herself did not speak Chinese. She gave them a place to meet on the school premises and the first service was attended by fifteen men and five women; this stirred the Anglicans and Presbyterians to do something similar.

Sophia's work was wide-ranging and imaginative. With a Brethren missionary she initiated a "Sailors' Rest" in 1882 to provide a haven for the numerous seamen passing through in various states of need, and this was later taken over by the "Agnes Weston" Homes. She set up a monthly Bible study for her graduates and other Chinese women. She also held weekly meetings for soldiers and policemen, and many of them responded to the Christian message with changed lives: when some of them died of tropical illnesses, she personally wrote to their families. With other ladies she formed a Bible and Tract Society, and this later led to the appointment of an agent for the British and Foreign Bible Society. She was a catalyst in many areas, setting up new initiatives which were taken up and continued by various international organisations after her death in 1895. The Chinese Girls' School still continues today as St Margaret's School, the oldest surviving school in Singapore, and its staff and students still have a concern for the poor.

A friend travelling in Fujian province in south China said her name "has been for many years a household word among all who possessed an intelligent knowledge of Christian work, especially in South China and in the Malay Peninsula. Again and again we come across in the wives of Christian native workers, the most cheering fruit of the labour expended by Miss Cooke and her colleagues in her boarding school in Singapore."[21] On her death, someone wrote, "Her influence was by no means confined to mission circles, but has been a power for righteousness among all classes in Singapore. She occupied a somewhat unique position, possessing great social influence, yet showing herself a friend to all Christian people, to whatever rank or denomination they belonged."[22]

## China at last! – Mary Ann Aldersey

In 1843, Mary Ann Aldersey was the first single Western woman to set foot in China. She was accompanied by her twelve-year-old adopted daughter, Mary Ann Leisk, whose Scottish parents in Java had committed her to Miss Aldersey's care. A few weeks later she was joined by the two Javanese teenagers, Ati and Kit, who had become Christians at her school in Surabaya. They had run away from their hostile homes and courageously made the long boat trip to Hong Kong alone. From there the little group went north to the port of Ningbo.

Ningbo was the largest of the Treaty ports, with a population of 300,000. It was situated at the meeting point of two broad rivers, twelve miles from the sea. One river bank was lined with foreign consulates, another with foreign warehouses for trade. Yet another section was full of logging yards, and the famous Bridge of Boats, using pontoons, linked the two banks of one river. The bridge was high enough to allow boats to pass underneath.

It was an unhealthy place to live: most Chinese farmers fertilised their crops with night soil, and those in Ningbo were no exception. Refuse went into the rivers and water for bathing, laundry, cooking and drinking came out. It was little wonder that "liver complaints" were constant, and dysentery, typhoid and cholera stalked their lives. In one terrible year no fewer than nine missionaries died, mainly from dysentery. The summers were intolerably hot, reaching 38°C. Once Mary Ann Aldersey had moved into the city centre, she would escape to the fourteenth-century pagoda with a few girls to catch what breeze there was in the stifling heat. In those days, with no electricity, no fans and no air-conditioning, the extreme heat often led to short tempers and riots. When dis-aster struck in epidemics, flood or drought, the Chinese assumed that someone must have offended the spirits, and the foreigners were the obvious scapegoats.

The ancient walls of the city were five miles in circum-ference, and rose 20 feet high. The top was broad enough for a carriage to be driven along it, and there was a path round the base of the walls. It was said that only beggars, soldiers and missionaries walked along the top: Miss Aldersey aston-ished the Chinese by taking daily walks at dawn, both winter and summer, clutching a bottle of smelling salts to ward off the odours that rose from the narrow streets. She had been warned to look after her health and took this very seriously all her life. The Chinese decided she communed with the spir-its of the night!

Moreover she wanted to teach their girls, and everyone knew that was a waste of money: girls married and left home, and they were a burden on the family from the day they were born until the day they married. Rumours abounded that Mary Ann had murdered all her own children and now wanted theirs. They said she took out her pupils' eyes before killing them.[23] One mother went to check on her "murdered" daughter and even when the living daughter was produced she was unconvinced: Miss Aldersey must simply have raised her from the dead. It was from this swamp of ignorance and superstition that Mary Ann and many missionary wives worked to try and extricate the girls and educate them for the future.

In such an atmosphere of apathy and even hostility, she could get pupils only if she clothed and fed them; they were often poor and unwanted, and some homeless. In return for the education, food and clothing, Miss Aldersey took advantage of Chinese custom by engaging in legal contracts to ensure that the girls had at least three years' education – she sometimes had to insist that such contracts were not broken. Then she might be able to arrange marriages for them, and if they became Christians, she could endeavour to find Christian husbands for them. Margaret Burton later summarised the situation:

> Such were the pioneer schoolgirls of China; the children of the poorest of the poor whose parents had to be bribed to send them... the homeless foundlings whom no one but the missionaries wanted, and despised little slave girls. This was the material with which the believers in Chinese womanhood must prove to custom-bound, conservative China that her daughters were as capable as were her sons.[24]

The girls were taught "the common branches of education, with plain needlework and embroidery, with the endeavour to equip them for the active duties of life". It included Chinese as well as Western subjects. The school began in Ningbo with fifteen girls in a wooden building outside the walls on the further bank of the river, overlooking the city. The Chinese landlady lived in the same building, with her grandson and his future child-wife. The child's screams when she was cruelly treated by her future grandmother-in-law were audible to everyone, but Miss Aldersey could do nothing to help her until the husband died. Then the child-widow joined the school and later married a Christian teacher.

After the first couple of years, Miss Aldersey was joined by a Miss Semple, sent by the SPFEE to help in the new school. She did not find it easy and complained of the girls' screaming! It is not clear whether this was a reference to the unfamiliar sounds of the strong Ningbo dialect or the traditional rote learning, but she is not heard of again. However, the young Mary Ann Leisk was able to teach Western subjects to the younger children, and also study Chinese subjects alongside the others. She was soon fluent in the difficult Ningbo dialect, as well as in Javanese and English.

In those early years Miss Aldersey was able to support the whole work from her private income, but as numbers grew, she had to turn to her friends for help. She was never an "agent" of the SPFEE, but she remained in touch with the society, sending regular reports to their magazine, the *Female Missionary Intelligencer*; they supported some of her needy pupils over the years, and supplied her with teachers. In 1852, as the number of boarders reached 40, the school moved into the heart of the city within the walls.

## The Dyer teenagers

That same year, Mary Ann Leisk became engaged to William Russell, a young up-and-coming CMS clergyman in Ningbo who would later become the first bishop of north China.[25] Miss Aldersey wrote to Mrs Tarn on the SPFEE committee explaining her need of a self-supporting teacher. Mrs Tarn, with her husband, was guardian to the Dyer girls, and so Burella Dyer, approaching 18, was invited to join Miss Aldersey at the Ningbo girls' school.

The Dyer girls had spent several years at school at Polam Hall in Darlington, but they had always been aware of their parents' desire for them to continue their work among the Chinese. Burella agreed to go, and Maria Jane, who was approaching fifteen, did not want to be separated from her. They met the SPFEE committee twice, receiving first a grant of £5, and then another of £20 towards their expenses. In the eleven-month gap between the two visits, they may well have been sent for some teacher-training. No doubt the lively Maria had calmed down with the years, the benefit of Miss Buckland's "judicious training" and the profound loss of both parents and a baby brother, but she must have been a girl of unusual courage and independence. It was five years since they had returned to Britain from Penang on their mother's death, and they had never been to China. Maria's main concern was to "help China" and fulfil her parents' calling, but by the time she arrived, she had made her own spiritual commitment to Christ.[26] They travelled to China in the autumn of 1852 with the Cobbolds (CMS), who were returning to Ningbo.

During the tedious months on board ship, the girls got down to Chinese language study with Mr Cobbold, and by the time they reached China, they were able to make themselves understood. Broomhall comments, "From constant living among the girls in the school, and study with a teacher, [Maria's] knowledge of the vernacular of Ningbo became both extensive and idiomatic to the extent that she could read to the older girls from an English book, translating into Chinese as she went."

No one was idle in Mary Ann Aldersey's school, and a strict routine was kept; the local people who slept the cold winter days away found it very strange. Burella and Maria were soon caught up in the routine, which sometimes began before 5 a.m., walking the walls with Miss Aldersey daily, winter and summer, before prayers with the school at 7 a.m. The Dyer girls carried the teaching load in Western subjects in the morning, and Chinese teachers taught Chinese subjects in the afternoons.

As the years passed, Burella and Maria moved freely through the narrow streets of Ningbo, where windowless walls surrounded the homes, and large doors on the street opened into courtyards and homes inside. They had a regular Bible study for women, and gathered up the mothers of their pupils for weekly meetings. They spent a lot of time visiting the pupils' mothers and other women in their homes, reading the Bible with them: they could not go alone, so often took the older pupils with them. In spite of her youth, Maria's fluency and experience enabled her to help new missionary wives with Chinese, and take them out to visit local women. At different times she also helped others with their small schools. The Dyer girls had no English companions of their own age except for the new young wives who were arriving and working alongside them. Chinese girls their age were secluded at home awaiting marriage, or married.

In 1852, at 55 years of age, Miss Aldersey was one of the most senior residents in the small missionary community, and was held in high respect. For one thing, she was older than most of them. The local Chinese decided that, since Britain was ruled by a woman, the Queen had sent Miss Aldersey to rule the British in Ningbo, and even the British consul took his orders from her! Hospitality was generously extended from the school to the missionary community of fifteen to 20 people, and everyone met weekly for prayer. A visitor admired the way "the orderly and self-respecting habits of [her] early years remained unchanged". The white tablecloth was always removed before dessert was served! Miss Aldersey was a pillar of the establishment, in close touch with the missionary community, while continuing to work hard to support her girls, local evangelism, and the many Chinese men and women with whom she was involved in Ningbo.

These were early days for overseas missions. Arguments raged between those who believed in preserving their Western culture and dignity in other lands, and those who abandoned the trappings of the West and adopted the ways of the place where they lived. There was a gulf between the foreign secular community, which maintained its traditional lifestyle at a distance from the Chinese, and the missionary community who mixed with them. Many missionaries felt able to maintain a simple Western lifestyle in the Treaty ports, but those who ventured outside the ports found themselves less conspicuous if they donned Chinese dress.

Miss Aldersey was always the same, the product of an

upper-middle-class home, and accustomed to being in control, and she did not find some aspects of life in China easy. A gulf remained between her lifestyle and that of the Chinese, yet she welcomed many Chinese to her home and took an active interest in the outreach to the villages. Some 50 years later, a friend said she had expected to meet "a tall, masculine-looking person who had a mind and will of her own... I was greeted by one of the loveliest little women it has been my privilege to meet. She captured my heart from the start."[27] No doubt "the mind and will of her own" were still there!

A glimpse of Ningbo life in 1854 emerges from the pages of the diary of Robert Hart, a 19-year-old Irishman entering the consular service. On arrival, he was escorted round the foreign community of some two dozen people for the ritual introductions on two successive afternoons, and found it very tedious. The social prospects for a young man were not exactly exciting! After confiding to his diary descriptions and frank comments on the people he met (which included "a nice old lady" called Miss Aldersey – she must have been 57 then!), he was not impressed, but decided that "the sight of Miss Dyer has reconciled me to Ningbo". It is not clear which "Miss Dyer" he meant – the calm and gentle Burella or the lively, intelligent Maria, who could "put on an argument" – but he certainly proposed to Maria three years later. Whichever it was, he would have to contend with the "nice old lady" who was only too aware of the impact the girls had on lonely bachelors in the port, and who was perfectly capable of dealing with them – or most of them![28]

## James Hudson Taylor

That same year another young bachelor reached Shanghai. James Hudson Taylor was 21 years of age and only the second person to be sent out by the Chinese Evangelisation Society (CES) in Britain. A friend described him as "young-looking, fair, bright and very poor". Another close friend said he was "more deferential to the opinions of others in his later years than in his youth... as I remember him, there was room for change in those respects!" Unfortunately, the CES was incompetent and irresponsible: over the next three years the society utterly failed in its obligations to the people it sent out. The members made no arrangements for his arrival, sent him unsuitable instructions from London because they had no experience in China, and gave him only a meagre allowance, subsequently providing no further funds for the work. Letters took two months to reach London, and the society ignored his protests and requests. It was fortunate for Taylor that the London Missionary Society members gave him lodging, guidance and encouragement. When he arrived the Taiping rebellion was under way, Shanghai was under siege, and foreigners were still forbidden to travel beyond the five Treaty ports.

Within six months, Taylor had learned enough Chinese to arrange lodgings of his own, and found a Chinese man prepared to help him with preaching. He began holding meetings locally, and over the next two years he teamed up with various missionaries to itinerate outside the city limits to sell and distribute literature. Most Chinese people had never seen a foreigner before, and curious crowds gathered, drawn by the strange sight of their Western clothes. Some welcomed them, but others were hostile, for foreigners were supposed to live only in the Treaty ports. If the local officials complained, they did so to the consuls and then it became a diplomatic incident in which the Chinese had the law on their side. The missionaries felt called to take the Christian message to the Chinese, and they were determined to do this, even if it meant travelling a couple of hundred miles inland in the process.

Those first years were ones of uncertainty and loneliness. Taylor was hoping to marry a girl in England, but his correspondence with her over the months was inconclusive. He longed to settle somewhere permanently, but Shanghai under siege was too expensive. The CES in London (who did not understand conditions in China) insisted he must work inland, but the British consul in Shanghai told him it was forbidden under the 1843 Treaty of Nanking. Taylor longed for permanent fellow workers. He also longed for more adequate finance for the work, so that he did not have to struggle from one crisis to the next. If he had completed his medical studies, he could have opened a hospital and supported himself, but he had been encouraged to consider evangelism to be more urgent than gaining qualifications, so he had broken off his studies. He wondered whether he should return to Britain to complete his medical training and perhaps find the wife he needed as well. He also needed a society that would truly back him up and guide him.

When he ventured inland, veterans advised him to wear Chinese dress to reduce the uproar that foreign clothes attracted, and he found this worked.[29] The issue was to be a controversial one for decades to come in the missionary world. The towns on China's eastern coast were accustomed to foreign dress and lifestyle: foreigners usually had their own settlements in Chinese cities, and Shanghai was very cosmopolitan. However, the moment foreigners moved inland (it was still technically forbidden and very few did), a Chinese lifestyle made it very much easier to move around. He could do nothing about his blue eyes and Western face, but the dress did help. He decided it was a matter of courtesy and respect to adopt Chinese dress and the lifestyle and culture that went with it. He even tried dyeing his fair hair black, but concluded this was not essential. Instead, he had it shaved except for the top, which he grew into a *queue* (pigtail).

In 1856, at the age of 24, Hudson Taylor found himself unofficially confined to Ningbo through force of circumstances. He had come to buy medical supplies for Swatow, but on his journey everything he possessed was stolen, and he was forced to spend a month or so in Ningbo awaiting money to replace necessities. It was a large city, and there were already some fifteen missionaries there from four different denominations and both sides of the Atlantic. He was not made welcome: a foreigner dressing like a Chinese was not appreciated. He was glad of the companionship of another CES couple, John and Mary Jones, when they arrived in Ningbo (though the society failed to provide adequately for them, too).

## Courtship in Ningbo

In 1856, the Chinese Girls' School was also facing change. Miss Aldersey was approaching the age of 60 and planned to retire. She invited the widowed Mrs Jemima Bausum in Penang to take over the school, and Mrs Bausum arrived in Ningbo with her three children in October 1856.[30] At that point she anticipated having the continuing help of the Dyer girls (whom she had known ten years earlier in Penang), with their energy, experience, and fluency in the Ningbo dialect. Four days after she arrived in Ningbo, the 19-year-old Maria escorted her round the missionary community to make the formal introductions.

However, further change was already under way. Burella had received a "welcome letter" from a widowed CMS clergyman, John Burden, and they hoped to marry the following year. Maria's diary for this period records the daily details of comings and goings in the community. When not absorbed in the school, or reading the Bible with Chinese women, she was visiting the young missionary wives, sometimes staying overnight (walking home at night required an escort). On Sundays, local missionaries dined with them at the school.

Just before Christmas, the highly respected clergyman Joshua Edkins proposed marriage to her. He had spent six hard years itinerating and evangelising in China and was now 40 years old, twice her age. The proposal reduced the lively Maria to giggles, and a refusal, news of which soon circulated in the small community. Shortly after, the young Robert Hart from the consulate, whose stay in Ningbo had been made tolerable by "Miss Dyer", also proposed, at the age of 21. He also was turned down, and Miss Aldersey became suspicious that Maria's heart lay elsewhere. Good marriages were important, and the choice in a foreign city very limited, and Maria had now rejected not one but two good offers.

If Miss Aldersey had seen her diary, she might have found a clue. In the course of the social round in September 1856, the guests at Sunday lunch included the young James Hudson Taylor. Maria confided to her diary that she was moved to "take the matter to God" and, in the world of that day, she could do no more.

Taylor had occupied himself in joining the other men on evangelistic trips, and finally returned to Ningbo with John Jones and his son. Their journey had been a hard one: a Chinese helper had been drowned; John Jones was suffering severe attacks of renal colic; they were shipwrecked crossing the bay. What was normally an eight-day trip had taken three weeks, and they decided not to "rest" on the Sabbath but to head for home as soon as possible. Their arrival in Ningbo on a Sunday shocked their Sabbatarian colleagues.

At Christmas, Taylor joined the other English missionaries for a dinner of beef and plum pudding, after which the Dyer sisters entertained the other thirteen guests with piano duets. The following day Maria visited Mary Jones, and Hudson Taylor escorted her home through the narrow streets. The walk was probably memorable for Maria, if not for him, for he was still pining for Elizabeth Sissons in England. It was Mary Jones who finally encouraged Hudson to relinquish his hopes of Elizabeth, and suggested he give some thought to Maria Dyer instead.

Shortly after Christmas most of the missionaries were evacuated because of local unrest: Hudson Taylor was asked to escort the wives and children to Shanghai, but Maria and Burella chose to stay with the indomitable Miss Aldersey. Even when the situation was defused, Taylor and the Joneses were delayed in Shanghai. Towards the end of March 1857, Taylor decided to write to Maria and asked his friends to deliver the letter in private. He knew her parents were dead and assumed she was of age, though in fact she was only just 20. The letter took two weeks to travel from Shanghai to

Ningbo, and Mary Gough discreetly passed it over to Maria at school. Maria had been praying ever since she met Taylor the previous autumn, but had carefully concealed her feelings from all but Mary Jones. Now she was overjoyed to find that he cared for her. She confided in Burella, who was delighted with her sister's news. Then Maria told Miss Aldersey.

The news was received coldly. "She remarked that she supposed I would not think of accepting him", and proposed writing to William Tarn, Maria's uncle and legal guardian, asking him to find out more about Taylor. Miss Aldersey had many objections to the match. She accused Taylor of cant; he had approached Maria, a minor, without asking Miss Aldersey's permission first; he was a member of the Plymouth Brethren "sect", and a Sabbath breaker (because he travelled on a Sunday with a sick man after robbery, a drowning and a shipwreck). He had not completed his medical qualifications; he was not ordained; he did not belong to one of the mainline denominations, or even a respectable missionary society (and was shortly to resign from that, had she known it!); he had no fixed income, in contrast with Maria who had a small private income; and he insisted on wearing Chinese dress.

Against her will and her heart, Maria was forced to write a letter rejecting Taylor's advances and asking him never to raise the matter again (Miss Aldersey insisted on that). She tried to write a letter that would satisfy Miss Aldersey, and yet indicate between the lines that her heart was not in what she wrote. It was a difficult task, and Taylor was still 250 miles away (four days' journey by boat). Although Miss Aldersey had now retired from the school, and Maria and Burella were living with Mrs Bausum in the school house, Miss Aldersey was a person Maria loved and respected, and felt she was bound to obey.

In May, both Taylor and Jones resigned from the China Evangelisation Society. They had learned that the society was in debt and they felt this was wrong. They decided to rely on God alone, believing that, if he had called them to that work, he knew their needs and would provide for them. Taylor finally returned to Ningbo in June; Miss Aldersey was incensed that he had the effrontery to return, though Edkins and Hart, who had also sought Maria's hand, were still welcome to call. Eventually Taylor realised the extent of her opposition, and spoke to her himself.

When Miss Aldersey received him, he was shocked to discover that Maria was still a minor, though Miss Aldersey had to admit that she was not Maria's legal guardian. He was able to refute some of her criticisms of him, and was concerned to hear that they had been sent to Maria's guardians without his having an opportunity to answer them. He felt this was most unjust. He also discovered that Maria had written to him under duress, and that Miss Aldersey had dictated the sentence requesting him never to raise the matter again. He decided he would have to write to the Tarns himself if he wanted to see more of Maria, but hesitated to do this without her permission.

Eventually a meeting was contrived, and letters were sent to England: Taylor gave the Tarns the names of friends who would vouch for him. The young couple had to settle down to a long wait in a small community where convention forbade them to meet. Meanwhile, the missionary community was also split. The Establishment background of Miss Aldersey and William Russell (husband of Mary Ann Leisk) made them suspicious of the unordained, medically unqualified Taylor – if he were ordained, had completed his medical training and belonged to a "proper" church, they might have felt differently. Others sympathised with Taylor but tried to maintain harmony in the community by deferring to Miss Aldersey's seniority.

After Burella's wedding in November, Maria told Miss Aldersey that she and Hudson Taylor considered themselves engaged; twelve days later the Tarns wrote that they would not oppose her wishes. At last the engagement was made public, and they could spend each evening together. They were asked to delay the wedding until Maria came of age, and that was only five weeks away.

In spite of a final attempt by William Russell to confront Taylor and further postpone the wedding, it finally went ahead, and they were married by the Revd William Gough on

20 January 1858. Taylor wore Chinese dress – his friends commented that in daily life he wore the clothes of the *poor* Chinese. Maria continued to wear Western dress until they moved inland to start the China Inland Mission eight years later.

Helen Nevius, a good friend, commented:

> To those who knew Mr Taylor only in his later years, it may be a surprise to know that when he "fell in love", it was a headlong plunge and by no means a slight touch of evanescent passion. And his fiancée with her strong emotional nature was in this respect not unlike him.[31]

At the ages of 25 and 21 years, James Hudson Taylor and Maria Dyer had been through months of severe testing. The lessons they were learning would stand them in good stead for the future. There would be plenty more criticism, opposition, accusation and rejection in the years ahead. They would need firm convictions, and an unshakeable faith.

Some 40 years had passed since the first Chinese woman was baptised by her husband; 30 years had passed since Maria Tarn Dyer and the first LMS wives began sharing their faith with Chinese women in South-east Asia, and Maria Newell started the first school for Chinese girls in Malacca. Under Miss Grant and Sophia Cooke, Maria Dyer's small school in Singapore was going from strength to strength, and Mary Ann Aldersey's school was established in Ningbo. Foundations had been laid for the future; at last it was possible to live in the Treaty ports in China itself, and the infant Chinese church was quietly growing. The next major step forward for both Chinese and missionary women would come through James Hudson Taylor and his wife Maria.

**Notes to Chapter One**

1   Abigail Beighton and Joanna Ince started a girls' boarding school in Penang in 1821, and Abigail continued till her husband's death

in 1844. Maria Dyer arrived in 1827 and opened schools in Penang, Malacca and Singapore over the next fifteen years. Mrs Eliza Medhurst ran Malay-language boarding schools in Malacca, Penang and Batavia from 1822 to1843, until she moved to China. Mrs Thomsen ran the first school for Malay girls in Singapore as early as 1823, supported by the expatriate community. Christine Doran, "A Fine Sphere for Female Usefulness: Missionary Women in the Straits Settlements, 1815–1845", *Journal of the Malaysian Branch of the Royal Asiatic Society*, vol. LXIX pt. 1 (1996).

2  In her first letter from Malacca, Maria Newell commented, "All my Chinese goes for nothing. Malay and Portuguese are most wanted. I am studying both." Council for World Mission Archive, China, Malacca, Penang, 1805–1861, Box 2: 1821–1829. She was in touch with Robert Morrison, so she had probably been in his ladies' Chinese class with Maria. In a letter to the Anglo-Chinese Boys' College, Morrison said he had been instrumental in her decision to go to Malacca, and regretted the fact that she was not staying at the Anglo-Chinese College.

3  Robert Morrison had a vision for this, and his LMS colleagues founded the school, hoping that, even if China remained closed to foreigners, some of these boys might be converted and take the Christian faith into China themselves.

4  When Maria Newell Gutzlaff died, her widower later married Mary Wanstall, also from the Malacca school.

5  Samuel Dyer, 2 March 1832. LMS, Malacca, Box 2, Folder 2.

6  Hence Morrison's desire for the Anglo-Chinese College to provide accommodation for Maria Newell. E. Morrison, *Memoirs*, p. 403.

7  Within two years only two were left – the others had married or died. Jocelyn Murray, "Anglican and Protestant Missionary Societies in Great Britain: Their use of women as missionaries from the late eighteenth to the late nineteenth century", Lecture, *Exchange 21* (1992), pp. 1–28.

8  Suter, *History*, pp. 275–76.

9  See Appendix.

10  Annual Report of the SPFEE c.1879, quoted in Daggett, *Sketches*.

11  Aldersey White, *Woman Pioneer*, p. 17.

12  Ibid., p. 18

13  Broomhall, vol. 1, pp. 226–27, 238. Scott W. Sunquist, "Dyer, Samuel" in Lewis, *Dictionary* vol. I, p. 338.

14  Personal letter after Maria's death in 1870. CIM Archive.

15  Davies, *Memoirs*, p. 215.

16  Ibid., p. 295.

17 Ibid., pp. 235, 236, 244.

18 Broomhall, vol. 1, p. 278.

19 Ibid., pp. 275–80. Davies, *Memoirs*, pp. 250–58.

20 Weldon Tarleton, in the *Female Missionary Intelligencer* (April 1856) p. 129.

21 Walker, *Sophia Cooke*, Introduction, pp. viif.

22 *The Malaysia Message* (October 1895), quoted in Sng, *In His Good Time*, p. 67.

23 Aldersey White, *Woman Pioneer*, pp. 30–32.

24 Burton, *Education*, p. 51.

25 Mary Ann Russell became one of the most honoured CMS wives in China, renowned for her fluency in the Ningbo dialect, and her loyalty and love for Chinese women. Stock, *History*, vol. II, p. 295; vol. III, pp. 367–68, 559–60. The Russells later provided a base for Miss Laurence to operate a CMS school in Ningbo.

26 Samuel Dyer had written to his wife from Hong Kong just before he died: "From our window we look upon the lofty summit of the Chinese hills... The sight is almost overwhelming. In my happiest moments just two thoughts seem to concentrate [my] every feeling... One is that the name of Jesus may be glorified in China; – and the other, that you, and each of our dear children... may live only to assist in bringing this about... Cease to serve the cause of Jesus... I never can while I have a head and hands to work." Quoted in Broomhall, vol. 3, p. 40.

27 Aldersey White, *Woman Pioneer*, p. 9.

28 Wood, *No Dogs*, pp. 36–39.

29 The Roman Catholic priests had done this. The veteran, Medhurst, used it as a disguise and recommended it. Edkins also used it outside the city. Broomhall, vol. 2, pp. 146, 278.

30 As Jemima Poppy, she had been sent to Batavia by the SPFEE in 1839; after five years there, she moved to Borneo to help Mrs Thompson in Pontianak, but Mrs Thompson died the following year. In 1845, Miss Poppy then transferred to the girls' school in Penang, to assist the widowed Maria Tarn Dyer. Soon after, Maria Dyer married Mr Bausum, an independent German missionary, and died herself a year later. Mr Bausum married Jemima Poppy in Penang in 1847. When he died eight years later, Mrs Bausum stayed on in Penang with her own three children and continued to help the Chinese church in the town.

31 Helen Nevius, Letter to Mary Guinness Taylor, Maria Memoirs, CIM Archive, Box 5, Folder 58.

*Chapter Two*  # The China Inland Mission

When Maria Dyer married Hudson Taylor in 1858, she had already packed more adventure and achievement into her 21 years than most Victorian ladies experienced in a lifetime. Born in Malacca in 1837, she had grown up in one of the very early London Missionary Society families, with parents who were totally committed to bringing the message of Jesus to the Chinese nation, at a time when no foreigner was permitted to live in China. After the deaths of her parents and baby brother she spent time in England, but at the age of fifteen she set sail for China – an unknown country – with her older sister. She taught at Mary Ann Aldersey's school in Ningbo until her marriage, and later she was part of the team that produced the romanised Ningbo dialect New Testament.

Travelling abroad in the nineteenth century was fraught with danger: medical knowledge was still extremely limited by today's standards and, even in the West, premature death from illness or injury was common. Life was yet more precarious for women, who had to contend with the perils of pregnancy and childbirth. Maria had nine pregnancies – most of them with complications – in thirteen years of marriage, at a time when birth control was almost non-existent. Only three of her children reached adulthood, but all three later served in China. She suffered from tuberculosis, and the normal tropical diseases struck at intervals, yet throughout her life she not only supported her husband and cared for her family and extended household, but took a leading role in running the new China Inland Mission. Through teaching and example she trained the first generation of women who were called to take the good news about Jesus into the homes of the Chinese.

Maria was driven by her calling and commitment to the women of China and the needs of the new mission. In spite of her increasing weakness, throughout her life she was active in evangelism and translation, and in her husband's absence she took overall responsibility for the mission administration. She deserves to be better known and respected for her sacrificial ministry.

Maria's health was always a concern: on her honeymoon she contracted typhoid, which probably damaged her health permanently, and she miscarried her first child at seven months. In the autumn of 1860 the young couple and their fifteen-month-old daughter, Grace, returned to London from China. The three-month journey home round the Cape had been a nightmare: another baby was due in the spring, and Maria tended to be extremely ill in the early months of pregnancy. She had also developed severe gastro-enteritis, but an unsympathetic captain made no provision for suitable food, and refused to let them leave the boat at the Cape. Hudson Taylor had feared for her life.

In London, their future looked bleak. Taylor himself was probably suffering from amoebic hepatitis and jaundice when he left China and, after six very stressful years there, he was physically exhausted. Medical diagnosis was still very limited but he was finally told that his nervous system, liver and digestion were severely damaged and he must give up all thought of returning to China in the near future.[1] He needed prolonged convalescence in a temperate climate. In fact, colitis continued to strike him whenever he was under stress (which was often) for the rest of his life.

It was a heavy blow for a couple who cared so deeply for China. At long last, in 1858, the Treaty of Tientsin allowed foreigners to travel hundreds of miles inland up the Yangtze River, and more Treaty ports on the Grand Canal and inland waterways were opened for trade. Moreover, both Chinese and foreigners now had freedom to propagate and follow their own beliefs. And yet, as these doors swung open, there were only 112 Protestant missionaries in the whole of China – five years later, the total number would shrink to 93. Now, just as the possibilities for missionary work were beginning to open up, Maria and Hudson were prevented from returning.

## Getting on with the job

Yet there was plenty to do. If they could not return themselves, they could put the needs of China before the existing missionary societies and churches, pleading for more prayer, more recruits, and the necessary support. In China, there was good co-operation between the few missionary societies represented in Ningbo, and Taylor's concern now was to stir up the mission boards in London. When sail still predominated over steam, and mail from China could take four months one way, it was hard for people in London to keep in touch with events. Taylor was among the first to return to Britain and report personally on the Chinese situation.

In spite of her youth, Maria had more experience of China and a better grasp of the language than her husband, but they were both of one mind in their commitment to the cause; Maria was closely involved in all that Hudson did. They began praying for five more men as reinforcements for the Ningbo mission where they had served with John and Mary Jones. Taylor came from a Methodist background and had experience of local lay preaching: he had already written from China to his parents, urging them to look for young working-class men, like the Methodist class leaders and local preachers, who could spend five years in China. Carried away by his enthusiasm, he even claimed that "the language is of the simplest nature" and could easily be acquired by the average person. Reading and writing Chinese ideographs was considerably harder, but this was less important. Few Chinese were able to read, so it was the spoken word which would convey the gospel message. Taylor suggested that if men could give five years to China, they could start the language on the four-month voyage, and begin to preach after six months. They would then have at least three and a half years to do something useful. Nowadays most missionaries expect to spend two years in full-time study to get a good grasp of the language, but Taylor was driven by his sense of urgency to see the gospel proclaimed.[2]

## The Ningbo romanised translation

In addition to recruiting more people for China, Maria and her husband were tackling another urgent project. The most recent scholarly translation of the Bible, written using Mandarin ideographs, was incomprehensible to ordinary people. It could take many years to master the four thousand or more characters required to read it. The new believers needed to access the New Testament for themselves. To this end, a New Testament in the Ningbo dialect had been produced, using a romanised alphabet, but it required considerable revision, correction and marginal references, which had to be worked out from the Chinese text. The Ningbo New Testament was a major undertaking, and Maria and her husband began working on it with the Bible Society. Taylor was appointed editor and Maria had a significant role because of her fluency in the dialect.

In the event it proved more complex than they anticipated. They were joined by an old friend, Frederic Gough, but his scholarly approach slowed the pace of progress. Then another CMS missionary arrived from Ningbo: William Russell, who had opposed their marriage so vehemently. Russell had his own views about the translation, and urged that it should reach a high literary standard – suitable for educated Chinese, rather than the man in the street. The situation was very difficult. While the team worked on, regularly spending six to eight hours a day on the project, they also had to spend time and energy defending their case to the

Bible Society and CMS committees. The whole project was almost brought to a halt. Meanwhile the Ningbo Christians were enthusiastic about the text so far, and Taylor was impatient to complete it as soon as possible.

Taylor also had his own unfinished business. His sense of urgency in getting to China with the gospel had led to his departure from Britain six years earlier before qualifying as a doctor. Although he had run the Ningbo hospital successfully for some months, he needed to complete his medical training.

In April 1861 Maria gave birth to Herbert, and within days they moved into their own home near the London Hospital so that Taylor could study and work and follow up his other concerns as well. Moving house within days of having a baby was hardly ideal, but Louisa, Taylor's younger sister, joined them for some months to help. Maria's home became the hub of the translation work, as well as lodgings for a constant stream of visitors: fellow missionaries returning from Ningbo stayed there, together with an ever-increasing number of possible recruits and friends.

James Meadows, one of the recruits, later recalled his arrival at the Taylor home:

> Mr Taylor... his utter indifference about his uncomfortable and poverty-stricken surroundings... Scarcely a dozen hot coals in the firegrate and it was bitterly cold too. The crockery was all odds and ends and the cutlery at sixes and sevens! Even (Mr Taylor's) personal appearance struck me as being very untidy for a man of his position, the bottoms of his trousers were bespattered with mud... He and the Rev Mr Gough... were intensely absorbed all day long... I had to patiently wait for hours before Mr Taylor could attend to me. The next thing I was struck with was the gentle, earnest piety of Mr Taylor and dear Mr Gough... I found that the good man was in poverty himself and had no means nor money to send me out to China!... His strong yet quiet faith in the promises of Scripture, his implicit confidence in God, this it was which compelled submission on my part to whatever he proposed for me.[3]

In Miss Aldersey's home in Ningbo, all the habits of civilised society had been preserved. She would have been horrified to see the "poverty-stricken" conditions in which Maria was living, and would probably have felt that her original opposition to the marriage was justified! Maria had turned her back on the refinements of Victorian life to identify with her husband and the Chinese; they had lived very simply in China and they did the same in London. They had no guaranteed salary, never went into debt, and never asked for money. They believed that if they put God first in their lives, they could bring their needs to him and he had promised to meet them. Later they employed a girl to look after Grace, setting Maria free for work on the Ningbo translation. Grace was reacting badly to the ups and downs in the household interspersed with visits north to grandparents, and they hoped the girl they employed would "calm her down". (Some 20 years earlier another governess had reckoned that Maria, her mother, would need some judicious training when she was three!)[4] As the household expanded, so did their financial needs, and Hudson and Maria had to watch every penny. And then there was an ominous note – at Christmas, Maria had "a troublesome cough".

## Reinforcements for Ningbo

The first recruits sent out to Ningbo to help John and Mary Jones were James Meadows and his wife Martha. They arrived early in 1862, in the middle of the Taiping rebellion, at a time when John Jones was already desperately ill with tuberculosis. That November Maria gave birth to Frederick Howard (for once she seems to have had a pregnancy free of major illness), and the three children must have kept her very busy. John Jones died on the journey home to Britain early in 1863, and the Taylor household was then augmented for some months by the widowed Mary Jones and her three children, before they rented another house in the same street. With his medical studies completed, Taylor could give more time to trans-

lation with Gough, though the discouraging criticism continued. The two men plodded on with their work day after day,
surrounded by all the distractions of a busy household.

Those distractions included occasional recruits from the
Church Missionary Society, the Baptist Missionary Society
and the Free Methodists. Taylor gave freely of his time to
them too, starting them on Chinese language study and giving them hand-copied lists of Ningbo vocabulary before they
sailed. One day in December 1863, Taylor spent eight hours
on the New Testament and Maria spent all day copying a
vocabulary. He joined her at 10.30 p.m. and they worked on
till 4.30 a.m. as the recruit was leaving at 9 a.m. that day.
Maria was three months pregnant with her fourth child, but
the couple continued with their punishing schedule: Taylor
regularly worked into the early hours. They literally poured
out their lives for their work.

In June of 1864, Taylor took Maria, their three children
under five and their nurse, to Yorkshire for two weeks' holiday. The next baby was due at the end of the month. They visited grandparents and went on to Scarborough, where the
children played on the sands while Hudson wrote letters,
caught up on reading, and proof-read the translation. They
missed their train connection back to London, so returned to
the long-suffering grandparents in Barnsley, where baby
Samuel was born. Taylor then had to leave Maria and return
to London with the two older children. It was scarcely a restful family life.

At the end of the year they were able to send Jean Notman
out to Ningbo to help Mrs Lord (Mrs Bausum had married the
widowed Dr Lord in Ningbo in 1861) at the girls' school. Since
Martha Meadows had already died of cholera, Jean was the
second of the "men" they were praying for as reinforcements
for Ningbo. In decades to come they would regularly pray for
men – and for pioneer work, they usually meant men – but in
a strange way, which they were slow to accept as a divine
answer to their prayers, a considerable number of women
usually completed the numbers.

Hudson and Maria were now coming to terms with the situation. For four years in London, Hudson had done all he could to encourage others to go to China through the existing societies. Nevertheless, in 1864, some 20 years after the first Treaty ports were opened to foreigners, LMS and CMS had only ten people each in China, and together with all other missions a total of 189 people. Everyone was overstretched and no one could consider extending the work into the other unoccupied provinces. In spite of the Moody revivals sweeping across the country, missionary societies were short of both recruits and the money to send them. China's interior provinces, with 100 million people, still remained unreached by the gospel, and this lay heavily on the Taylors' hearts. However much Hudson tried to work through the existing societies and help their recruits, little was happening. He agonised over the situation, talked to prominent lay leaders, and founded a Foreign Evangelists' Society to encourage more people to offer themselves as missionaries. In the spring, two more young men sailed for the Ningbo mission: Stephan Barchett from Germany and George Crombie from Aberdeen, and Crombie's fiancée followed shortly after. They completed the five for whom the Taylors had prayed for the last five years, but the needs of China's interior loomed large, and the recruits were far too few.

Taylor was now spending time dictating letters, articles and a book on China, pacing up and down the study as Maria wrote. She also had to make handwritten copies of many of the letters he dictated. In his absence she handled all the correspondence and also gave Chinese lessons to hopeful recruits. Some young men and women were being drawn into the weekly prayer meeting, and they might be accepted by other societies which worked in coastal China, but how could people be encouraged to work in the interior?

## Crisis point

In June 1865, Taylor found himself walking and praying on Brighton beach on a Sunday morning – he was too troubled to attend the morning service. As he prayed, he finally reached the conclusion that a new mission to the interior would have to be established, and he would have to lead it. So few people had any experience of China. He had always seen himself as an enabler of others and a colleague, first among equals perhaps, but no more. He shrank from the responsibility, until he realised that if this was from God, God would provide for all situations – his own task was just to obey. For several years he and Maria had lived without any visible means of support, and God had supplied their needs from various sources when they prayed. Now he believed God was asking him to lead the first missionaries into inland China.

The Chinese philosopher Lao-tse said that a journey of a thousand *li* begins with the first step. So that day Hudson took his first step and asked God to provide 24 willing and skilful helpers. That number would let him place two people in each of the provinces unoccupied at that time, and two more in Xinjiang, and he hoped to be able to send an equal number of Chinese fellow-workers with them. He was also wondering whether to place a couple of men in Burma to access the south-west province of Yunnan from there. It would be a drop in the ocean, but it would be a beginning. He returned to London with a deep sense of peace in his heart. Two days later he took another step of faith and opened a bank account in the name of the "China Inland Mission", depositing £10. It represented the small gifts that came their way, sometimes augmented by larger ones from wealthy friends – but nothing was guaranteed, nor even remotely adequate for the task that lay ahead.

## Establishing foundations

In the coming months Hudson and Maria discussed the ground rules for the new mission with their trusted friends, William and Mary Berger. They spent many weekends with them, thrashing out policy. Hudson did not want to draw money away from the other societies, and determined never to take collections or appeal for money. They would make their needs known to God alone, and encourage people to pray for guidance before they gave. William Berger was a businessman, and became home secretary of the new mission when the Taylors left for China; Mary, as a mother figure, kept in touch with Maria and the other women who sailed, sending letters of warmth and encouragement which were all the more welcome when some of the girls were as young as 21 years of age and had little family to support them.

At the ages of 32 and 28, Hudson and Maria carried the responsibility for leading this new team, and Taylor recognised the crucial role Maria would play. Of necessity he would often be away from home in China shepherding the team and caring for the sick. In his absence, Maria would have to be in charge, and he insisted that the team should agree to this. She was the only other person with language skills and experience of the country. While the treaties now allowed foreigners to move inland, no one knew what the reactions of the Chinese would be. It was vital that people should avoid stirring up trouble and be willing to listen to those with experience – in this case, himself or Maria.

Neither Hudson nor Maria was a charismatic leader. Hudson was small in stature (Maria was the taller of the two) and people who knew only his reputation were often disappointed when they actually met him; however, those who heard him speak were profoundly influenced. Maria occupied the traditional role of wife and mother, but in addition she had considerable gifts, skills and experience for such a young woman. Visitors to their home described her as a tower of strength and wisdom, calm, unruffled, and deeply spiritual.

Both of them were totally committed to China and all that involved, but when Taylor was overworked, ill, or away travelling, a huge amount of extra work descended on Maria's shoulders.

As discussions moved forward, basic policies emerged. Taylor was in charge, and decisions would be made in China. In his early years he had had enough of societies and their boards, far away in London, deciding what people must do in China. He was prepared to send out to China those who were called of God, who showed some ability to learn the language, and who had a good knowledge of the Bible and a concern for evangelism. He was more concerned that they should have spiritual gifts than an academic education and training, and in this he differed from some of the other societies. He was prepared to accept people regardless of their church affiliation, provided that they could agree on the fundamentals of the Christian faith as found in the Bible, and be content to differ on less important things like church order.

Where finance was concerned, he could guarantee his colleagues nothing. He would keep his own finances separate, and share out whatever money the new mission received, but it was God who called them, and they must trust him to supply their needs. They must not go into debt. They could pray directly to their heavenly Father, the giver of all good things.

Since they would be heading into inland China, where almost no foreigner had set foot since Marco Polo, 700 years earlier, the recruits must be willing to respect the Chinese by wearing Chinese dress, eating their food and speaking their language. Gutzlaff and others had recommended this, and Taylor had found it a great help, but the policy seemed scandalous to the insecure and those who believed in asserting British superiority, and the policy would be hotly contested once they reached China.

Several of these policies were radical, but none more radical than his decision to encourage single women as well as men to go to China as equal members of the mission. He scandalised Victorian Britain, just as Florence Nightingale had done ten years earlier when she took nurses to the Crimean War. In England, unmarried women lived with their families and never set up house on their own. However, Taylor had already seen how effective the young Dyer girls and the Ningbo wives had been, and he knew that without the help of Christian women, the women in China were inaccessible.

The call went out for single women to be equal members of the mission with men, and before they sailed, he realised that since he expected the married women to work alongside their husbands, they too should be recognised as full members. Later he would spell it out even more clearly to recruits:

> It is most important that married missionaries should be *double* missionaries... unless you intend your wife to be a true missionary, not merely a wife, homemaker and friend, *do not join us*. She must be able to read and be master of at least one Gospel in colloquial Chinese before you marry. She must be prepared to be happy among the Chinese when the duties of your calling require, as they often will, your temporary absence from home... [5]

Taylor was indeed breaking new ground.

Among those who responded to this call were some young women, barely out of their teens, who were to become very significant to the China Inland Mission in the years to come. Jennie Faulding and Emily Blatchley attended the weekly prayer meeting, and Emily took over as governess to the Taylor children. Both girls embarked on Chinese. In the autumn, Grace Ciggie joined them from Glasgow.

## Preparations

With her husband away travelling round Britain, Maria found herself at the heart of a growing household, and before long they rented an adjacent house to have space for everyone. There was a cook, and a nurse to look after the four children, but Maria was supervising the household, children, catering and laundry, teaching Chinese to the new recruits and helping with New Testament translation, and by the autumn of 1865, she was pregnant once again. In November her pregnancy was threatened with a possible *placenta praevia*, and she needed bed-rest for three weeks. She already had a perpetual cough and temperature, which threatened "lung disease". "Weak lungs" or phthisis seemed to be regarded by the Victorians as a physical tendency one could do little about, and Hudson accepted that this condition would probably become permanent. He told his mother she had been failing since September.

Now there was an added complication in the pregnancy: "The haemorrhage now scarcely ever ceases and is at times serious. She is very thin and weak..."[6] (There were, of course, no blood transfusions until blood was refrigerated for the first time in 1916.) Then the cook went down with typhoid. Taylor sent the three older children and their nurse back to his parents in Barnsley, isolated the typhoid patient in one house, enlisted Jennie's help and moved Maria to the second house. He finally called in a top consultant, who insisted that the baby be induced immediately to save her life. It was a difficult breech delivery and baby Jane lived for only half an hour.

Christmas came and went and the children were still away. In the New Year, Taylor took Maria to the quiet of the Bergers' country home and Emily Blatchley stayed with her. Within days Maria was coughing up blood. Taylor had a string of appointments and could not visit her but sent medicine, though many of the supposed cures for tuberculosis at the time were no more than bizarre superstitions.

They were now planning to leave for China in mid-May, but Taylor had lost Maria as his secretary. Jennie helped with correspondence and Emily ran the home as best she could. In order to give his time to the task ahead, Taylor resigned from the final stages of the Ningbo translation. He and Maria had done the cross-references between them, and he had worked on it for five or six hours daily for the previous four years in addition to everything else. Maria rallied a little in February, though she was easily overtired, and she helped to check the proofs for a new edition of Taylor's book, *China's Spiritual Needs and Claims*. She was well enough to accompany her husband on a speaking tour in April, continuing to rest in the homes of friends, but they kept her away from London and the turmoil of preparations.

It was a massive task to educate the churches and encourage them to pray for China, when newspapers with pen-and-ink sketches were the only medium of mass communication. Taylor understood the power of the printed word and his small book, *China's Spiritual Needs and Claims*, affected many people. It had a hundred pages and sold for sixpence: the first edition sold out in three weeks. Over the years the CIM always ran an extensive publishing programme to keep people informed, and their books about China are still to be found on second-hand book shelves today. Taylor was also quick to grasp the value of the earliest portrait photographs as an encouragement when praying for individuals.

Preparing clothing for the party was an immense undertaking, even if they were planning to adopt Chinese dress once they arrived. Typically Taylor made himself responsible for their outfits and was busy buying cotton socks for recruits or asking Maria to get them, as if neither of them had anything more important to do. The efficient Jennie had organised a team of 40 church ladies to make the clothes: sewing machines were only just becoming available, so most of them were probably hand-stitched.[7] The girls now lived in a separate house in Coburn Street under the care of an older lady, in Maria's absence. In March, a Swiss governess called Louise Desgraz joined them. Grace Ciggie was busily involved in all the preparations, but developed bronchitis so severely that her departure was deferred. In all his careful researches, A. J. Broomhall failed to discover any suggestion that Maria was thought unfit to go. Fresh air was prescribed for lung disease, and the hazardous four-month sea voyage would give her plenty! At least they would leave the cold and damp of London behind.

## The *Lammermuir*

The *Lammermuir* party (named for the ship in which they sailed) gradually came together. There were eight members of the mission already in and around Ningbo. The new group would include 17 adults. In addition to the Taylor family with four children, there were Mr and Mrs Nicol and five single men; of the eight single women one was a fiancée and Mary Bausum, only fifteen, was rejoining her mother (now Mrs Lord after marrying Dr Lord in Ningbo). It was the largest missionary party ever to land in China. At that time there were only thirteen other unmarried Western women in the whole of China, and seven of those were in Hong Kong. Back in Britain, William Berger undertook to process new recruits, keep churches informed and praying, and forward any financial gifts that came for those in China.

They were able to take all the passenger accommodation of the *Lammermuir*, a clipper due to sail on 26 May 1866. The voyage to China under sail was incredibly tedious and uncertain, but it provided several months for welding the assorted group together, and daily Chinese language study could be started. Conditions were spartan, and the diet on board was restricted, though it would be varied by the sheep, pigs, geese, ducks and chickens that were kept on part of the deck. The ten passenger cabins opened on to one living area, and inevitably the confined space and basic amenities also provided opportunities for friction when such a diverse group was thrown together at close quarters. They also had to get on with the crew,[8] some of whom were far from happy to learn that they had a group of missionaries on board. Taylor needed people of independence who could function alone in China when necessary, but he also needed people willing to learn, take advice, and work together. It was not an easy combination.

The journey took four months round the Cape of Good Hope, and they did not touch land until Anjers, in the Sunda Straits of Indonesia. During that time they were becalmed on the equator for a week, and survived two typhoons, though the second destroyed much of the rigging. It was a demanding voyage for everyone, but one of the young men described the convalescent Maria as "quieter, in some ways perhaps more mature – such rare judgement; calm sweetness about her face always; most restful... She gave a good deal of time to the children."[9] In truth she was still ill, and had been separated from the children for months because of her illness. Then, in June, she began vomiting severely again, and threatening another miscarriage. Towards the end of the voyage she was "not as strong as she was in Britain", and "laid up for five or six weeks".

## Shanghai at last

They reached Shanghai on 30 September, a party of 22 with nowhere to stay. Since the *Lammermuir* needed to repair the severe storm damage, they were able to remain on board until the women were invited to move into a mission house. A warehouse was found where they unloaded their 268 boxes and packages from the hold, and Hudson, Maria and the men slept there.

Typically, Louise Desgraz took over the next stage. She was always willing to shoulder whatever work had to be done and, in a lifetime of service in China, this was typical of her: loyal, faithful, humble, versatile, always there when needed. Now she organised a team to handle four months' laundry, unpacking, washing and drying everyone's salt-soaked baggage from cabins and hold. They were also organising Chinese clothes for everyone, and the men had their heads shaved and the traditional *queue* attached. Then they held a reception where the 22 missionaries already resident in Shanghai were invited to meet the new arrivals before they disappeared upriver. Only ten supportive friends turned up. Some were away; others were already critical of Taylor for bringing the eight single women, and encouraging them to wear Chinese clothes.

Maria took the lead in donning Chinese dress, though she had never worn it before. One person commented that it was "a very real trial to her". Hudson had adopted Chinese clothing soon after he began to travel inland. As one writer put it:

> (Taylor's) missionary colleagues dressed and behaved like European clergymen. They belonged, visibly, to the same world as the merchants, administrators and soldiers whom the Chinese collectively classed as "red-haired foreign devils". The first step was obviously to get out of devildom by looking and behaving as much like a Chinese as possible... He could travel into the country districts without being conspicuous... [10]

Maria had her reservations where the women were concerned: her close contact with Chinese women and girls in Ningbo enabled her to see things from their perspective. Firstly, knowing how the local women were despised, she was afraid that Western women who dressed like them would lose respect. Secondly, she knew it was not simply a matter of donning their clothes, but of living their lives, with all the appropriate manners and conventions that went with the outward appearance. A foreigner could be forgiven many discourtesies, but one in Chinese dress could not. Dress represented a way of life. "The nearer we come to (the Chinese) in outward appearance, the more severely will any breach of their notions of propriety be criticised."[11]

Both men and women found the loose-fitting jackets and wide blue trousers difficult to begin with. Mary Bowyer, writing home to Mrs Berger, said she did not admire the clothes but admitted that they were comfortable, and they were all getting used to going out hatless! Jennie confessed that the outfit had some advantages, "but it feels clumsy... I very gladly wear it... but I shall never like it."

Taylor planned to make an initial base at Hangzhou, 80 miles up the Qiantang River estuary, but it was no easy thing to provide for this large party of foreigners in an uncertain situation. He decided to take a month instead of the three days usually required, and hire houseboats to follow the inland waterways. It gave people time to see the countryside, adjust to Chinese clothes and food, and get on with language study. Boats provided a retreat from the crowds, curious or angry to see foreigners in their country. Taylor was familiar with the area from his first period in China, but the recent Taiping rebellion had devastated towns and villages since he was last there.

## Hangzhou

In the derelict streets of Hangzhou winter was approaching fast, and they were thankful to find a ramshackle old mansion, once the home of a wealthy family, with 30 rooms, albeit no ceilings, doors or windows, "resembling most a number of barns or outhouses", as Emily cheerfully described it in a letter, "with a superabundance of both dust and of ventilation. Before us is one wilderness of ruins." They had brought five Christian men from the Ningbo church to help in the initial work, and there was room for everyone and also a clinic and dispensary, a print shop, chapel, and separate quarters for single men and women, and families. There was also sufficient space to accommodate the large number of foreigners in privacy without appearing to be a threat to the local people.

Maria was ill again as her pregnancy drew to a close, and this was not helped when she fell down the staircase ladder. Her second daughter was born in February, bringing the number of their children to five. Louise Desgraz now supervised the large household and staff, while Emily acted as secretary to Taylor and governess to the older children. Jennie Faulding and Mary Bowyer were already befriending Chinese women, receiving invitations to their homes, and gaining confidence daily in using Chinese.

In the spring, Maria started an "industrial school" for women where they could meet and sew, and while they sewed, she would read them stories from the Bible. When the other girls could spare time from language study, they dropped in to chat to the women. Maria was not only reaching the women by helping them develop skills while she shared God's love with them, at the same time she was drawing the new recruits into the work. Broomhall saw her as the key figure who laid the foundations for reaching Chinese women, and trained the new arrivals for their future ministry. She had, after all, embarked on it herself when she was a teenager in Ningbo.

It was a delicate task trying not to offend the Chinese. They were a proud and ancient nation, and treaties with foreign nations had been forced on them at gunpoint. Chinese families and communities were being driven into destitution through opium, which Britain in particular forced on them. (For the first 60 years of Victoria's reign, Britain exported half a ton of opium from India every hour.)[12] Foreigners now had the legal right to move inland, but it was not surprising that some cities still refused to allow them to live there. They could not know that missionaries were protesting against the opium trade and doing all they could in high places at home to bring the trade to an end. The Chinese also feared the effect of foreigners living within their walls and flouting their ancient culture and religion. They believed it would bring trouble on the whole community if the foreigners did not conform to the superstitions that pacified the spirits. These included *feng-shui*, which dictated how houses, rooms, and streets should be built – its observance held up the development of the railways for decades.

## Lies and half-lies

Further opposition to the infant China Inland Mission came from missionaries in other societies. They were still critical of the adoption of Chinese dress, and of the close relationships with local believers that developed when the CIM missionaries identified with them, living and eating Chinese-style. The Western lifestyle of other missionaries in the Treaty ports separated them from the Chinese: in Hangzhou the other missionaries wore Western dress when they went out and were carried in sedan chairs; Taylor's team wore Chinese clothes and cloth shoes and walked. He found his team influenced by the criticism, to the extent that one couple and several single people resisted the policy of identifying with the Chinese in their dress, even though they had promised to do so in London. Taylor was also accused of unseemly behaviour and worse – keeping so many single women under his roof, when he was their leader, pastor, teacher and also doctor. He had promised Jennie's parents she would be part of his family, and Emily, without parents, had been included too. Sadly the half-truths, spread by critical members of his own team to other missionaries, turned to lies, and were then reported back in Britain. The accusers ignored the fact that Maria, his wife, was there with him.

The accusations went to and fro for months and Taylor still had to travel, sorting out problems, encouraging isolated missionaries in new towns, and visiting some who were seriously ill. In the midst of all this, they endured one of the greatest tragedies of all. Maria had been ill again, and so had two of the boys. They escaped from the summer heat to the nearby hills, but, as the boys recovered, their eight-year-old sister Grace became ill. Once again Taylor was called away and then delayed by the sickness of others. By the time he hurried back to his family, it was clear to him that Grace had meningitis, and there was little he could do but wait for the end. The Chinese were so frightened of the spirits of the dead that they had to take Grace back to Hangzhou in secret at night to bury her in the garden. There was no other place available.

Jennie Faulding described Maria at this stage as "always ailing". Her cough and raised temperature continued, but these did not stop her from working. With her husband under so much pressure, Maria took over the correspondence with the Bergers at home, explaining the true situation with the younger women so that the Bergers could answer the accusations in Britain. The single women also produced a signed statement to the effect that there had been no impropriety. Finally, in 1868, one couple was asked to leave the mission and three of the single women went with them. It was a sad time for everyone, but there had been so much dissension and criticism that it seemed to be the only solution.

## A church is born

In spite of the painful relationships within and outside the team, there were great encouragements in the infant church. A month after they arrived they had begun meetings in the chapel, where a high partition down the middle made the presence of men and women in one room acceptable to Chinese culture. Missionaries strongly disliked this custom – keeping the women out of sight appeared to reinforce their "inferiority" in Chinese culture – but without it the women could not attend and keep their reputations. It was Emily who described the scene in the chapel.

> I do wish... friends in England could see... the crowd of faces changing gradually from their expression of mere curiosity and wonder to that of interest – even earnestness... as Mr Taylor, mounted on a chair in order to throw his voice further, first explains to them the nature of our meeting and of our worship, how there is no visible form to bow to, no incense, no silver paper, no candles; but the great invisible God Himself present, seeing and hearing all that we do and say and think. Then... Mr Taylor explains and illustrates bringing each point in it home to them with peculiar adaptedness... Yesterday a man who attends the services told Mr Tsiu that he believes in our Christ; and today another man asserted his belief... [W]e cannot yet vouch for the genuineness of these cases... [13]

Taylor opened a clinic on the premises and was soon overwhelmed by the crowds that came. He began the afternoon sessions with a short service, and when the McCarthys arrived from Britain, they found him standing on a table explaining the gospel to the crowd before starting the afternoon clinic. In a couple of months, the chapel services were crowded with the curious, and Jennie and Mary Bowyer were busy establishing friendships with the women. In May, the first four men and two women were baptised. Three men followed in June, and in July, two of Jennie's women and another man. In the summer they appointed Wang Lae-djun as pastor and, with some of the Ningbo believers working in Hangzhou, the number of believers rose to 18, with more being prepared for baptism. Lae-djun's Christian wife was set free from the restricted life of Chinese women and became a valued co-worker with Jennie and Mary, and they were already leading women into the church. At the same time, Jennie was running the school for the new generation of church children. Elders were appointed, and the church was on its way to becoming independent. Taylor believed that the presence of too many foreigners could hinder the growth of the indigenous church, so it became the more urgent for the other missionaries to move away from this new church and scatter in new towns. Jennie and Mary were to remain in Hangzhou with the McCarthys.

By this time, Maria was writing home to say that she was now convinced they had made the right decision over national dress. She felt their foreign clothes had commanded fear, rather than respect, and she had not felt any loss of respect since wearing Chinese clothes. They attracted much less attention as they went through the streets. One critic had claimed the single women were wasting their time; on the contrary, Maria said, they had plenty to do. Taylor wrote:

> In every direction our sisters have free access to the women in their own homes... In its actual influence on the people at large, I am strongly inclined to consider it the most powerful agency we have at our disposal.[14]

At the same time, they had a delicate relationship with the national church leaders, many of whom had minimal education and were first-generation Christians. On leaving Hangzhou, Taylor wrote to an anxious 25-year-old Jennie:

> You cannot take a Pastor's place in name, but you must help Lae-djun to act in matters of receiving and excluding as far as you can. You can speak privately to candidates, and can be present at church meetings... Then after the meeting you can talk privately with Lae-djun about them and suggest who you think he might receive next time they meet. Thus he may have the help he needs, and there will be nothing that any one could regard as unseemly.[15]

Because the "women's world" was so separate from that of men in China, the single women missionaries were able to support and encourage the local pastors without undermining their status in the church. If Western men were present, the pastors shelved responsibility and relied on them. This became an important factor in the growth of the national churches.

However, they still faced the major problem of where the single women should live: neither in Britain nor China was it acceptable for them to live alone. Taylor had hoped they could live with married couples, but Chinese houses were small and the walls thin, and young married couples were not keen to share their homes. This was a real obstacle – they were needed, but how could they be housed and mobilised? The *Lammermuir* women were doing a great job, but what would happen when they went inland? How safe would they be? No one knew, because scarcely any foreigner had been there before, and certainly no woman. For the moment Taylor asked Berger not to send out more single women until the future was clearer. In the five years after the *Lammermuir* sailed, only four single women joined them – a sister, a nurse for the children and two fiancées.

Their first year had been traumatic in many ways: as well as eight-year-old Grace, one man had died from smallpox. But as 1867 drew to a close, there was much to thank God for. In

Hangzhou, the printing press was busy, numbers trebled in the women's industrial school and class, and Jennie's boys' school had 17 pupils, nine of whom had committed themselves to staying for five years. This would be significant for the church in the future. They were building a chapel on newly acquired land to seat 200 people. They had added the adjacent house where the McCarthys could live with the single men. They now had centres in six significant cities, and five other towns. Until then the London Missionary Society had been the largest in China with 30 members; now the CIM had reached 30 members and there were five more on the way. Numbers alone mean little, but it was a remarkable beginning for such an apparently insignificant group which had arrived only fifteen months earlier.

While some voices advised Taylor to pause and consolidate at this point, he could not forget his calling to evangelise the unoccupied provinces, and this drove him on to make journeys of exploration inland. Even the Chinese were vague about towns more than 40 miles (or two days' journey) away. The roads were little more than tracks, unsuitable for wheeled vehicles. People and goods travelled by boat on the innumerable waterways and rivers. Taylor's goal was still to place two missionaries and two Chinese in the chief city of each province and work out from there to other places, but they also needed strategic mission centres en route as supply bases. They could expand south of Ningbo into Zhejiang province, south-west of Hangzhou up the Qiantang River, and north up the Grand Canal through Jiangsu and Anhwei. For some weeks Taylor, his more experienced men and local believers, explored these areas, while Maria held the fort in Hangzhou for the infant mission. In 1868, with the coming of spring, they prepared to scatter.

## The Yangzhou riot

Taylor had decided to move his family and the CIM headquarters to Yangzhou. Some of the single men and couples moved out to other cities along the 1,100-mile Grand Canal: some were able to rent accommodation without problems, but in other places either the landlords refused, or the people strongly objected to the presence of foreigners. Where they did find premises, local riots sometimes forced them to retreat. The missionaries deplored the way treaties were forced on China by the Western countries, but took advantage of the legal right to live inland that the treaties conferred. In the spring, the Taylors slipped quietly into Yangzhou with their four children, the children's nurse, and Emily Blatchley. They had a difficult summer with all the children ill with measles, and two of them at death's door. Taylor was away legalising rental agreements when he himself went down with a dangerous case of dysentery. Meanwhile he deluged Maria with quantities of mail and instructions, although she was two months pregnant and nursing a very sick infant. Maria commented, "My brain seemed almost to reel after reading [the letters]. May the Lord help me..." Their resources were few and they were very overstretched.

For a few weeks all was quiet in Yangzhou – it was the lull before the storm. The Rudlands and Louise Desgraz were due to move to Zhenjiang with the printing press and local staff, but arrangements for premises were delayed, so they moved temporarily to Yangzhou. The people of Yangzhou city soon heard that Zhenjiang had prevented the foreigners from staying, thus inflicting them with an increased number of "foreign devils" with a large quantity of luggage. Then Duncan and Reid, living alone in Nanjing, also dropped in, and this seems to have been the last straw. Local emotions ran high in the stifling heat of summer, and the trouble-makers converged on the mission property. Taylor notified the authorities but they did little to restore order. When things got worse, Taylor and Duncan went to the *yamen* (city office) in person but were kept waiting for hours.

Meanwhile the women and children retreated to the mission house while Rudland tried to barricade the doors of the rambling building to keep the crowd outside. Finally it became impossible to keep them at bay and they swarmed in to loot the rooms. Reid was left downstairs as the others went upstairs and tried to secure a trap door at the top of the stairs. The crowd then set fire to the ground floor. Taylor and Duncan were still away, and no one came to restore order. The missionaries threw mattresses out of the window to make a soft landing below, made a rope out of sheets and lowered Mary Rudland (who was heavily pregnant), Louise Desgraz and the three older children to the ground. The nurse made a quick escape by the stairs with baby Maria. Then the crowd set fire to the mattresses and rope.

Maria, who was now five months pregnant, escaped to the roof with Emily and Rudland. Rudland was attacked and almost thrown off the roof, but Maria and Emily held back the attacker and, when Maria spoke to him in Chinese, he turned back. They now had to jump from the roof, a drop of twelve to fifteen feet. Reid, left below, tried to break Maria's landing, but he was being pelted with stones and had been injured. She twisted her leg badly, but her unborn baby was unharmed. As Reid tried to catch Emily, a brick hit him in the eye and blinded it permanently. Emily landed on her back, fracturing her elbow, but her Chinese hairstyle probably protected her head from serious injury.

Taylor and Duncan finally returned to find the buildings empty, wrecked and smouldering. They had been told the crowd was around 10,000 strong, and that all the foreigners were dead. It was a while before they found everyone in hiding at a neighbour's home. When the officials finally dispersed the crowds, the neighbours had put out the fires and the missionaries were able to go back to their beds for what was left of the night, but they had to transfer to Zhenjiang for three months until repairs could be made.[16]

One of the young men visited them soon after the riot and found them in makeshift accommodation in Zhenjiang, their possessions strewn around their one room. Hudson Taylor was ill in bed again with enteritis.

Mrs Hudson Taylor was sitting down in the middle of the room amidst all this confusion as composedly as possible, going on with the composition of the Ningbo dictionary. She had a wonderful power of concentration... She struck me as remarkable for her faith and courage. She had a delicate, sweet face – a fragile body but a sweet, expressive face of indomitable faith and courage.[17]

They were finally able to return in November, after formal enquiries by the British consul and the Chinese authorities. There was an official procession to lead Taylor back, and the heralds who led the procession announced to the people that they must take care not to hurt the foreigners, or to call them "foreign devils", but give them the title of "great men". An engraved stone at the front of the house announced that foreigners had the right to live there and propagate their religion. Maria and Emily returned at the end of the month. Maria had been unwell since the riot and her lungs were in a bad state, but she gave birth to another son a week after her return. Yangzhou was still a difficult place in which to live, but Louise Desgraz also returned and started two schools for boys and girls. Some 20 years later the girls' school was still functioning, and the language training centre and home for all the new single women was established in Yangzhou.

They learned some valuable lessons from the experience, for they would meet resistance in other places in the future. The ordinary people were so steeped in ignorance and superstition that they readily believed the persistent rumours that foreigners would steal and murder their children. The missionaries determined that in future they must avoid gathering too many foreigners together at one time, and also avoid starting work in several places in one vicinity. They should also keep their luggage to a minimum. Where local people were so fearful, it was wiser to visit at intervals, so that they became known and accepted before they settled in a town.[18]

## The growing seed

In the following year, four years after the arrival of the *Lammermuir* party, the mustard seed of the church was quietly growing. By 1870, some 33 missionaries were working in four provinces based on thirteen "stations" and eight outreach centres. There were 160 baptised believers in twelve churches and many enquirers in addition. For the next fifteen years the CIM would continue to be the only mission working in Anhwei province. The Cardwells began moving up the Yangtze River to Jiujiang, as a base for exploring Jiangxi province and the Guangxin River too. Where married men were involved in making such surveys, it meant many lonely weeks and months for their wives left at home.

In spite of these encouragements, life was still very hard and the demands on Taylor were colossal. They were two days' journey from Shanghai and his medical help was in demand by all the missions and even some Western business-men. Characteristically, he did his best to help everyone, though disease was rife, especially among the many children. He was tireless in his devotion to his fellow-workers, travelling incessantly, visiting each station in turn, encouraging, exhorting, advising, preaching and caring for the health of all. He once made a journey of 500 miles to visit a sick colleague. This was in addition to the heavy administrative work for which he was solely responsible (and there were no type-writers in those days). No one was surprised when he suffered a breakdown.[19]

## Sending the family home

As 1870 approached, three issues were concerning the Taylors. Firstly, their family: the two oldest Taylor boys were approaching eight and nine and needed schooling, and five-year-old Samuel was ill with tubercular enteritis. He was haemorrhaging and in constant pain when eating and drinking, and so frail that they wondered whether he could survive a long journey, but they hoped he might have a better chance of survival at home. Little Maria was three. Where health and education were concerned, all the children would be better in Britain.

Secondly, Emily Blatchley was also growing weaker, as tuberculosis spread through her lungs. Several of her family had died from this in Britain. She, too, might regain some health in Britain. Thirdly, the Bergers, who had taken responsibility for CIM in Britain for the first four years, needed help. They had never been to China, and found it hard to assess the situation and needs there: they had sent out some unsuitable candidates.

It was an agonising decision for Hudson and Maria to part with the four older children, though Charles, at 18 months, would remain with his parents. Samuel died early in 1870, before they were due to leave. Emily was heartbroken to be leaving China, but her health required the move. They also thought she could be a second mother to the children, which, incidentally, shows how very little was understood about the spread of tuberculosis. In addition, Emily's long relationship with the mission meant that she really understood the principles on which the CIM was based. Her knowledge and experience would be an invaluable resource to William Berger. As Taylor put it, she "will be better for you than 20 letters; being more intimately acquainted with mission matters than any other members".[20] She was still only 25 years old but knew far more about China than the businessmen on the London Council. In the midst of his grief over the departure of the children, Taylor was relieved that for the first time there would be someone at the London end of the enterprise who really knew what was going on in China. Maria wrote to the grandparents asking them to welcome the bereaved Emily as one of the family and use her first name.

## A life laid down

That summer the temperatures again soared into the nineties. In June there was friction between the French and Chinese, which led to atrocities and a massacre of French diplomats and Roman Catholic workers, both men and women, in Tianjing in the north. There were reactions across China, and Yangzhou and Nanjing missionaries were evacuated to Zhenjiang. Maria was still there in the heat, in a CIM house crowded with missionary refugees, when she went down with "English cholera". She was a little better two days later when she gave birth to Noel. However, a severe haemorrhage followed the birth, and Noel was born with diarrhoea and died two weeks later. Maria died peacefully three days after Noel. Her husband identified her illness as tubercular enteritis only as she was dying, and even then he expected her to recover.

Hudson Taylor was an extraordinary man who poured himself out in serving others, but perhaps he failed to recognise both his own and his wife's limitations. All his activities seemed to cascade down on to Maria. Yet, in those early days, they were the only two people in the mission with the language skills and experience to lead the work. Without them, inland China would not have received the gospel for many years to come. Maria, at 33 years of age, had laid down the foundations for the women of the China Inland Mission. She trained her successors, setting the pace for the young women, and working with them. In accepting women as missionaries on an equal basis with men in 1865, Hudson Taylor and Maria led the way in mobilising men and women to work together in evangelism and church-planting. Within fifteen years, the CIM women, both married and single, would move across China with the men to the distant borders.

> Unless a grain of wheat falls into the earth and dies, it remains just a single grain; but if it dies, it bears much fruit. Those who love their life lose it, and those who hate their life in this world

will keep it for eternal life. Whoever serves me must follow me, and where I am, there will my servant be also. Whoever serves me, the Father will honour (John 12:24-26).

## Notes to Chapter Two

1  Broomhall, vol. 3, p. 246.
2  Ibid., p. 196.
3  Ibid., p. 270.
4  Ibid., p. 273. Miss Buckland, unpublished letter, CIM Archive 1870.
5  Dr and Mrs Howard Taylor, *Hudson Taylor*, p. 155.
6  Broomhall, vol. 4, pp. 90-91n.
7  The first Singer machine was produced in 1851 and Mrs Berger gave one to Maria when she sailed in 1866.
8  The crew numbered 34 from Sweden, Germany, the West Indies, the South Sea Islands and Britain. Broomhall, vol. 4, p. 171.
9  Ibid., p. 178.
10 G. Woodcock, *The British in the Far East*, p.105, quoted in Broomhall, vol. 4, p. 226.
11 Ibid., p. 230.
12 *China's Millions* (January 1899) p. 2.
13 Broomhall, vol. 4, p. 293.
14 Ibid., p. 351.
15 Dr and Mrs Howard Taylor, *Hudson Taylor*, p. 397.
16 Broomhall, vol. 5, pp. 93-101.
17 Ibid., p. 106.
18 Ibid., p. 160.
19 Lyall, *Passion*, p. 43.
20 Broomhall, vol. 5, pp. 233-34.

*Chapter Three*     # Inland Pioneers

The first four years of the China Inland Mission had not been easy. The young team had to adjust to Chinese language, culture and climate. Life was precarious enough in Britain when medical knowledge was limited, and inoculation almost unknown. In the tropics Europeans were very vulnerable as they had no immunity to tropical diseases. The team also had to learn to work together: Taylor had accepted a more diverse range of people than most other societies.

His radical approach to mission involved the deployment of single women, identification with Chinese culture and penetration into the inland provinces, and it brought bitter criticism from his compatriot missionaries, the diplomatic corps and the newspapers, both in China and in Britain. Taylor was publicly criticised, scorned and derided, even by those who should have known better. He was an affectionate and sensitive person, albeit stubborn and single-minded, and stress always brought on an attack of dysentery. With the loss of Maria and two children in five months, he hit rock bottom, yet he was still carrying all the responsibility for the leadership and pastoral and medical care of the others.

A year later his mother was writing to him about remarriage. He needed a wife; his children needed a mother. She suggested Emily Blatchley, who was now caring for the children in Britain, and who had been part of the family for so long, but Taylor knew she was far too frail and ill to fill the gap Maria had left. In the summer of 1871, a year after Maria's death, he was still far from well. The Goughs had been caring for his son Charles, now aged two and a half, and when Taylor collected him after a separation of several months, at first the child did not recognise him. Together, father and son returned to Britain to rejoin the other three children. Taylor knew that with William Berger's imminent retirement from administration, an alternative homeside leader must be found.

However, the churches continued to grow, and there was much to encourage him. There were now 160 baptised believers gathering in twelve churches scattered across four provinces. The young men were exploring inland. The Hangzhou church, led by Mr Tsiu, Wang Lae-djun and McCarthy, had 50 members. The Chinese staffed four outreach centres and McCarthy rotated them round the other centres so that he could spend time with each in Hangzhou in further Bible teaching, using the romanised Bible. At times, training could occupy eight hours daily. Meanwhile Jennie Faulding supervised schools for 30 boys and girls: four years in a Christian school was educating the new generation of young people in the church. She also found time to work closely with Wang Si-mu (sister), the pastor's wife, visiting Hangzhou women.

## Moving forward

After five years in China, Jennie Faulding was also exhausted and struggling to overcome severe malaria. She left for home in the summer of 1871, travelling with another CIM family. Her anxious mother had agreed to her spending five years in China but enough was enough, and she sincerely hoped that Jennie would now settle down at home. Unexpectedly, Hudson Taylor and Charles ended up on the same ship, and by the time they reached London, Taylor and Jennie were engaged. One of Taylor's hardest tasks was to break the news to Emily Blatchley by letter before they reached home. She was heartbroken.

There was one final hitch. Jennie's mother insisted that her 28-year-old daughter should postpone marriage for a year, although Taylor was already 40 and an old family friend. This must have come as a shock to Jennie, who had lived an independent life in China for the last five years. Taylor must have recalled Miss Aldersey's intervention between himself and Maria, thirteen years earlier. Mrs Faulding had always been possessive and anxious about Jennie going to China, and not without reason. She said they both needed to be in a better state of health before they married. She may rightly have been concerned that Jennie's health was at a low ebb, and wanted her to be fully restored before embarking on sharing the pressures of Hudson Taylor's lifestyle, as Maria had done. She also had to face the fact that, once married, Jennie was going to be in China for life.

All this caused both Taylor and Jennie, unwell as they both were, a great deal of stress. Taylor was in the embarrassing situation of having to establish a home where Emily could look after his four children, while he was engaged to Jennie. He had to get his mother to come and help until Mrs Faulding capitulated, and then they married within days. There was no possibility of a honeymoon at that time, and it was only two years later, back in China, that they suddenly realised they had a house to themselves for the first time since they were married!

Before returning to China, Taylor organised a small Council of Management in London with a treasurer and two businessmen to take over William Berger's work as honorary secretaries. Emily, at 28, looked after house, children, and the mission office. Taylor had charged her when she first went home with the children:

> May He make you so conscious of His indwelling... that you may realise... that in Him the weak is strong, the ignorant wise, the mute eloquent, the incompetent all-sufficient, and that in *Christ Jesus* there is no male or female, that so far as moved *by* Him, and acting *for* Him, you are no longer a girl whose place it is to keep back, retired and silent, but His instrument, called to adorn Him who is your adornment.[1]

Unfortunately the two businessmen did not appreciate the amount of work involved, or the need to keep Taylor informed about the financial situation so that the mission, which had no regular income, did not go into debt. They failed to forward money to China and the treasurer did not bother to check the accounts. They were happy to leave as much work as possible with the "competent, reliable Emily", who edited and distributed the *Occasional Paper* with reports on the work for friends, and dealt with the mail and everything else in the office without the necessary authority to do so.

Before long she also discovered that the council of eminent men did not even fully understand the financial basis of the mission – praying for money was not exactly familiar ground to them when there was no income! She had to be Hudson Taylor's "mouthpiece". She wrote, "I cannot be blind to the fact that as yet the real responsibility of the work at home rests on me. Mr Challis told me the other day that the Council do depend on me." It was the old story – it was all right for her to use her gifts to do a "man's job" so long as it was not official. This basic dishonesty was never faced by the leaders. Emily was in effect running the CIM home department in Britain, and doing it efficiently, and her authority rested on the experience and expertise which she alone possessed in that situation. She was the only one in London who knew what it was all about, but her strength was ebbing away. Taylor urged her not to overdo things, and to employ extra help.

In the autumn of 1873, Taylor was travelling by boat in China when he fell down some steep steps on board. He injured his back and ended up on crutches. By the following summer, Emily was dying. He and Jennie began the long journey home in July to relieve Emily of the care of the children and the office, only to hear that she had died before they arrived in England.

# The appeal for "the eighteen"

Over the next few months Taylor's paralysis spread until he was confined to bed, and Jennie thought it unlikely they would ever return to China. The mission office was moved to his bedroom and volunteers came to help. Once again they faced a desperate situation, but Taylor still could not forget inland China. Eight years earlier he had accepted a call to proclaim the Christian message there. They had been building the foundations, getting a support team together and establishing bases in the eastern provinces; now at last it was possible to go forward. As 1875 dawned, he asked people to pray for 18 men – two to pioneer each of the nine remaining provinces.

> Will each of you Christian readers at once raise his heart to God, and wait one minute in earnest prayer that God will raise up this year 18 suitable men... warm-hearted young men, who have a good knowledge of business, clerks, or assistants in shops who have come into contact with the public and learned to cover the wants and suit the wishes of the public, are well fitted to this work. They should possess strong faith, devoted piety, and burning zeal; be men who will gladly live, labour, suffer or if need be, die for Christ's sake.[2]

His description was interesting. He was still looking for the traditional Methodist lay worker, but past experience had taught him the value of "people skills"!

The members of the Council of Management were startled when they heard this. They thought it was hardly the time to expand and move forward when a number of missionaries were ill, the leader was paralysed and bed-bound, and the London base was so fragile. With Taylor injured, there were no major speakers who could tour the country to encourage support. Yet Taylor was convinced again that God was calling them forward and trusted him to provide the answers. Was this foolish credulity or was it really a leading from God? The CIM had received a large gift of £4,000 for the new venture. Five men sailed in 1875; by the autumn of 1876, ten more young men had set out for China and it was possible to reassign six men already there. The strategy was up and operating, and language study was the first priority. Meanwhile, slowly, as the spring of 1875 moved into summer, Taylor's paralysis receded.

Taylor returned to China alone in the autumn of 1876. Jennie remained in Britain to care for their six children – her twins had been stillborn, but she had given birth to another son and daughter, and then there were Maria's four children. The two teenage boys were a lively handful. With Emily gone, Taylor delegated the CIM administrative responsibilities to members of the Council of Management. Jennie usually opened the CIM mail and continued to handle what she could, and passed the rest on to the others. Like Emily, she was the only one with first-hand experience of China. The monthly *China's Millions* had been published for the first time the previous year; Taylor had drafted the coming issues and Jennie was to sub-edit. As A. J. Broomhall later put it,

> Jennie could not be in charge, she had to be Emily Blatchley all over again, the life and soul of the London Headquarters while appearing not to be.[3]

Like Maria, she too would be at the receiving end of a stream of letters and instructions from her husband.

By the time Taylor returned to China, the experienced men had already set off for the interior and the first new recruits were ready to go. The miles they covered in the next few years were formidable. More settled missionaries accused them of wasting their time, doing nothing properly. But, as they went, they were selling books, giving out tracts and exploring the vast hinterland of towns and villages. They had to identify the main cities and industries, and assess whether or not people made them welcome. As they covered thousands of miles, they were laying down the foundations for the future expansion of the work.

However, one question mark still remained. Half the Chinese population was female, and traditional culture decreed that women's feet were bound, so they still stayed at home. Wherever European men went, they could not plant churches with Chinese men alone – they needed women to work with Chinese women. But how safe was the interior for married European women, let alone the unmarried? Could Western women be placed inland to do what they had done in the coastal provinces, and who would help and train them in the early days? Taylor arrived in Shanghai with six new women recruits, making a total of eight that year – a large increase considering only eight altogether had arrived since the first *Lammermuir* party ten years earlier, but most of those had married fellow missionaries. There was only Louise Desgraz and one other experienced single woman available to train the new women on the team.

In 1875, two men had established a base at Bhamo in Burma, hoping to enter south-west China from there, and the veteran John McCarthy walked across southern China to Bhamo, only to be forbidden by the British consul to return that way because it was so dangerous. The first exploratory journeys had also been made into the central provinces of Henan and Hunan. The following year, the new recruits moved north and south to enter four more provinces and later a start was made in the remaining three provinces of Guangxi, Guizhou and Sichuan. The journeys continued over eight years until they were able to establish a permanent centre in each province.

In those days a CIM missionary was not allowed to marry until he and his fiancée had both completed initial language study, and he had established a base to which he could take her. Before long the rule was introduced that marriage must be delayed for two years after arrival, in order to reduce stress on the women. The "marriage rules" were resisted for years afterwards, but the fact was that many young wives were so exhausted by the climate and sickness when they first arrived, that the added stress of marriage and childbirth resulted in the death of many mothers and babies. It was not uncommon for the early missionary men to marry two, if not three, times.

## The Shanxi famine

Shanxi province was nearly twice the size of Scotland, with a much bigger population. It was mountainous, dry, without irrigation, and very cold in winter. Northern China had rain for only two months of the year at the best of times, and famine was frequent. In 1876, there had been no rain for three years. By the time news filtered out to the West, people were dying of starvation; the dogs ate the corpses, and the people ate the dogs and other animals. The roads were jammed with refugees moving south.

The famine reached its peak in January 1878. There was no seed, and the animals had all been killed for food. All the stored rice, all plants and even the bark of the trees had been eaten. People were living on cakes made from soft, ground stone and husks – not surprisingly they were said to taste like mud. In some areas people resorted to eating dead bodies, and before the famine was over some were killing others for food. Grain had to be transported on pack animals, and the starving people attacked the animals for their meat. Even when they finally managed to obtain seeds to plant, the poor would be too weak to pull the ploughs without the help of animals. Only the strongest of the poor survived. Across the northern provinces it was thought that 75 million could be destitute. An estimated 5 million people had died, including, in one district, one third of the population. The famine-stricken area covered 70,000 to 100,000 square miles. Suicide abounded.

People had sold everything they had to buy food, and that included children: speculators were willing to buy both women and children. Many women would end up in brothels. Domestic slavery was already a fact in China, where poor children could be sold into domestic service and set free when they married. An inter-mission famine relief committee had been formed, and missionaries who ventured inland for the first time found a ready welcome for food and literature. However, when famine fever (typhus) broke out a dozen or more missionaries involved in relief work caught it and died, severely hampering relief efforts. Some 400 orphan children had gathered in the northern city of Taiyuan, and Taylor alerted Louise Desgraz to be ready for an influx of orphans in her boarding school in Yangzhou.

Taylor himself was only just back in Britain after a gruelling fifteen months in China, joyfully reunited with Jennie and his six children. He did all he could to make the needs known through the new mission magazine, *China's Millions*, which contained graphic pen-and-ink drawings of the suffering caused by famine. The mission contacted newspapers and churches, and collected money for the relief fund. Several of the CIM men had gone up to the famine area to distribute what they could, but women and children were still in desperate need and there were no missionary women to help them. The CIM had two young women ready to travel north, but no experienced woman to accompany them; Western women had never been inland before. Perplexed, Taylor and Jennie discussed the situation and finally, reluctantly, Taylor asked Jennie whether she would return to China herself to escort the young women up to the famine area.

Her initial response was negative; the children had to come first. She felt she could not go unless the children were cared for, as they were her first responsibility, so she prayed about it, asking for a sign that it was God's will that she should go. That afternoon someone gave her money towards expenses, and a few days later she received a larger gift for the same purpose. As for the children, when Taylor's sister, Amelia (who lived next door), heard about it, she said that if God had called Jennie to go back to China, then she was called to look after her children. Amelia already had ten children of her own and the Taylors had also made a home for the orphaned Caroline Duncan. Amelia was also running the mission home and caring for new recruits while her husband, Benjamin Broomhall, ran the London base of the CIM. They did not have many servants, but the Broomhalls had a nurse and a governess, and the Taylors' nurse stayed on to help. The neighbours thought she had started a school! It was not an easy decision for Jennie to leave her two toddlers for a long period; it would be two and a half years before she saw them again.

Jennie arrived in China in June 1878, to face the furnace of a Chinese summer on the Yangtze River. Typhus was already spreading across north China in the wake of famine, and Jennie herself contracted cholera, but she recovered. Refugees were moving south, and she planned to offer refuge for 200 orphans in CIM schools, but as the women and children arrived, they were rapidly sold and disappeared. Someone needed to make contact with them before they set out on the journey south. Jennie decided to venture north with her two companions: she had already written to some of the men working on famine relief, and they welcomed her as an answer to prayer. With a male colleague to escort them they sailed from Shanghai to Tianjin, and then travelled by boat, cart, and mule-litter over the mountains to Taiyuan. The journey took a month.

Shanxi had first been visited by two CIM men from October 1876 to January 1877 (Taiyuan), and the mission in P'ingyang was opened in 1879. It was a very courageous step of faith for the women to go there, and critical for proving that the CIM wives and single women could live inland in safety. When they arrived the men had already distributed money and clothing to over 100,000 needy people. Jennie and her colleagues opened an industrial school where destitute women could learn to support themselves, and organised an orphanage. By the following February she was able to leave the two younger women in charge. The rains had finally arrived that winter, crops were growing and food was once more available, but the months of April and May 1879 still saw the highest death rate of all from malnutrition, typhus, dysentery and smallpox. Although the CIM did not usually open orphanages (though some orphans might end up in the mission boarding schools), there was a great need to be met. The following weeks saw a steady stream of refugees arriving, until the refuges for boys and girls and the elderly were full with no less than 1,156 people.

The greatest breakthrough of all was the evidence that Western women could live inland and minister to others in safety, 500 miles from the coast. In fact, Jennie's two junior workers were able to continue working peacefully in Taiyuan, where the men had previously met with a hostile reception. This would not be the last time that women, apparently less threatening than men, gained access to places when men could not. It suggested that where the young men were pioneering, the women would very soon be able to follow.

Hudson Taylor was reunited with Jennie in China in February 1879. His health was still fragile and they retreated north from the summer heat. However, in spite of his physical weakness, he was overseeing another burst of missionary activity, this time undertaken as discreetly as possible. The first couples were about to move far into the interior, and possibly single women too. It was all perfectly legal, but Taylor did not want a public furore in the press in Britain or China, and especially in diplomatic circles, until the women had settled and demonstrated that it was safe – as he hoped, prayed and trusted God that it would be. He instructed the couples to keep records of all they did and discover all they could about the towns and people, the industry and agriculture, the good inns for travellers, and the reception they met. He gave them instructions for treating the most common diseases, and Broomhall surmises that the husbands were also given some information about helping at childbirth. They would need it. Humanly speaking, these couples would be on their own.

## To the north-west – Shaanxi province

Emily King had been in China for only six months when she married George King in the summer of 1879. He was 23, and had been in China pioneering with the other men for four years. Within weeks of their wedding they were heading back to Tianshui (Tsinchow) in Gansu. They were the first couple to move inland, and travelled to the north-west by boat, slowly hauled up the Han River with its rapids, carrying 18 boxes of books for Easton who was already in Tianshui alone. From the mission centre at Hankow on the Yangtze River they took three months to reach Hanzhong near the Gansu border, and decided to stay there for the severe winter ahead. They were fortunate to find a house to rent – the alternative would have been a local inn.

In the following weeks George King found himself preaching in the courtyard almost daily to crowds of men who gathered there; many of them wanted help in giving up the opium which had led their families to destitution. Other people came for medical help. Meanwhile Emily received the women in her home on her own. They crowded in to look at the first foreign woman they had ever seen, and stayed to listen to what she said. By the spring, around 100 people would gather in the courtyard for the Sunday services, and half of them were women. That was extraordinary in China, and the response was such that George and Emily settled in Hanzhong and did not move on further. When George was near breaking point from exhaustion, Easton rushed south from Tianshui to help, covering 150 miles in three days.

There was no other couple available to support them, so, in February 1880, two single women set off on the 1,000-mile journey across China to join them in Hanzhong, escorted by two Chinese Christians. Elizabeth Wilson of Kendal had arrived in China four years earlier, at the age of 46, when she was described as "well past middle life"! Although she worked hard at learning Chinese, she never achieved the facility in the language that the younger people did, but her grey hair won her the respect of the Chinese people. As a senior person in a young mission, she had a unique ministry of support and encouragement to the younger workers. Fortunately she proved able to cope with the long, exhausting journeys. She took a new recruit, Annie Faussett, with her, and they travelled mainly by boat. If they met hostility in some areas, the women could remain hidden inside. Mostly, there was enormous curiosity to catch a glimpse of the foreigners. One enterprising group of Chinese even cut the mooring ropes, hoping the women would appear when they found they were adrift!

Emily must have welcomed the companionship of the two ladies, especially as Annie was close to her own age. By the time Emily gave birth to her first child the following winter, she had seen 18 Chinese women baptised, and the church was growing fast. It was a heavy blow to all of them when she was struck down with typhoid in the spring of 1881 and failed to recover.

## To the west – Sichuan province

A month after the Kings left for Hanzhong, George Nicol and George Clarke married their brides in a double wedding. The women had both arrived in the previous year, and two months later, in November 1879, they all set off together on the long slow journey up the Yangtze River for Chongqing in the western province of Sichuan (Szechwan). George and Fanny Clarke were to move further on to Guiyang in Guizhou province. The Yangtze was more hazardous than the Han River, and the gorges, rapids and currents far more dangerous, quite apart from pirates and hostile crowds en route. From Hankow they continued upriver for 350 miles, then transferred to a Sichuan junk for the Yangtze rapids, and navigated a further stretch of river to Chongqing. They were shipwrecked twice in the icy waters of the Yangtze rapids in December, and spent Christmas Day out in the open on the river bank trying to dry out boxes of books and literature that had been soaked with water. Lives could easily have been lost, but they reached Chongqing safely after a journey of ten weeks.

For Mary Ann Nicol and her husband, this became home. The CIM house was in a narrow street in the heart of the large city; it had been obtained by the pioneer bachelors two years previously. The entrance led into a hall used for meetings, and beyond that a courtyard surrounded by a guest room and living rooms. As the New Year approached, the local women were busy with preparations, but even so, once they knew a foreign woman had arrived, curiosity prevailed. Around 200 women called each day, and after the New Year, the numbers grew to 500!

> For nearly two months past, I have daily seen some hundreds of women. Our house has been like a fair. Men have also come in large numbers to hear the Gospel. They are spoken to in the front of the house; the women, I see in the guest hall at the back, and in the courtyard before it... [O]ften indeed while seeing one company out at the front door, another has been found coming in at the back.[4]

Inside the room was full of the smoke from the women's pipes, and the lane outside was jammed with their sedan chairs and bearers. Mary Ann's language skills improved by leaps and bounds, but as the crowds continued month after month, and the summer heat increased, she became more and more exhausted. She would snatch moments during the day to write letters home in the midst of the crowds, or else she would write late at night. She was often called out to the opium suicide victims, sometimes two or three times in a night.

After Fanny Clarke moved on, Mary Ann did not see another European woman for two years, but the local women gave her their friendship and support. One elderly lady saw her plight in the summer heat and would take her back to her own home to rest and relax, and sit and fan her while she slept. Mary Ann had open access into the upper-class homes of the Mandarins, and women confined to their homes welcomed her and listened to the Bible stories she told them.

## To the south-west – Guizhou and Yunnan provinces

After a week's rest in Chongqing, George and Fanny Clarke set off on the next leg of their journey to Guiyang. The two couples had travelled together for five months, so parting could not have been easy. For the Clarkes it involved another 17 days of travel over the mountains in January to join two single men in Guiyang; the almost incessant winter rain made the trails slippery and dangerous, and Fanny was badly bruised when her mountain chair was dropped. She was the first Western woman ever to reach the province of Guizhou.

Within three months she was joined by Jane Kidd, who became the first single woman to go so far inland, and the recently widowed Ellen McCarthy, who had arrived in China only the previous year. Escorted by a male colleague, they travelled the more dangerous route overland through Hunan, which had been hostile to foreigners in the past. However, a Christian boatman took them up the Yuan River (where the boat was holed in the extensive rapids), and in most places they received a warm welcome. The journey took seven weeks on the boat, and a further nine days crossing a mountain range.

While the bachelors itinerated, the Clarkes started making friends in the town. George tried to start a boys' school, but only one boy turned up! The Clarkes planned to stay in Guiyang for a while until their baby son was old enough to travel, but he died at five weeks old, and after that there was nothing to detain them. With the arrival of Jane Kidd and Ellen McCarthy, they felt free to make a further six weeks' journey west into Yunnan, a province of 12 million people. The men had been unable to get permission to pass through it earlier. The nearest missionaries were now 500 miles away, and as the mail took five months from the coast, there was little news and no medical help.

Fanny Rossiter Clarke had grown up with her sister in a prosperous merchant home on the shore of Lac Léman in Switzerland, near Lausanne. Her parents were furious when she told them she wanted to go to China, and the whole family ridiculed her, but she stood firm. She visited the CIM in London and spent several months with Jennie Taylor before sailing in May 1878. At some point she met George Clarke, but then he was sent up to Shanxi to help with the famine relief, and they saw little of each other until the double wedding in September 1879. George Clarke and George King were two of "the eighteen" who went to China in 1875.

Their surroundings at Tali were incredibly beautiful, with snow-covered mountains rising 15,000 feet around the great lake. The town was quite a different matter. A house had been rented for them, but the other occupants refused to move out and they had to share it for six months. Further attempts to rent a house were blocked, and the whole atmosphere was one of rumour and suspicion. For the first year George and Fanny concentrated on printing Christian literature: Tali was a great examination centre and at certain times of the year hundreds of scholars would arrive eager for reading matter of all kinds. They produced 6,600 booklets under twelve titles.

Fanny was mobbed if she went out, so she received women at home. At first she could get no house help, although such a person was always invaluable as a source of information and contacts when settling into a new place. She felt as if she were up against a brick wall, and achieving nothing. What she learned of the town was depressing, and very different from the situations of Mary Ann Nicol and Emily King. In a letter to Jane Kidd she wrote:

This is a terrible place, Sodom and Gomorrah could not have been more wicked. Just as I write, the husband of my woman has come – a wretched opium smoker – and taken her little girl away. Last year he sold her two other children; this one is only three years old. We can do nothing to prevent it. God help them, he wishes to sell his wife as well. One of our neighbours went further and was going to kill his wife and child. My husband and three women held him. I never before witnessed such terrible scenes. Oh, what a land! Nothing but sorrow and sin.[5]

It was hard to bear the strain, loneliness and their helplessness in the face of such evil.

After six months, they were able to start a small school and employ a local teacher, but their house help spread lies about them and the teacher was interested only in his salary. They moved to the provincial capital at Kunming for twelve months while two bachelors did language study in Tali, but Kunming was harder, if anything. The women there were fearful and withdrawn, and would not go near Fanny or invite her to their homes. Finally the Clarkes returned to Tali, where Fanny gave birth to her second son, named Samuel. She never regained her strength and died some six weeks later, in the autumn of 1883.

As Fanny lay dying, she felt she had achieved very little, but she said, "Others will come after us." In the circumstances they were words born out of faith, and she was right. This was only the beginning. In his diary George recorded that he had bought a plot of land to bury her, and "scores" of women came to see her before she was buried, and heard the Christian message of forgiveness through Jesus, and life after death for those who trusted him.

> I had to conduct a short service at the graveside myself, and mostly to myself, because the coolies and other onlookers were so indifferent. Oh, it was a hard time, yet there is the blessed hope of a glorious resurrection, and meeting my beloved again.[6]

He walked home alone, carrying his six-week-old son. Five months later he baptised the first boy who had enrolled in the small boarding school he had started four years earlier. Three years after Fanny's death, George remarried; he went on to lead the CIM work in Shanxi province, and his daughter Agnes also spent her life in China.

## To the far north-west and beyond

There was one more newly married couple who moved inland. George Parker had arrived in China in 1876, and made several long journeys of exploration in the north-west. He then caused consternation by announcing his intention to marry a Christian Chinese girl from the Yangzhou Mission School (supervised by Louise Desgraz). The anxiety arose because of the obligations George must assume if he married into a Chinese family. There was also another concern. When her father sent her to the school and agreed that the mission could handle her future marriage, he was anxious lest she marry a foreigner and leave China. Hudson Taylor had actually given him his word that this would not happen. The mission members were divided – some for Taylor, others for the couple. Some feared that there could be repercussions for other schools too. In the event, her father (an opium smoker) was quite happy to receive some financial compensation for the expense of bringing up a daughter, and the couple were married in 1880. For Shiao Mian-zi (Minnie), who was probably still a teenager, marriage to a foreigner must have been a major undertaking, and she could not have known then how very far away they would travel. But she served faithfully with her husband in pioneer work, and outlived him to become one of the longest-serving and most highly respected members of the CIM. Her daughter also joined the mission later and had a long and significant ministry of her own.

In 1880, George and Shiao Mian-zi followed the Kings up the Yangtze and Han Rivers to Hanzhong, and there Elizabeth Wilson joined them for a further two weeks of travel by mule, covering the 150 miles across the hills into Gansu province. Elizabeth became the first Western woman to enter Gansu province. Tianshui was on the ancient Silk Road leading from Xi'an city across the deserts of Xinjiang and Central Asia to the west. Elizabeth and Shiao Mian-zi "took Tianshui by storm" and were warmly welcomed into their homes by the women. Soon there was "hardly a lane or a courtyard where they were not known or welcomed".[7]

Elizabeth returned to Tianshui early in 1882, taking the 23-year-old Hannah Jones with her, and they kept Minnie and her son company while George was away for five months in north-eastern Gansu and Ningxia. Minnie was almost as much a stranger in that area as the Westerners. She was over a thousand miles from her home and family, and showed tremendous courage and faithfulness in the work. When George returned, he promptly took Minnie and Hannah to meet the wives of the Mandarins and Tibetans on the Qinghai border to the east, leaving them at an inn while he went further inland to sell Bibles and distribute literature at some of the large Muslim and Tibetan centres. They covered 1,000 miles in 78 days. He was deluged with requests for Arabic and Persian Bibles which he did not have. In their absence, Elizabeth held the fort at Tianshui with one of the younger men. Everyone had to be prepared to buckle down and do whatever needed doing, whatever the opposition and difficulties they faced, but the women showed themselves equal to the task.

George and Minnie then moved on to Lanzhou, which later became a major mission centre with schools and a hospital. In 1887 George moved his family another 500 miles north up the Silk Road to Jiuquan, where Mildred Cable and her colleagues were later based. He left Minnie there on her own while he went on to Ürümqi, a further 800 miles away, to make a home for them. Minnie joined him with the family the following year; they were several weeks' journey from the nearest missionaries. While there, George covered the thousand miles west to Kashgar and also went north-east to the Barkul Lake and the Mongolians there. It was from there that they made their way across Russia to Britain. In 1890, Minnie addressed the CIM annual meetings in London – in excellent English.

In 1876, the first six young men had begun itinerating in the nine interior provinces. Five years later, in spite of hostility, sickness and many deaths, all those provinces had been explored, even if it had not been possible to settle in some. There were now three married couples, seven single men and four single women living and working in the interior, and for the most part they were welcomed. Latourette, the mission historian, pointed out that the safety of women inland was in fact a great tribute to the Chinese, as well as to the women themselves, who were courageous enough to do what they were not allowed to do in their own country; namely, live independently away from the protection of their families.

In the next two decades there would be a huge increase in the number of women recruits, until the married and single women together formed two thirds of the mission membership. Working with their Chinese sisters, they found themselves set free from a great many of the restrictions on their ministry that they would have faced in Britain. They demonstrated that, when such restrictions were removed, they were able to exercise remarkable gifts of teaching and evangelism, breaking down traditional Western boundaries of gender. People were astonished at what missionary women were able to do and to endure. It was because of these women's sacrificial willingness to live and work in remote places under the most primitive conditions that the women of China were able to hear and respond to the gospel.

### Notes to Chapter Three

1  Broomhall, vol. 6, p. 233.
2  Broomhall, vol. 5, p. 429.
3  Broomhall, vol. 6, p. 61.
4  Guinness, *Story*, vol. II, p. 326.
5  Ibid., p. 341.
6  Clarke, *Lausanne*.
7  Broomhall, vol. 6, p. 249.

# Chapter Four

# The Guangxin River Women

It was now possible for women to move inland in China, but they needed to work alongside married couples, and there were not a large number of these available. Taylor still needed many more missionaries.

## Moving forward – with Chinese co-workers

As the first young men were sent inland in 1876, the newly married Douthwaites were sent up the Qiantang River from Hangzhou to Qü Xian. Taylor urged them to visit the city initially for a few days at a time, so that people did not feel threatened by foreigners and they could win their confidence. He continued:

> I should be glad if eventually you were able to live there and take permanent oversight of the work... in process of time occupying all the *xian* (county) cities of the districts and *extending into Jiangxi province.*[1] This would be the work of years... Read the Word with much prayer with (your Chinese fellow-workers). Hold much communion with our Lord; then, fresh from His presence, minister *Him* to them... Tell them what you are finding there. You will not be kept *long* sowing *thus* before you are rejoicing over the firstfruits.

Douthwaite acted on this advice and there was real progress. The CIM had no formal Bible school at that time. Some of the Chinese evangelists had very limited education, and had not been Christians for very long, but were eager to share their faith. At a provincial conference of evangelists and church elders, Douthwaite suggested some simple guidelines to help them in their spiritual growth:

- They should write comments on their daily scripture readings, sending a copy to Douthwaite.
- They were to send him copies of their prepared sermons.
- They had to keep a monthly record of places visited, meetings held and books sold.[2]
- They should write a monthly essay on a given subject for Douthwaite's comment.[3]

It was a very early example of what is better known today as "theological education by extension"! They were learning to study the Bible for themselves, prepare their messages, be accountable for their time, and develop their thinking, not in the ivory tower of a college, but in the ups and downs of daily life and ministry. This approach laid the groundwork for the initial training of the first national workers, who then moved into new centres in the area. Within two years, Chinese evangelists from the emerging churches in Zhejiang province on the east coast had crossed the hills to the west into Jiangxi province and settled in three towns along the upper reaches of the Guangxin River. At the same time, others from the Poyang Lake area in the west moved into two centres at the lower end of the river.

## Jiangxi province

Jiangxi had once been a significant province in China, famous for the large and beautiful Poyang Lake. A network of rivers flowed into it from the southern mountains, and then on to the great Yangtze River. The Grand Canal then linked the Yangtze with Beijing in the north, so Jiangxi lay on a very significant trade route by boat from Guangzhou (Canton) in the south, to Beijing, the northern capital.

The province was prosperous, known for farming on the plains, mining silver and making porcelain china. The Guangxin River was an important short cut to the coast. Light goods could be taken upriver, carried across the hills and then taken downriver to Hangzhou and the coast. The rivers provided safe transport at a time when travel on land could expose foreigners to hostile crowds. Moreover, the Guangxin River was only some 200 miles (but seven days' journey) from the east coast – an escape route if civil unrest flared up and they had to evacuate.

When Hudson Taylor visited the Guangxin River four years later, in 1880, there were small groups of believers coming together, but they were all men. The wives stayed at home, hostile to this new religion and clinging to their familiar Chinese folk religion, a mixture of Buddhism, Taoism, Confucianism and ancestor worship. Church leaders asked for missionaries to help, but there were none to spare. Yet Taylor always had his eye on the future, and even then he wondered if the Guangxin River valley might be an inland area suitable for single women.

## Moving forward – with D. L. Moody's new Christians

After another four years in China, Taylor returned to London in 1883 to find that D. L. Moody's evangelistic campaigns had had a widespread influence.[4] Moody had spent six months in Scotland in 1882, and then held missions for Oxford and Cambridge students in the autumn. After initial mocking and ridicule from the students, his message finally got through and many young people responded. The following year he spent eight months in London, and hundreds more people, both rich and poor, responded to the Christian message. These home missions depended heavily on ordinary Christians for counselling and evangelism, rather than professional clergy. There was a growing concern among church members for evangelism in Britain, and this developed into a concern to spread the Christian gospel overseas as well. In

1884 applications for overseas service increased, from women as well as from men. The climax came when seven young Cambridge men sailed for China early in 1885: China had a high profile in the churches, and there was a surge of interest across Britain. Taylor was approached by the Quakers and the Bible Christians (Methodists), among others, who wanted to send out their own missionaries with the CIM.[5]

He returned to China in 1885 convinced that his prayers for reinforcements were about to be answered in a significant increase in recruitment. He was not mistaken. Over the four years from 1879 to 1882 the mission had received only fifteen single women, but in 1883 eleven had reached China in one year, and the following year this rose to 27. Taylor chose Yangzhou as the base for a women's training home where the newly arrived women could spend six months studying Chinese and adjusting to the culture. He put Mariamne Murray in charge and for the next 38 years, until she retired in 1922, she was friend and mentor to the hundreds of single CIM women who passed through her hands. Within a year of establishing the home, the CIM received 100 more recruits, half of whom were women. But how could such numbers be deployed? Where were the senior women missionaries who could help them adjust to living and working in China, after their first six months in the training home?

## The breakthrough on the Guangxin River

Katie Macintosh and Agnes Gibson were members of the 1884 group, and the following year, their initial language study completed, they were sent to work with a senior couple in Qü Xian near the Jiangxi border, where the Douthwaites had trained the first local men some years earlier. Katie was 25 and Agnes 21. They were kept busy over the winter with further language study, teaching in a small girls' school and visiting women in their homes.

By the spring, Agnes needed a break, so one of the

Chinese evangelists and his wife invited her to visit them some 25 miles away in the Changshan outstation. The small congregation there was entirely male. The arrival of the first Western woman to be seen in the town was a major event, and provided an excuse for the women to go out on the street to look. They turned up in crowds, curious yet fearful, but when Agnes, in Chinese dress, chatted with them in their own language, their fears were dispelled. Some even had the courage to turn up in church later. Agnes was so disarming that the church members raised money to repair some old mission buildings so that she could visit them again, bringing Katie with her. The two young women also travelled by boat along the Guangxin River, visiting towns where the evangelists were facing an uphill task.

In May 1886, when Hudson Taylor and Mariamne Murray travelled down the river, Katie escorted them. This time Taylor found women in the Guangxin churches as well as men. He also witnessed the first baptism in Guixi (Kweiki). In Yanshan (Hokeo), at least eight women had asked to be baptised, and the church leaders were now asking for missionary *women* to settle in the towns with the Chinese church couples.[6]

## A field for women

For 20 years Taylor had known that the service of single women was vital for the evangelisation of Chinese women, but the way forward had not been clear. They had been moving inland to join the married couples in the major centres, but with such small numbers in such a vast country they were widely scattered. Suddenly it looked simple: the women could fulfil a vital role in the growth of the churches by living and working alongside Chinese colleagues. Several of the 26 single women who had arrived in 1884 were ready to take on this responsibility. Their ages ranged from 20 to 26 years of age, and none had been in China more than two years, but they were gaining confidence in the language and adjusting to Chinese life. After travelling up and down the Guangxin River visiting the towns along the banks, Katie Macintosh and Jeanie Gray settled in Yüshan with Pastor Chang and his wife.[7] Within a year, 42 more people had been baptised and the Yüshan church had grown from 30 to 108.

In 1887, Agnes Gibson settled in Yanshan, "an unwalled town of the greatest commercial importance of any place along the Kuangsin (*sic*) river". She was 24, and she was to lead the team there until her death 20 years later.[8] Guixi was one day downstream from Yanshan. The Guangxin River made it easy for people to travel from one centre to another, to share in special occasions such as baptisms, gather for conferences and fellowship or just to spend a few days with friends.

As the teams grew, they worked in pairs alongside the Chinese evangelists and their wives, focusing their efforts on reaching women. The following year, Pastor Chang from Yüshan baptised six men and nine women in Guixi, four people in Ganren, and seven in Yanshan. The very first photograph (as distinct from pen-and-ink etchings) to appear in *China's Millions* was of Guixi (Kweiki) Christians and their children.[9] John McCarthy superintended the work from Yangzhou, 250 miles away. He was careful to explain in *China's Millions* that "from lack of workers, the stations and out-stations have had to be left with lady-workers only", but no one in China felt this needed an apology.[10] It was an exciting step forward, and a radical development as far as women's ministry in the churches went. Many years later Nellie Marchbank wrote:

> Quietly, very quietly, was the work begun. It was all new ground, but the confidence of the Chinese was gained, especially of the women, because things were gone about very gently and quietly. So the work grew.[11]

Florence Tapscott was 20 when she ventured to try to speak to some women with a noisy, clamouring, curious crowd outside the house.

I had given myself over entirely to the Lord, and told Him that I was trusting Him to help me speak so that I should be understood, and all at once I realised that there was absolute silence, and not a man spoke as I went on telling these dear women of the love of God. When I felt all eyes were on me, and knew the students were listening, I for the moment felt nervous, but the Lord strengthened me... He gave me such liberty in speaking and oh, such unspeakable joy in my own soul! I am quite sure the Lord gave me a message for someone there.[12]

Five years later, nine mission stations and a number of out-stations were strung along the banks of the river for 150 miles, all roughly one day's journey apart. In addition to the Chinese couples, there were now 16 single women, and five more at Nanchang on the Poyang Lake. The most senior had arrived in China in 1884, and five of these were 21 or younger, facing a first term of service of seven years. The team grew as new people reached China. Most of them arrived with only six months of language study, so for their first year they had to work hard on fluency.

## Nellie Marchbank

Nellie Marchbank arrived in Shanghai in December 1887. She could not have been more different from the "Cambridge seven" who had blazed a trail of media glory from England to China two years earlier. Her Scottish mother was a widow, and their resources were very limited, so Nellie had only three years' education before she left school and started work, probably at the age of eight or nine. She "continued to study a little" and read Christian biographies. She became a committed Christian at the age of eighteen. Later, the death of her mother left her alone in the world, but, as she made her way home after the funeral, she suddenly realised she was now completely free to serve God in China.

She applied to the China Inland Mission when she was 26. There were misgivings about her ability to learn Chinese, but her application papers were satisfactory and the reports of her referees were glowing. For whatever she lacked in formal education, she seemed to make up in character and natural (or God-given) ability, and she had shown particular gifts in relating to people. She was accepted and reached Shanghai in December of that same year. She spent only three months in the training home, perhaps because of the growing numbers of women arriving. Then she was sent to the Guangxin River where she spent the next 37 years, and left a record of these years in her diary.[13] In that period she rarely left the province, seldom went away on holiday, and only twice returned to Britain.

Her first two years were spent with Katie Macintosh in Yüshan. The navigable river ended there and the boats had to unload their goods for transport through the hills to the River Fuchuan. Katie had now been in China for four years and was the most senior woman in the area. Their report for 1889 explained that they had worked with two Bible women (Chinese evangelists) and they had visited 40 or 50 villages in the Yüshan area in the previous year: there had been thirteen baptisms.[14] It gives some idea of the systematic and time-consuming work done to reach the many women confined to their homes by custom and bound feet. Even missionary women could not travel alone, so the companionship of the Bible women allowed them to work separately, and in Nellie's case the Bible woman could talk to the women when Nellie's grasp of Chinese was still limited. It also meant that the two young European women could learn from their very much older Chinese sisters. These local women were usually elderly widows with little or no education, but they came to fill a very important double role, both in reaching local women, and in training the young missionaries in Chinese life and thinking. Two years later Nellie wrote:

> Nov. 24th. We have been a great deal among the people, I mean out living with them... I have been away all week visiting villages with one of the Bible women... I often think that when

someone like me can learn the language and is used in this land, it does bring glory to Jesus for I have nothing to recommend me, but just that I am saved, and that I love the Lord.[15]

In the spring of 1890 Nellie was asked to begin work in the small market town of Yangkou on a tributary of the Guangxin River. She took four others with her: Jessie Buchan, who had been in China less than a year; a Bible woman; a teacher; and an evangelist. The last two worked with the local men. The team goal was to share the Christian gospel with every person in and around the town, and in the first few weeks, Nellie visited a great number of houses, and also went into the country, leaving early in the morning and returning at night. The evangelist held daily meetings in their "chapel", and the market held every third day attracted crowds from the countryside to the town. "It is well worth leaving our nets behind to follow Him and do such work."

They were back in Yüshan in the August heat for a conference of the 17 women now working along the river, with their superintendent, John McCarthy, and Geraldine Guinness, who was visiting.[16] There was time for fellowship and prayer and rest, and Nellie reported that she returned to Yangkou refreshed in body and soul. She was now holding two weekly classes for women. In January 1891, Jessie Buchan reported on their first year there. The previous November Nellie had been moved to Guixi, so Jessie was now the only European woman until a new companion arrived. That was unusual for new workers, but sometimes unavoidable. She was still supported by the evangelist and his wife, three Christians, and two more preparing for baptism. "There are very few houses in the town which one or another of us has not visited... as this is only a small market town almost every inhabitant must have heard a little, and at least knows where to go to learn more." They had worked hard to visit every house in one year, and the two Christians were learning to read the romanised New Testament.[17]

Leaving Yangkou was a wrench for Nellie even though

she had been there for less than a year. She described the wet, dismal November morning when a small group of friends, new Christians, Jessie and the evangelist escorted her down to the boat. As they sent her off with gifts of chickens, oranges, dates, sweetmeats and potatoes, she was painfully aware of how few they were among so many who needed to hear the gospel.

Pastor Chang and Annie Say were on the quay to welcome Nellie to Guixi on 12 December 1890, and she found the women very friendly. It was now twelve years since the first Chinese workers had settled in Guixi; the women missionaries had begun visiting in 1886 when the first person was baptised. They continued to follow Hudson Taylor's strategy, beginning in the major towns and working out from these to smaller towns and villages. From the outset the new Christians were encouraged to share in witness and evangelism and take responsibility for reaching family, friends and neighbours: Guixi became an excellent example of this in practice.

When Nellie arrived, Evangelist Chang was acting as pastor, there was a literature worker, two Bible women and some 50 believers. That year they had agreed on a monthly rota whereby a different man and woman would be responsible each month for visiting and encouraging absentees. Nine men had volunteered for open-air work, and all accepted the responsibility for inviting people to services. They agreed to set aside the whole of Sunday for prayer and worship, although this could be costly for many in terms of lost wages or sales. They also accepted their responsibility to support the work financially as far as they could. Where a couple were Christians, they undertook to hold family prayers, and agreed not to bind their daughters' feet. (For caring parents, this was a step of faith: large feet limited a girl's marriage prospects, and could condemn their daughters to heavy work when they married.) The Guixi church members were actively involved from the beginning.

Chinese New Year was always a testing time for

Christians living in non-Christian families, and Annie and Nellie endeavoured to visit them before the New Year arrived. Meanwhile they spent some "pleasant, quiet evenings together talking and knitting. We are preparing little socks [for bound feet?] and things for New Year's presents." Jeanie Munro had joined an evangelist and a Bible woman in a rented house in Shangtsing, 25 miles away.

When Annie Say left some months later, Nellie Marchbank became senior missionary for the district. Only three years earlier she had been in domestic service in Scotland. It was a heavy responsibility and she commented many years later:

> I was then left alone, but was very happy, because there were some 50 Christians gathered in by this time; and our hearts were drawn very closely together. They helped me much and comforted me, and I think I was a help to them. Some of these early Christians are still with us and have been my fast friends all these years.[18]

She carried ever-increasing responsibilities for the next 35 years, apart from two furloughs. She was totally committed to the task of evangelism and church-planting in Guixi and the surrounding area, and committed to doing this alongside the local believers. She was probably less prepared for the imminent increase in missionary recruits.

## The decade for women

In 1888, Taylor had returned to China via North America, hoping to encourage Christians there to form their own mission to China. Instead, he sailed from Vancouver with a party of eight single women and six single men: against all the advice and wishes of the London Council, a North American branch of the CIM had been born.[19] Two years later he visited Australia by invitation and the same thing happened there. The first Australian party of thirteen included seven women, and reached Hong Kong in December 1890. There were already many more set to follow. It was well that Taylor had anticipated this to some extent by establishing a more adequate headquarters building in Shanghai, and extending the women's training home.

The third General Missionary Conference in Shanghai in 1890 had ended with an appeal from Hudson Taylor for prayer for 1,000 new missionaries in the next five years.[20] It would mean a massive increase for all the societies, but inland China was now open to foreigners and the need was great. The results of this prayer were remarkable.

In the 1880s, Taylor's writings and speaking had stirred churches in Scandinavia and Germany to think about mission overseas, and Taylor himself was always open to co-operating with others. As a result, some Scandinavian and German missions had become CIM associates. As separate branches, they were independent (in contrast with North America and Australia), yet shared the facilities and benefits of full members.

The Scandinavian missions were sparked off by a young Swedish pastor and evangelist, Frederik Franson. He had studied Moody's revivals and was a gifted evangelist himself. He was eager to see Taylor's prayer for 1,000 missionaries fulfilled. After conducting missions in Sweden, he returned to the Swedish immigrant churches in the USA and ran classes in evangelism. It was not long before the CIM were informed that 35 missionaries had boarded a boat for China, and when they arrived, they reported that fifteen more were ten days behind them. In 1890, nine more parties arrived from Europe, Canada and Australia. The training homes were already full and the CIM headquarters in China was overwhelmed. Taylor himself was administering the CIM alone, since one director was ill and the other had returned to the UK. Franson was blissfully unaware of the crisis he had caused.

The resourceful mission-home hostess in Shanghai turned her guest house into a language school for 50 recruits, and established a routine of lessons. After a few weeks of basic teaching, they were farmed out to mission stations to continue their language study. In time it was sorted out: a language school was established for Scandinavian women at Takutang on the Poyang Lake, and geographical areas for evangelism and church-planting were allotted to the different groups. There was plenty for everyone to do but it required planning and organisation.

That is why, in 1892, Nellie suddenly found herself leading a team of *six* missionaries instead of two! The new parties of women from North America, Australia and Scandinavia were arriving, one after the other, and hastily scattered for language study: some arrived just as the work on the Guangxin River expanded. The first eight North American women all started on the Guangxin River. Nellie's junior worker had arrived in China two years earlier, and two Australians and two Scandinavians the previous year. The last four were majoring on language study, but someone had to organise the housekeeping, find language teachers and later give the new arrivals opportunities to practise their Chinese on village visits. Most of the river stations became very busy.

## Florence Young

Florence Young from Australia reached China in 1891 and left a vivid account of life in Guixi in this period. At 35 she was considered "old" in those teams: she came from a well-known, wealthy Australian family from Bundaberg in Queensland. She had been concerned for the Kanakas (Solomon Islanders) working as migrant labourers growing sugar-cane on her brother's estate; wanting to encourage others to take up the challenge to share the gospel with these people while they were temporarily in Australia, she founded the Queensland Kanaka Mission.[21] When she heard Hudson Taylor speak about China on his first visit to Australia, she knew she had to respond to that call.

Her initial period of language study was interrupted for

five weeks when she was asked to care for a sick colleague, and by the time she was free the training home had filled up with a new group, so she had to join an overflow group 35 miles up the canal for a further fifteen weeks. Finally, in March 1891, a year after leaving Australia, she travelled up the Yangtze River by boat to Jiujiang. The missionary there organised the travel, stores and business for the area, and arranged for them to travel across the Poyang Lake to the Guangxin River with seven Swedish girls from the new Scandinavian training home. The journey required endless patience. The boat was becalmed for twelve days, then it hit a sandbank, and then it was nearly wrecked in a storm. When the boatmen refused to go further, the missionaries had to change ships with their 100 boxes of luggage and stores. Finally they turned up the Guangxin River and another six days brought Florence to Guixi. She later described the work as:

> carried on by single ladies, assisted by Chinese pastors and evangelists... It gives the Chinese workers fuller scope and responsibility; and yet provides the oversight, teaching and direction which is so necessary... Vigorous native churches were formed; schools opened for boys and for girls... and in the country districts many out-stations were opened.[22]

It will be evident that the relationship between missionary and national was delicate, but they worked in separate spheres with women and men, and with Christian grace and mutual respect, they all made it work.

A large meeting was held on her first Sunday in Guixi, and without warning Nellie Marchbank asked Florence to give her testimony. Nellie may not have realised that because of interruptions she had managed only five months of language study. Bravely, Florence launched out and did her best, but the Chinese were reduced to fits of laughter, which did nothing to boost her confidence. People in Asia are usually extremely polite, and laughter can mean different things in different cultures: it may be used to reduce embarrassment and tension – a gesture of sympathy; sometimes it is unavoidable when the wrong tone for a word produces an entirely different meaning from the one intended, with ludicrous results. Florence may not have appreciated any of this.

Her ordeal had not yet ended, for Nellie later asked her (in Chinese) to pray. Florence fervently hoped she had misunderstood the request! Praying in Chinese was complicated. For one thing, using pronouns such as "you" when addressing God was irreverent; you couldn't just translate from English. But the Bible woman kneeling alongside nudged her and murmured in Chinese, "she has asked you to pray". There was no escape. Once more Florence launched out and once more she reduced the Chinese to smothered amusement. That evening another Bible woman came to comfort her and offered to help. Every night she hobbled up to Florence's room on her bound feet to pray with her, and before long Florence found praying in Chinese easier than talking, and invaluable in sharing with the Chinese in their daily lives.[23]

By April she was weary with sitting indoors studying:

> I have not been out for eight days and am going with Miss Marchbank at 6 a.m. tomorrow for a walk. It is too hot later, and unhealthy in the evening, but I am sure we need to get out more. We get no fresh air, and are so shut in that it is depressing. Only it is not always easy to go out. Sometimes it is raining, and other days we can't get a companion, and sometimes we are too tired etc.... The temperature has been 95° by day and 92° by night... and not a breath of wind.[24]

In August the superintendent visited. He had walked the 180 miles from Jiujiang, but judging from Florence's earlier experience that may well have been faster than the boat! He spent time giving the team some Bible teaching – with limited Chinese they were glad of the opportunity to work in their own language. He suggested that Florence should begin making a weekly visit to the country with a local Christian woman as companion. The local dialect was different from Mandarin, and she needed the experience. She described one of these visits with her friend Mrs Hong. They travelled by local "barrow" (like a wheelbarrow) eight miles to a village where they spent the next ten days. The houses were like "mud-built stables" but the welcome from their hostess was warm. They shared the family meal of rice, stewed melon and vegetables, while the chickens picked up the bits under their feet. The floor was of earth, the walls of mud and the tiled roof black with smoke. There was a narrow passage with a pigsty on one side and the kitchen on the other. Their bedroom was next to the kitchen; the rubbish was cleared out and clean straw put on the large wooden bedstead.[25]

Writing soon afterwards to a friend who had applied to go to China, Florence wrote of the cost as well as the privilege of serving overseas. Too often missionary talks emphasised the romantic aspects rather than the negative ones, and she wanted to prepare her friend for both:

> The first six months in the mission field is often a time of great trial. The devil tempts in unexpected ways, and perhaps for those who are not very young there are special trials. Does this seem a sad view of missionary life? I do not mean it as such, but I think you often hear only the bright side, and there is a very bright side, and all the cost has a still brighter side. *It is for Him.*[26]

Three months later the superintendent reappeared. The main mission stations were always intended as centres for reaching out to smaller towns. Shangtsing was 25 miles away, a long day's journey, but it was significant as the main centre in China for Taoism. Over the previous two years a number of workers, both Chinese and missionary, had lived there; all had been evacuated with severe malaria. Of the three new Australians, who would be asked to go? Florence's heart sank. With so many cities in China unoccupied, was it worth losing one's health for this one?

That evening they had a communion service together in English – "a rare privilege": evidently this depended on the presence of an English-speaking man! (Ordination was not the issue, as few of the missionaries were ordained.) During the service Florence was reminded of the ear of wheat falling into the ground and dying, in order to bring forth fruit. Jesus' words also came back to her: "He that loveth his life shall lose it... if any man serve me, let him follow me; and where I am, there shall also my servant be" (John 12:25–26, AV). In 1892 she had no problems with the language of the Authorised Version of the Bible: "he" and "man" included "she" and "woman". She commented: "Every word meant – Shangtsing – to me, and all doubt and hesitation departed." When the superintendent mentioned Shangtsing to her afterwards, she replied that the Lord had been saying it to her all evening, and she gladly agreed to go. Of the other two Australians, Edna Bavin was not robust enough to go with her and Katie Fleming was needed in Guixi.

## Shangtsing

Florence travelled in January, three weeks before the snow came:

> Miss Marchbank escorted me to my new home. Shangtsing is a long day's journey by wheelbarrow from Guixi. In spring time and summer a lovely journey. The path leads over hills ablaze with red azaleas. Honeysuckle and wild roses scent the air; and ferns and mosses luxuriate in cool nooks beside streams hurrying over their stony beds to empty themselves into a clear and sparkling river. A certain high hill forms the dividing ridge, and for the last ten *li* (three miles) the track descends a valley terraced and irrigated for rice fields, which gradually widens out to the city of Shang-ts'ing on the banks of a river. There are hundreds of temples... Our mission premises were outside the city. The household consisted of a young evangelist and his wife; a dear little Bible woman, over 70 years of age, frail and nearly blind from past tears, but loving and faithful to the core; an equally faithful woman servant; and her son as barrow-man.[27]

The evangelist held a daily service to which people dropped in. Florence's priority was still language study, but the household met in her room each evening to study the book of Joshua together. When the snow came three weeks later, she kept warm wrapped in a rug with a foot-stool filled with red-hot cinders covered with ash. There was no English speaker within a 25-mile radius, which was good for her Chinese. Every week or ten days a messenger arrived from Guixi with the mail and bread.

That summer the day came when Tong-li, the barrow-man, went to Guixi and found that the superintendent had arrived to supervise Florence's second language exam. Tong-li insisted on returning immediately to bring her back himself. (There were no telephones!) Nellie Marchbank remonstrated – he had already walked 25 miles that day – but he was adamant. He would not allow anyone else to transport Florence. Sitting in an unsprung barrow for 25 miles over rocks and stones could be torture if the barrow-man was not careful, and he wanted to take her himself. He went straight back to Shangtsing that night, accompanied by a second man Nellie sent, arriving in pouring rain at 4 a.m. Florence also objected, for he had now covered 50 miles, and she tried to hire a substitute barrow-man, but no one would go in such bad weather. Tong-li's mother finally assured her that he was young and strong and *wanted* to do it, so he did. He wheeled her back to Guixi in the barrow (75 miles in 36 hours!) and the other man towed. They were all soaked and took an hour to get across the swollen Guangxin River, but they made it. The story speaks volumes about the devotion and faithfulness of the Chinese Christians. Nellie once got exasperated with a barrow-man who was unable to memorise Bible verses. He replied he didn't have time to do things like that because he spent all his time thinking about how to get her to places!

During her five months in Shangtsing, Florence commented in letters home to friends that she had expected sickness and trial but she had never anticipated such isolation. Yet later she looked back on her time in that simple household as the happiest of her life. In spite of her initial fears, she was never ill for a single day in that period. A family tradition says that one of "the Cambridge seven" proposed to her, but she turned him down. Some years later she reluctantly returned to Australia (with Hudson Taylor's blessing): the Kanaka Mission was crumbling, because Australia's "all-white" immigration policy had forced the Solomon Islanders to go home. Florence founded the Solomon Islands Mission (subsequently the South Sea Evangelical Mission) and worked with the Kanakas in the Solomon Islands for the rest of her life.[28] The foundation for all her future work had been laid down on the Guangxin River.

Nellie herself set the pace for the team. She was indefatigable, and her colleagues later recalled how they had gone out visiting daily, rain or shine. Missionaries were expected to keep diaries for the superintendent, reporting what they had done each day (this was common in Victorian times and accountability was useful for people who enjoyed the freedom to arrange their own timetables). Nellie had stated on arrival in Guixi that she wanted every person in the area to hear what Jesus had done for them. The Guixi church members threw themselves into evangelism. They understood the emptiness of Chinese religion, the endless search for merit through monthly fasting, the visits to temples, the fortune-telling and superstition, and the fear that had dominated their lives as they tried to placate the forces of evil and searched in vain for security.[29] In the Christian faith they had found a God who loved and cared for them individually, and set them free from the terrible burden of trying to earn merit for the future. They found that the living God offered for-giveness of sin as a gift to those who would take it, because his Son Jesus had laid down his life for them. Now they were learning to walk in this new way – and sometimes failing – but those who had found the answer to their search longed to make the message known in their family villages.

## Liukia – a local initiative

Meeting places in the villages were always difficult to find because the houses were small. However, sometimes families moved to the town but still owned a village house, and were able to loan premises where an evangelist and his family could live and witness.[30]

The village of Liukia, ten miles from Guixi, became an outstanding example of this. Mr and Mrs Liu, an elderly couple, lost their only son when he was 22, and the son's one regret had been that he could not give his life to evangelism. His parents were challenged to make the best use of their remaining years, and they decided to retire to Liukia, their family village, to live there as Jesus' witnesses. It was a small place with about 30 families. The Guixi church contributed towards turning the house into a preaching hall, with "Jesus Hall" written over the door. In the event, the Lius were needed by the church in Guixi, so they undertook to support an evangelist, Mr Li, and the missionaries supported his wife. Their work bore fruit, and after six months a number of people had given up their idols and came to worship each Sunday. Two of Nellie's language students, Katie Fleming and Edna Bavin, went to spend two weeks in Liukia. News travelled fast when the two foreign women arrived, and the whole village downed tools to have a look, and give them a welcome. Then the men went back to work and the women stayed to chat – Katie and Edna were able to put their elementary Chinese to good use and experience village work under the guidance of the Chinese couple.

During the week the two girls visited women in the smaller villages around – work which could only be done by women. Katie later reported, "There are about 40 people who regularly attend the Sunday services, most of them are just like children, knowing nothing beyond the barest facts of there being a true God, whose Son Jesus Christ, died for their sins."[31] When the CIM superintendent visited a few months later, he examined 29 people and, of these, fourteen were baptised. They included four couples, the oldest couple being 80 and 75 years of age, with thirteen other members of their family interested. Another 22 were baptised in the outstations of Fukia and Kikia.[32]

This picture is typical of the work on the Guangxin River, and the way the local Christians were taking responsibility for outreach at an early stage of the work. It also reveals how missionaries and nationals worked together in teams as brothers and sisters. If missionary men had been around, oriental culture decreed that the nationals would have deferred to them. The missionary women, however, provided someone with experience and wisdom who could be consulted, but still allowed the local leaders to take responsibility in the churches. The women's sphere was primarily among women, though when need arose they also taught men. The men often pleaded to be allowed to attend the women's meetings, and this sometimes happened in the evenings, but it was important that the women should have their own sessions. Their lack of education and restricted lives required a very simple approach. Some 50 years later, Bishop Frank Houghton commented that only women missionaries had the patience needed to reach out to them and help them to understand the Christian message.

Outstations were slowly established around Guixi with Chinese evangelists and their families in charge. The women missionaries could be sent to help new groups for a week or two, or live there for a while. Ideally they went in pairs but, as the work expanded, some went alone to join their Chinese colleagues.

Guixi became one of the busiest stations on the river. It had an unusually high number of elderly people, particularly women, and in consequence conducted far more funerals than the other centres. Nellie recorded each one in the back of the diary that she kept for the 35 years she spent there. The women also outnumbered the men in church – something unusual in China: usually men predominated in the CIM churches, because the women were housebound and more difficult to contact.

When the annual statistics were collected, Guixi usually

had more baptisms than the other stations in the area, too. The superintendent or Chinese pastor would interview each person to decide whether or not they were ready for baptism, and this was no mere formality: the missionaries sometimes commented on the difficulty of the questions posed (though no doubt they varied according to the ability of the person concerned). Baptisms were often deferred so that candidates could receive more instruction. In areas where education was minimal and illiteracy widespread, it says much for the teaching that the churches grew as they did.

In 1895 Nellie had been in China for seven years. Most missionaries were ready for home leave after their first seven-year term, but Nellie stayed on for another five years. This was not because she had nowhere to go – she had many friends in Britain – but Guixi was now her home. Her life was not easy: she would get tired and stressed in the hot, oppressive summers; she felt the weight of her growing responsibilities; and her companions, mostly much younger than herself, were constantly moving out of Guixi to live in the villages. She could only confide to her diary:

> Am so tired – Oh for someone to understand, someone to lean on just for a little while to feel real human sympathy. But there is more need to sympathise than to get sympathy. Oh Master, at such a time Thou art the One I need. [33]

As the churches grew there was an increasing need for church workers; they had to train their own. There was still no public education system – although by 1895, there were some Chinese who believed that the country should modernise and introduce public education and democracy as soon as possible. However, opposition from the imperial family was so great that heads would roll – literally – before the necessary reforms could be introduced. Meanwhile, if the churches needed leaders, both male and female, who could read the Bible for themselves and be able to teach others, they had to start with the education of their own children.

In the autumn of 1896 a day school was opened in Guixi with six boys. The following year it was enlarged to take 30 boys, and a small house was rented for a girls' boarding school. On the whole the Chinese did not waste money educating daughters, who would marry and bring no financial return to their families, but Chinese Christians began to take a longer view. The missionary women were significant role models, demonstrating that women had options beyond their courtyards, and were capable of more than most Chinese women had ever imagined. There were soon 30 girls setting out to prove that it was possible to educate girls! Fanny McCulloch had been in China for four years, and she was able to supervise the school and the local teachers.

The two schools did not cater for all the needs of the growing church in 1897. Life in China was precarious, and even those who had once been prosperous could be brought to poverty through sickness, death of the wage-earner, war, robbery, injustice – the list was endless. In her work among elderly Christian women, Nellie met many who were very poor and had no family to support and care for them. True to character, she did not act alone.

> We gathered [the Christians] together and studied the Word about it, and saw what God said about caring for the poor, and our people were very much interested.

As a result, a small home was built for six poor, elderly women (the oldest was 93), where they could live out their days in peace and security. There were plans to extend the home the following year: the Christians increased their giving from monthly to weekly to help finance the venture, and it was a testimony of loving care to the whole town.[34]

In June 1899 Henrietta Soltau, who was in charge of the CIM women's training home in London, visited China for the first time. She travelled across the famous Poyang Lake to visit the Guangxin River stations, and left a description of a Sunday in Guixi typical of most of China. The day began as the country people came in on foot or in carts or by boat at 7 a.m., and the courtyard filled up with fathers, mothers and children chatting, reading aloud (to the illiterate?) and memorising verses, for the first hour.[35] Then the men, women, boys and girls met in separate classes where they brought their gifts – eggs, vegetables, money, whatever they had. At 11 a.m. everyone assembled in the large, newly built chapel (more building!) where the pastor took the morning service. The men and women sat on separate sides and Henrietta counted about 70 men. The children were perfectly quiet for the two-hour service (a remarkable thing when so few had the discipline of schooling). People provided their own lunches and could cook their rice outside.

The afternoon was spent in further instruction until 5 p.m. when the country people started homewards. An evening meal was followed by the evening praise service, attended by men from the town, which finished at 9 p.m. Both Christians and non-Christians were eager to learn. In June the CIM superintendent examined and baptised 76 people from Guixi, and 35 from Ihyang. In Yanshan a crowd of three or four hundred people watched quietly from the river bank as 44 more were baptised. Remarkable things were happening along the river. [36]

In September 1899 political trouble flared up in Guixi when the Roman Catholic church and other buildings were burned down. The Roman Catholics were unpopular for various reasons, and British and American men could also provoke hostility because of the way their governments had treated China in the past. By contrast, the missionary women were highly respected by the authorities as well as the people. Nevertheless the anti-Christian feeling made it an anxious time for Chinese Christians, and Nellie and a colleague visited friends in the town and the villages to encourage them to trust God and stand firm against opposition.

Meanwhile, a hostile force of some 50 men from Ihyang attacked the Roman Catholics in Yanshan, 50 miles from Guixi. The Mandarins were unable to prevent them burning the Roman Catholic church, and when they invaded the CIM mission premises there and began looting, the officials personally escorted Agnes Gibson and her two colleagues to the safety of the *yamen* (city office). They and the local people were very apologetic, and publicly took the women home later, and organised the repair of the buildings. It was not long before a quantity of the stolen goods was returned. Agnes Gibson commented that the officials "could not have done more for us. We will ever remember their kindness. No foreign gentleman could possibly have acted more wisely, or befriended us any more."

The most fearful time for the women at Guixi was when Dr Judd and his wife proposed coming upriver to help them – they really feared the consequences of a white man appearing on the scene. As it was, the officials felt responsible for protecting the women and there was a lot of goodwill. Nellie wrote:

> We have to go very carefully for a little while, and I did not want any foreign *men*, as they are not in favour with the people just now. Our peace and our safety lies (under God) in the fact that we are women. I sent a letter to be given to Dr Judd... asking him not to come up. But God was working for us, and next evening we just looked at each other when a letter reached us from Ganren (Pehkan), saying that the Judds had returned; their boat was too large, and the water too low for them to come on. That is what they thought, but we knew it was the Lord. Praise God, the Christians and the Jesus doctrine have a good name everywhere. It is not because we are bad, people want to get rid of us. On one side it is because we are foreigners, and the other because they want our things.[37]

For the moment calm was restored, but the storm clouds were gathering.

The following spring, Nellie Marchbank left for Britain after twelve and a half years in China, ten of which had been spent in Guixi. She had seen great things happening: it was just fourteen years since the first baptisms had taken place in Guixi. The statistics for 1899 recorded eight women missionaries working in the district, two pastors, four Bible women, five local schoolteachers and three schools. There were now eight other churches established in the villages around Guixi, 233 church members (76 men and 157 women) and 76 new people had been baptised. This made the work the most extensive one on the river, and indeed in the whole province. Only one other station had two churches, and Yanshan came next in the number of baptisms with 44. Yüshan and Guixi each had boarding schools for 30 girls.

## The second decade

While Nellie was away, China was in turmoil. An imperial edict went out from the Empress Dowager ordering the deaths of all foreigners, and the rebel "Boxers" were ready to put it into force. They swept across northern China intent on destroying everything foreign, including the Chinese Christians. The full force of the Boxer Rebellion affected the northern provinces, but it provided other dissident groups with the opportunity to fight their own private wars while the official forces of law and order were preoccupied elsewhere. Katie Macintosh Lachlan had married some years earlier, and then been widowed. She was back with her two daughters in Yüshan where she had pioneered the work at the beginning, this time with a team of seven single women. In July 1900 the Yüshan team heard rumours that the Roman Catholic priest had left in haste, and that the Jesus Hall would be burnt. Christians were warned to stay away but they refused to be intimidated, and the eight women knew their flight would destabilise the city further.

The people had expected them to flee but, instead, they carried on as normal. It was said that one Mandarin had hidden the imperial edict to kill them. Soldiers who were sent to help the town in the event of an attack came to the mission and were glad to be given books and medicine; some of them even came to services. Rumours continued to circulate that an army was advancing against Yüshan. A sudden uprising in the province to the east cut off their escape route to the coast, and Yüshan was trapped.[38] The city gates were shut to keep out any spies, and people were terrified. Few bothered turning to the temples for help, but they knew that the Christians were praying.

The threatened attack did not come, and more people left the city in panic, many of them urging Katie and her team to do the same. The missionaries stayed on: the local Mandarin assured them of protection in the city, as long as it was not occupied, and in any case many more people were willing to listen to the Christian message in this time of danger. A few days later they heard that eight CIM missionaries and three children over the provincial border had been murdered. Even so, Katie waited two more weeks until the situation was somewhat calmer. Then she took her small daughters and one of the ladies and slipped downriver early one morning. The loyal boatmen never revealed their presence to a soul. When they reached Yanshan in safety, they sent for the other women from Yüshan. It would be eight months before they could return.

Meanwhile Nellie was on leave in Britain, and finding it hard to adjust to the change of culture. She travelled to meeting after meeting, saw old friends, made new friends, and, as usual, worked herself to the point of exhaustion. The CIM Home Director kept her in Britain for another year to rest. By this time the Boxer Rebellion was raging, and the daily atrocities against Christians, both Chinese and missionary, were too awful to comprehend. Nellie wrote in her diary, "The thought of going back is not easy these days. What if I should be called to suffer so? Am I ready?"[39]

Her diary says that she spent some time at home with her "mother", though she lost her father in childhood, and her mother before she sailed for China. Did she have a stepfather who remarried, or an adoptive mother? It is not clear, but when she left them to return to China, her heart was heavy because "they know I have the best, but they grudge to give up the world". Those at home were not fully in tune with her. She sailed from London in September, and visited old friends in Yangzhou before reaching Guixi in December 1901. Once back, she rarely left the province.

After the Boxer Rebellion, the other missionaries went back quietly to Guixi in 1901, not knowing what to expect, but Nellie believed the Lord had given her a promise for the future in the verse "I...will do more good to you than ever before" (Ezekiel 36:11), and so it was. Throughout China increasing numbers of people were turning away from the old religions, which failed to address the issues of a new century, and beginning to attend meetings in the small churches. Guixi was no exception. Soon, every meeting was crowded out and the old buildings were inadequate. No one was rich, but the Christians had learned to pray for what they needed and to give what they could. They prayed for land to build on, and then prayed for money to put up a building. The new chapel cost £230 and the Christians gave £120, a lot of money for them at the time.

The new chapel, opened in 1905, seated 600 people. There were 344 believers in the district and many enquirers, and the country folk from the eleven worship centres over a wide area travelled into Guixi on Sundays when they could. On the day the church was opened the collection was so heavy they had to hire a coolie to carry it away in a barrow! The process of building was exhausting for those in charge; materials and methods had to be checked at every stage and there were endless problems. Nellie did not want the distraction of supervising the building, and she had no experience in that area. Her priority was evangelism, but the church leaders could not manage without somewhere to meet and to live. No sooner had they provided for Guixi than the outstations outgrew their buildings and the process started all over again.

The following year the boys' school was built, and a more adequate home and base for the women missionaries: all the new buildings were Chinese in style. Nellie was overstretched and needed a rest from building, but the need for a new girls' school was urgent. National schools for girls in China were only just beginning to open in the largest cities, and the Guixi Christian boarding school for 30 girls was the only one in the region. They lived and taught in an old, crowded house by the river, vulnerable to flooding in the autumn and too small: many girls from Christian families were being turned away. They had prayed for a plot of land adjacent to the boys' school, so more building began.

In 1909 the new school opened with room for 50 girls. Five years earlier Mary Blacklaws had written, "While we seek to train the girls and want them to become useful women, our chief aim, of course, is that they should know and serve the Lord Jesus, and in the future be helpers in His work."[40] There was increasing pressure in China, even from Chinese Christians, for prestigious Western education including science and English. Some missionaries believed that education in Western culture was the first step towards embracing the Christian faith, but most CIM missionaries firmly resisted this, identifying themselves as far as possible with Chinese life. They were in China primarily to share the good news of Jesus, and they were intent on educating the children about their own culture in their home areas. The girls learned to read and write, to make basic Chinese clothes for their families, and to do Chinese embroidery as a means of supplementing the family income.[41] They also learned the basic tenets of health and nutrition. The churches needed educated, literate women as wives, mothers, schoolteachers and Bible women, but they did not need English speakers.

The girls in the school were aged from nine to 17. Things had changed since the 1840s, when the girls left school to be enclosed at home until they married. In the summer of 1903 Mary Blacklaws had travelled 100 miles round the area, visiting the girls in their homes and interviewing new pupils for the autumn. Some schools elsewhere in China accepted a small proportion of girls from homes that were not Christian, but the Guixi schools could barely cope with all the children from Christian families.

Alongside growth and development, there was also tragedy: the close-knit team of women working on the Guangxin River suffered illness and many deaths. Susie Parker, one of the earliest Americans, had died soon after reaching Guixi in 1888. Lucy Smith died from typhoid in 1902, just after Nellie returned from her first furlough. Agnes Gibson, whose success at 22 years of age had led to the opening of the whole Guangxin field for women, died in 1908 at the age of 44 after surgery in Canada. She had served on the Guangxin River for over 20 years; Nellie pressed some geranium leaves from Yanshan in memory of her, and they are still in her diary. Katie Fleming, one of the early Australians, petite and full of natural vivacity and humour, died of cholera in 1908. In 1912, a new worker died from dysentery only four weeks after reaching Guixi. The toll was similar at other stations; today, rehydration would probably have saved many of them, but medical knowledge at the time was limited, and their resources were few.

As the work grew, the women moved to the outstations on their own to work with the church staff. Mary Baxter found herself without even that local support. There was no one but her to be "pastor, elder, deacon, preacher, teacher, visitor, settler of family disputes". She was leading all the meetings and asked for prayer that the believers would have the courage to help her. The obvious solution was to appoint people to these functions, but that was not always easy. If they were young in the faith, or frail and elderly, or illiterate and unable to read the Bible for themselves, they could not be pushed too fast. In addition, she was helping at two other outstations west and south-west of Guixi. Jeanie Anderson was responsible for three stations to the south, and Louisa Seymour for four stations to the north. In Guixi, while the pastor cared for the church work, Annie Sharp supervised the new schools, and Nellie and Agnes Leith did everything else.

# The third decade

From 1910 to 1920 the work continued to expand, though the Great War also had an impact: new recruits were few, and furloughs difficult to arrange. Nellie went home for her second furlough in 26 years, but illness overtook her and she needed surgery which left her very weak. She was at home for nearly two years, and returned to a rapturous Chinese welcome, which Annie Sharp described. The "Pleased to welcome" committee of young and old had planned it for weeks beforehand, and everyone from town and country contributed money for the expenses. The women spent hours cutting out Chinese characters and sewing them onto banners. The country people began moving into town, some arriving five days early, and the church looked after them all. News of Nellie's progress overland travelled ahead, and they sent two men 80 miles down the Guangxin River to meet her – one to cook and the other to look after her. On the great day several hundred people gathered in the church and processed to meet her off the boat:

> Can you picture it? Leading the way, the Union Jack and the Chinese flag, next to them the city band, playing its very best music, followed by a large, red, satin banner, with "The Goodness of God is past finding out." Then the banner of the boys' school, and right behind it all the schoolboys. Following them, the Church banner, with all the men Christians following it, more Chinese scrolls and banners followed by the Chinese gentry, teachers etc. Next the girls' school banner, followed by the schoolgirls, the young women and older women. And in the rear, the beautiful Chinese tablet which was to be presented to Miss Marchbank, about two feet broad by four feet long, with the four large Chinese characters in gold, "Denying Self, Loving Others"... Right at the very rear came the "state chair" which was to carry Nellie in triumph through the city... As she stood on the side of her boat, the long cavalcade passed slowly before her, all bowing and smiling – in a long procession of 500 to 600

people. Miss Marchbank got out of her boat, into her chair, and passed right through the city, all the shop keepers and people en route turning out in great number to witness the sight – such a procession had never been seen in Guixi before. "That is she, that is Ma kiao-si, the one with the white hair."[42]

That was only the beginning of a long day of speeches, feasting and praise services, all coming from the hearts of the Chinese whom she had served for 28 years.

## The closing years

In 1890 Geraldine Guinness, as a young missionary, had travelled down the river to the Poyang Lake. She had spent several days in Yüshan, taking part in a small conference of the young women who were just settling along the river, and one of them she had never forgotten: "the well-remembered face and form of the young Scotch (*sic*) missionary", Nellie Marchbank. Some 30 years later she travelled that river once more, but this time with her husband, Dr Howard Taylor, son of Hudson Taylor, the founder of CIM. In the intervening years, Geraldine had become an outstanding writer and historian for the CIM. She travelled widely, and never stopped writing. Her account of Guixi in a letter to a nephew showed that the changes astonished her.

The "young Scotch missionary" was still tall and spare, but stooping a little, and the brown hair had become "a silvery white". Nellie was now 60, and had been back to Britain only twice in 30 years, and had "rarely, if ever, taken a summer holiday" in spite of the extreme summer heat. Geraldine and her husband were led through the great gate and first courtyard to the chapel, where everyone gathered to welcome them, and the pastor, now 80 years of age, prayed. A crowd had already met them off the boat, and escorted their two ornate sedan chairs through the town with the choir from the boys' school in front making a cheerful noise. (One chair belonged to the church for weddings, etc. and the other was loaned by the Mandarin! Howard Taylor was, after all, Hudson Taylor's son.)

Nellie then took them through the "beautiful, well-ordered mission premises – all in absolutely simple Chinese style". There were prayer halls for men and women, guest halls, a pastor's home, servants' quarters, a boys' boarding school with beds for 60, a girls' school for 60 girls, and a kindergarten. There were playing fields and drill sheds, kitchens, store houses and gardens. There was an old folks' home with individual rooms for 30 elderly church members (seven were over 80 years of age), and a Christian burial ground outside the town. Broad eaves and verandas protected everyone from sun and rain as they moved from building to building. It emerged that the buildings had cost $22,000 over the years, but the CIM had needed to contribute only $2,000. Gifts had come, unsolicited, from the homelands, and the Chinese themselves had given generously. Another $8,000 had been spent on chapels and houses for the thirteen out-stations. Over 1,350 people had been baptised over the years, and 700 church members remained in the area.

Geraldine commented:

> We had never imagined anything like the station and work we found in Kweiki. And it is all the expression of this woman's soul. How well I remember meeting her for the first time 30 years ago. I wondered then whether she would ever learn the language, and get in touch with the people. I little realised then that she was already far more of a missionary than I. She had been out a few months longer, but was so reserved, that I, taken up with dear Katie Mackintosh – my ideal of all a missionary should be – was wholly unconscious of the depth and power, the inward largeness and practical possibilities of this life.[43]

In spite of her age and failing strength, Nellie continued to join the younger women on visits to the villages. On one trip she was away for 17 days at three outstations: she visited 33 villages and 66 homes. She wrote, "Hai Ing [her Chinese helper] goes with me now to take a bit of care of me for I am not strong or particularly well but daily strength is given and Hai Ing is such a comfort. I am off again today to the south country." Nothing would stop her.

The church's witness continued to expand across the Guangxin River valley and the surrounding hills, but for Nellie the end came in May 1925. She had been in poor health for some time and an infection finally brought her life to a close. Around 800 people attended her funeral, including many public officials and a representative of the Mandarin. The church could receive them all – it now seated 1,000 people – and a large procession wended its way through the city to the North Gate and the Christian cemetery which lay beyond the walls.

It was the end of an extraordinary life – a life which began with a young woman, orphaned in her twenties, setting out for China. She was already known for her humility, her love for people, her compassion for the sick and dying, and her concern for people's practical and spiritual needs. These were the very things that continued to mark her life in China. She was most at home, even in the poorest of homes, sitting round a table listening, sharing people's troubles, and telling them of the love and forgiveness of Jesus.

To these people she gave her life unsparingly, and day after day her diary records her visits to these women who rarely left their homes. She expected the same dedication from her team. The very fact that so many new arrivals were sent to her for training indicates the respect in which she was held by the mission leaders. Over 37 women of many nationalities were associated with her over the 35 years she served in Guixi. They remembered the relentless programme of activity, setting off for villages ten or even 20 miles away, come rain or shine, on foot or in barrows. Was she too hard on them? If so, she was hard on herself too, and they spoke of her with affection, respect, and concern as she grew more frail. The young women who started their training and language study at Guixi later served in mission stations across the whole province and beyond. By the time Nellie died, the 50 believers meeting in Guixi had become 796 believers throughout the area, with eleven more churches based on the outstations.

## Reflections

The Guangxin River became known as "the women's field" and it became one of the most successful areas of church-planting in the CIM. If asked, Nellie would have said that she was only a willing instrument: what happened there was achieved not by human effort, but by the God who called them all and sent them. The workers, both Chinese and Western, tirelessly sowed the seed, and the one they served gave the harvest. In human terms the workers were nothing: few of them had much education, even the Western women. Some had been teachers or governesses; one had been a clerk; some had worked in factories; some were dressmakers; and a few, like Nellie, had been in domestic service. Their level of education reflected their social background but not their intelligence. Some were barely 20 years of age when they arrived, but they were totally committed in their Christian service, and most of them spent their whole lives in China.

One of the strengths of the work done by the CIM missionaries was their commitment to mobilising ordinary Chinese Christians. When Nellie died, there were only three pastors for the whole province of Jiangxi, and two of these were in the Guangxin area. The new Christians knew very well that if they wanted to share the Christian good news which they had found, they would have to do it themselves: they could not wait for the "professionals" to do it. They took the initiative in offering the use of their homes in villages and towns; they were not dependent on official buildings, and if these were destroyed (and many were), the message was still passed on from mouth to mouth. The Christians did not realise it then, but roots were being put down which would feed a different system many years later, when the buildings were taken away but the churches refused to die.

Another strength in the Guangxin valley was the partnership between the Chinese couples and the missionary women. In accordance with Chinese culture, the Chinese men reached out to the local men and led the emerging churches. The women, both Chinese and Western, concentrated on the huge task of taking the message to the local women in their homes. Each outstation could be surrounded by hundreds of villages, and one missionary might be responsible for three or four outstations at a time. The Chinese were able to develop their leadership abilities rapidly because they did not assume that women missionaries would take charge – but the women were there to talk to, and they could give support and encouragement to the young, emerging church leaders.

Today many people are critical of the large mission stations, which could so easily become ghettos where Christians could congregate, cocooned from the outside world.[44] It is scarcely letting your light shine from a prominent place for all to see. But the earliest Christians in these places were often beleaguered individuals, attacked and ostracised by family, neighbours and the authorities for embracing a foreign religion. They needed the support and encouragement of the Christian family. The schoolchildren were no angels, and though they came from Christian homes, they did not all follow their parents in believing; they were given a Christian environment as far as possible, and protected from some of the moral evils around. The elderly were cherished and cared for, and the small group of widows and orphans no longer feared the poorhouse, or landlords who demanded money they did not possess.

In Guixi the whole community was open to the town. Everyone could go in and out, and Nellie's room was by the main gate so that she was available to anyone who wanted a listening ear. She shared their troubles – and they had many – over three decades. Every Sunday people poured in from the country, and there could be two or three hundred enquirers at a time, who wanted to learn more about what it meant to become a Christian. The church members still lived and worked in the towns and villages, where they shared the love of God with others and lived it out in their community. The local people could not fail to see the difference.

> Consider your own call, brothers and sisters: not many of you were wise by human standards, not many were powerful, not many were of noble birth. But God chose what is foolish in the world to shame the wise; God chose what is weak in the world to shame the strong; God chose what is low and despised in the world, things that are not, to reduce to nothing things that are, so that no one might boast in the presence of God. He is the source of your life in Christ Jesus (1 Corinthians 1:26–30).

## Notes to Chapter Four

1 My italics.
2 Missionaries were also expected to keep such records. Accountability was taken very seriously.
3 Broomhall, vol. 6, p. 396.
4 Over these four years Taylor had travelled some 15,000 miles himself in the interior. Ibid., p. 442.
5 Ibid., pp. 349, 400.
6 *China's Millions* (September 1886) p. 115.
7 Chang Sien-seng was listed as an evangelist ten years earlier. He became pastor for the chain of churches along the Guangxin River. In 1886 Katie Macintosh was 26, and Jeanie Gray 22.
8 She died in Canada following surgery at the age of 44, in 1907. Obituary *China's Millions* (September 1907) p. 140.
9 Ibid. (May 1890) p. 59.
10 Ibid. (September 1887) p. 115.
11 Ibid. (June 1914) p. 91.
12 Ibid. (December 1888) p. 160.
13 CIM Archive, School of Oriental and African Studies, London, UK.
14 *China's Millions* (June 1889) p. 96.
15 Ibid. (May 1889) p. 73.
16 Better known later as the writer Mrs Howard Taylor.
17 *China's Millions* (September 1890) p. 128; (May 1891) pp. 57–60; (January 1892) p. 6.

18  Ibid. (June 1914) p. 92.

19  Most of the women ended up on the Guangxin River as the work expanded.

20  Four years earlier there were 891 missionaries in the whole of China. Broomhall, vol. 7, p. 137.

21  Piggin, *Christianity*, p. 69.

22  Young, *Pearls*, p. 72.

23  Ibid., pp. 78–79.

24  Ibid., p. 74.

25  Ibid., p. 75.

26  Ibid., p. 77.

27  Ibid., p. 78.

28  Piggin, *Christianity*, p. 71.

29  Even today, non-Christian Chinese are fearful. Some nurses find night duty particularly hard, if they fear evil spirits.

30  Even the New Testament churches were very dependent on the homes of a few wealthy people.

31  *China's Millions* (January 1892) p. 6; (November 1892) p. 145; (March 1894) p. 32.

32  Ibid. (May 1893) p. 64.

33  Marchbank, *Diary*, 9 June, 1895. Personal Papers, CIM Archive, School of Oriental and African Studies, London, UK.

34  *China's Millions* (May 1897) p. 70; (June 1914) p. 93.

35  Many were illiterate and literacy became a priority later.

36  *China's Millions* (June 1899) p. 85; (October 1899) p. 156.

37  Ibid. (January 1900) pp. 4–5.

38  Broomhall, vol. 7, pp. 392–94.

39  Marchbank, *Diary*, 3 April, 14–15 June, 1901. Personal Papers, CIM Archive.

40  *China's Millions* (December 1903) p. 170.

41  As early as 1885, Hudson Taylor realised that the early boarding schools prevented the children from acquiring from their parents the agricultural and domestic skills needed in daily Chinese life. The school terms were adjusted to allow the children to study in the winter and return home for the summer months to help their parents. It is not clear how long this continued. Broomhall, vol. 6, p. 385.

42  Annie Sharp, "The Kweiki Welcome Home", *China's Millions* (May 1915) p. 74.

43  J. Guinness, *Web*.

44  The early Celtic Christians gathered into communities around the monasteries for fellowship and teaching.

*Chapter Five*      # The Gift of Reading

Susie Garland was just 21 when she sailed from Australia for China with her older sister Annie. Hudson Taylor had paid his first visit to Australia the previous year, and the first two groups of Australians had left shortly afterwards. The Garland sisters had also heard him speak, and left for China in 1891 in a party of fifteen women and seven men. Genuine fears were expressed that the two girls would be too frail for the rigours of China: they came not from the tough Australian outback, but from a godly middle-class home in the suburbs of Melbourne, where they had organised a local Sunday school. In the event they both served in China for over 35 years, during which they returned to Australia only three times.

After a year in the language school, they were designated to the distant border province of Gansu – an area larger than Britain with a population of only ten million. The ancient Silk Road ran through it, moving north-west for several hundred miles through a long, high valley bordered on the west by the snow-covered Qilian Mountains rising to 22,000 feet, and on the east by the ranges of Mongolia. Here, on the edge of the Gobi desert, the Great Wall ended, and the ancient fort of Jiayuguan guarded the narrow pass against invaders.

The area included an extraordinary mix of peoples and cultures, for the Han Chinese mixed with Tibetans, Mongolians and Central Asian ethnic groups who moved down from the mountains and in from the deserts for pasture and trade, bringing Islam with them. Most of the time they

lived at peace with each other, but at intervals political rival-
ries stirred up civil war, and then the slaughter and destruction were terrible.

## Life in Tianshui

Susie and Annie spent most of their lives in the city of Tianshui
(Tsinchow) and later, Hui Xian (Hweihsien) in the south-east
of Gansu. George Parker and his Chinese wife Shiao Mian-zi
were the first CIM couple to settle in Tianshui in 1878, when
it was "a city made up of six townships unified by one main
three-mile street".[1] Five years later they had three Chinese
colleagues working with them, had baptised ten believers and
were teaching another fifteen.[2] A few years later, Hannah
Jones wrote of the snow-clad mountain ranges between China
and Tibet, the green hills, the roads beautifully shaded by
large trees, with a rich variety of fragrant wild flowers, a
place where a bowl of milk could be bought for a farthing.[3]

From the language school in Yangzhou, the Garland sisters had travelled across China from the coast, first by river
and then overland for three months. As the crow flies, it was
about 1,500 miles, but by river it was a different matter. The
journey by boat was more comfortable (apart from the occasional rapids) and cheaper than travelling overland, and the
women were less exposed to curious, over-friendly crowds,
and hostile bandits. However, engine power was not yet in
use, and the boats could be delayed by wind, rain and strong
currents as they were hauled upstream. At one point the
women covered less than a mile in three days. In her diary
Susie wondered whether they would ever develop the
patience of the Chinese; yet as the weeks passed they learned
to ignore the clock and accept each day as it came, and get on
with their language study on board. In the larger cities they
found mission centres from which they eagerly collected
their mail.

When they left the boat at Hanzhong they faced a further
trek of at least two weeks through the mountains with pack

animals to Tianshui. There they joined a married couple and two other single ladies. The senior couples changed at intervals, and a succession of junior missionaries arrived for initial experience and training. The Garland sisters were to provide continuity in the area for the next 35 years.

Annie soon found herself supervising a school for fifteen boys. If the church in Tianshui was to become independent and take the Christian message to the surrounding towns and villages, it was essential for the children of Christian families to be educated to provide future leaders. Few adults could read: it was a massive task involving memorising several thousand Chinese characters. Annie was glad to have the support of her Chinese language teacher, who became a Christian shortly after their arrival in Tianshui and began helping her in the school.

## Village work in Gansu

Susie, on the other hand, devoted her time to the women, especially in the countryside. As usual they had to be visited in their homes, and this required long journeys travelling round the villages. They worked in small teams: sometimes the sisters travelled together, but often Susie was accompanied by Mrs Chao, the church Bible woman (evangelist), or by other local Christians. At first, they could visit only towns that had inns where they could stay. It was some time before there were Christian homes where they could find a welcome.

Susie described a three-week spring tour she made with Annie and a Chinese Christian who was anxious for them to visit her friends. A local Christian man accompanied them. It took them three days to travel on horseback the 60 miles to the city, where they stayed at the local inn. They were welcomed by the local Mandarin, who put up official notices "permitting people to look at us and not hurt us"! He also provided a guard to control the local youths, and an escort to the next town. At first crowds thronged the inn where they were staying, but as the local women gained confidence they entertained the foreign women in their homes; finding that they would not accept gifts of money, they invited them to meals. While the women visited, Mr Hsu sold Christian books and preached on the streets. Everywhere they went, they tried to explain the Christian faith as simply as they could. They were well received, and remained there for ten days before moving on.

They were unable to hire any extra animals, so they had to walk most of the way, with their baggage on the one horse they had brought. In the next town their reception was less friendly. Once again people thronged their inn to look at them, but they were too timid to invite them to their homes. Rumours abounded that the foreigners blew wind into their listeners' faces which turned them into snakes; superstition, fear and ignorance dominated their lives. Fortunately the missionary party were able to hire the extra horses for the 30-mile journey home, and they were grateful for the help of the two men sent by the friendly Mandarin. The road was in poor condition, piled with deep snowdrifts, and crossing high, bitterly cold mountains. There were another 21 cities within a 50-mile radius of Tianshui, as well as smaller towns and villages for which they felt responsible.[4]

The following year found Susie undertaking a four-month tour with her co-worker, Eleanor Holme. They covered 400 miles, passing through cities, towns and villages in all weathers. There were no vehicles or trains, and in that mountainous area horses were the only alternative to walking.

> The road was so steep and slippery that it was scarcely possible to keep one's footing. I was constrained at last to give in and follow the advice of the coolies and hung on to my horse's tail, till I was splashed from head to foot with mud. This was going up-hill; though not so tiring, progress downhill was in some ways more difficult, many were the unintentional rests I took by the way. That 30 *li* (seven miles) seemed interminable, but having started walking, we were soon too wet and muddy to ride, and so had to keep on.[5]

If she had been frail when she sailed for China, she was doubtless developing stamina in Gansu! This experience in the villages laid the foundation for Susie's life's work. In the early days it was hard, and the inns primitive, but as time went on there were more Christian families with whom they could stay. Living in Chinese homes brought the sisters into close contact with the local people. As they all lay together on the heated platforms, wrapped in their quilts, the missionaries listened to the gossip far into the night, and developed a deep understanding of people's daily lives and problems.

After two years in this remote province, Susie and Annie were delighted to meet a party of four new missionaries who were passing through, who brought with them the latest news from the outside world. Susie commented:

> It has been such a joy and a help to meet them fresh from intercourse with the Christian world, which seems so far away as to be quite unreal, we get so taken up with our own little circle. If we continue to narrow down during the next six or seven years I wonder what we shall be like.[6]

She was 25 and expecting to spend the rest of her life in that corner of China. The first term of service for new missionaries was seven years – the next could be anything from ten to fourteen years. It was natural, even inevitable, that they should focus on the situation in which they lived. There was no telephone, radio or newspapers, and mail probably took months to travel overland. In 1894 they heard that war had been declared between China and Japan, and that France and Germany had joined in, but with no indication which side they were supporting. The Garlands would have liked "fresh, reliable news, but it is enough that our Father knows and has all his own in safe keeping".[7] Under cover of the Sino-Japanese War the Muslims staged a rebellion against the Chinese in Gansu itself. Slaughter and atrocities swept across areas north of Tianshui, and many missionaries were temporarily evacuated. Susie's comments reflect the reality of living each day in the light of God's sovereignty: their response was one of active trust rather than passive resignation. In fact, Susie did not need to fear the "narrowing" of her life, because she never allowed herself to be bound by her circumstances. Her understanding of the needs of the Chinese church was so far-reaching that, in spite in being confined to that far corner of the land, she came to wield an influence across China that few have equalled.

In 1898 Annie contracted typhus fever, from which far too many missionaries died. She made a slow recovery and the sisters went back to Australia for their first leave in 1899. Their return to China was delayed by the outbreak of the Boxer Rebellion in the north of China, when 188 missionaries and children and a far greater number of Chinese Christians lost their lives. In 1902 they returned and made the same long journey inland up the Han River. Gansu was still considered dangerous, and it was another four months before they were allowed back to Tianshui. Instead they stayed in the border town of Mien-Hsien, ten days' journey from Tianshui, and made the most of their time there by visiting and preaching in that city. Finally they reached "home" in July, to find that in spite of the danger the church had survived. There was increasing interest in the Christian message, and opportunities to share it were greater than ever. Susie went back to her work in the villages: years later the writer of her obituary traced "her accurate Chinese, and intimate knowledge of folklore" back to the many years she spent in grass-roots evangelism and teaching in Gansu.

## The first resources

In 1908 Susie wrote to the *Chinese Recorder*, a monthly journal in English which circulated in the missionary community throughout China. Apparently various small hymn books for children had been produced by different groups for their own use, and she suggested that the time had come to produce a larger book for wider use among Chinese children, "a kind of

*Golden Bells*". (*Golden Bells* had broken new ground when it was produced in Britain in 1890 by Scripture Union, and later gained worldwide acceptance.) She invited people to submit suitable hymns for this project; two years later a hymn book of 200 hymns was in print, compiled by Susie and edited by F. W. Baller. Evidently things happened when Susie suggested them.

Meanwhile, perhaps during those long treks on horseback, Susie's mind was busy with other problems. She was concerned about the vast numbers of illiterate women in Gansu, and indeed throughout the whole of China. It was rare to find any women who could read; if they learned at all, they learned by rote. They loved to listen to Bible stories, but very few could read the Bible for themselves. When the missionaries tried to train the Bible women as evangelists, they realised that the reading and Bible study which was taken for granted in the Western world was impossible. They needed extremely simple illustrated booklets for these women. By 1911, Susie was producing her own booklets: the first was *A Guide to Christian Women in Scripture*, and later she worked on *The Biblical Teaching on Women*.

## Braille for the blind

Another of Susie's concerns was the estimated one million blind people in China. How could they ever hope to read the Bible? In the West, Braille was in use in many languages, but Chinese presented special challenges. Many Chinese words are very similar in sound, but distinguished by different tones, and, to complicate life further, dialects use different numbers of tones. Braille has only a limited number of symbols with which to express these. People in other areas of China had been struggling to develop a form of Braille for different Chinese dialects. The Hankow system had been in use for 25 years and was excellent for the Mandarin spoken in Hubei province, but inadequate for Mandarin elsewhere.

In 1906, it was reported that Susie had "devised a new

system of teaching blind Chinese to read. It is based on a combination of initials and finals (symbols), and has been taught with success."[8] Susie had systematically analysed and included the 443 Chinese sounds in her system, reserving the simplest written forms for the most-used sounds. In 1912 the Institute for the Chinese Blind was opened for Mandarin speakers and the decision was taken to use Susie's Tsinchow (Tianshui) system, as it was called.

That same year, she and Annie returned to Australia for some well-earned leave, after having completed a second term of service of twelve years. The following year, 1913, Susie was back in China in time for a conference in Shanghai for workers among the blind, convened by the Bible Societies. There had been considerable progress. Schools for the blind were increasing, and some five or six hundred pupils were now being educated, but each school was laboriously producing its own texts by hand: this was not only costly in time and energy, but also vulnerable to error. The Bible Societies invited teachers and workers among the blind to try to produce a Mandarin Union Braille system from the two existing ones.

They agreed that the Hankow system was best for school use (providing it could be expanded to cover all forms of Mandarin), but they also recognised that Susie's system was better for those who had to learn it at home, since it could be taught easily by sighted people. As comparatively few blind people had any hope of specialised education in the near future, they decided to adopt Susie's system, revising it to incorporate the best from the Hankow code. The resulting "Union" code covered 443 sounds with 54 radical characters. The way ahead was clear to produce the scriptures, literature and reading primers nationwide in Mandarin Union Braille.[9]

By that time Susie was back in Gansu, once again busy with village evangelism and teaching. When harvest time came, and the villagers were busy, she pressed ahead with transcribing the book of Psalms into Braille. It was checked in China before being posted to Bible Society in London for printing. The Braille Bible was on its way.[10]

A blind girl from Jiangxi province in south-east China, one thousand miles away, wrote to Susie:

> To Teacher "Chia" [Garland], peace!
> Many thanks to the Teacher for preparing for us these books. Truly I thank (you) Teacher for taking this trouble for us. May God keep Your honour and daily give you much strength to work for Him. Thank God I have now read *The Heart's Eye Enlightener* (Primers), also the *Travellers' Guide from Death to Life* all but three chapters. Since then I have read John's Gospel, chapters 1–4.
> *Wu Ho-hua*, 6th moon, 20th day. [11]

## The China Continuation Committee (CCC)[12]

After the World Missionary Conference in Edinburgh in 1910, Continuation Committees were established across the world to take forward its work. In 1913 the committee in China broke new ground by drawing a third of its members from the national churches, at a time when they were only just beginning to attend major mission conferences. They were commissioned to foster church unity by encouraging the use of uniform terminology within the churches, a common hymn book, and the *China Mission Yearbook* to be published annually. In 1914 Susie Garland was invited to join the committee. It is not clear why she was invited from one of the most distant corners of China, or how she took part when travel from Gansu was so arduous, but her experience, first with the children's hymn book and then the adoption of her Braille system across China, had made this "frail" Australian woman's name known throughout the land's Christian community.

That same year she wrote an article for the *Chinese Recorder* appealing for people to target China's women with the gospel. The Chinese church was still a "man's church". The majority of Chinese women were still rarely seen on the street, literally known as "keepers at home", immobilised by their bound feet, uneducated, and isolated from public life. Susie challenged the churches not to forget them or treat them as second-class people. "Woman is a force in China as in other lands. How can we convert this force into a power which shall work for righteousness?"[13]

In 1916 there was a memory competition in Tianshui. Chinese education was based on "learning by repetition" as it was called, and some became highly skilled at this.

> Three women and one girl have this year repeated the whole of Philippians, Colossians, and 1 and 2 Thessalonians. A number of others have only repeated Philippians and Colossians... Some have committed to memory only one chapter. But this represents very great effort and much real prayer. Some who have seemed as if they were quite incapable of learning anything correctly, have done wonders.[14]

When the majority of women were still illiterate, memorising Bible passages was a very significant way of learning for Christian women. How much more might be achieved if only they could read and study the Bible for themselves and then teach others.

## The phonetic script

The development of the Braille code was a great step forward, but China faced an even greater problem than the one million blind. There were 324 million who were unable to read and write, and this included the majority of the women. It was estimated that 90% of the non-Christian population was illiterate (the figure was 40% in the churches). Reading Chinese was a difficult skill to master: more than 50,000 characters were used in writing, and the average person needed to know at least four or five thousand in order to read. If readers came across an unknown character, they could not even pronounce it.[15]

For the churches this was a formidable barrier, and dif-

Maria Dyer

Nellie Marchbank in
Chinese dress

The first group of CIM missionaries who set sail for China on 26th May 1866, on board the *Lammermuir*

Jessie Gregg's mission trips across China (taken from the cover of *China's Millions*, the CIM magazine, November 1920)

China

The nine unoccupied provinces (Chapter Three)

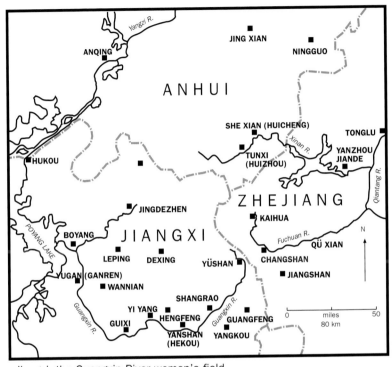

Jiangxi: the Guangxin River women's field

Travel by wheelbarrow was common, even for long distances

Women of Honan, returning home after the spring Bible school at Yencheng. A donkey, an ox, and a pony are yoked together to the farm cart. The small boy stopped eating his stick of sugar cane to be photographed

Christian Chinese women teaching other Chinese women to read

**Left:**
Jessie Gregg after 40 years of service in China

**Below:**
Margaret King

ferent solutions had been explored. Some of the first New Testament translations in local dialects (like the first Ningbo translation prepared by Hudson Taylor and his team) printed the Chinese text in the romanised alphabet. Another system endeavoured to use a basic 1,000 characters instead of the usual minimum of 4,000. The subject surfaced again in the *Chinese Recorder* in 1917. The following year the Revd C. Y. Cheng, chairman of the Continuation Committee and an outstanding national leader, went to the heart of the matter: they had once expected missionaries to evangelise China. This could be done only "when every man and woman takes up his and her full part in making known the Glad Tidings to those in China who are yet in darkness and sin".[16] It was, therefore, all the more pressing to have an educated, literate church if Chinese believers were to take full responsibility.

Christians were not the only ones concerned about language. In 1911 Sun Yat Sen had established the new Republic, and the following year, as China moved towards representative government, a group of 70 leading scholars was appointed to unify the Chinese language as a basis for a modern educational system. Different regions pronounced the written characters according to their local dialects. In the absence of an alphabet, the scholars developed a phonetic script based on simplified Chinese characters, using only 39 symbols. This was intended as an academic tool for a limited purpose.

When the China Continuation Committee (CCC) met in 1918, they appointed a sub-committee to make recommendations on a written script, and the scholars' phonetic script seemed to be ideal. It had been devised by the Chinese themselves and was approved by the National Ministry of Education. (Chinese scholars were less than enthusiastic about the idea of teaching the masses to read, fearing that the phonetic script would replace the traditional ideographs.) The Continuation Committee endorsed the script and immediately launched a programme to teach it throughout the churches. It required reading primers, using typewriters (previously unusable when thousands of characters were needed) and employing new printing techniques for the production of the Bible in that script. The CCC approached the China Inland Mission and asked for the secondment of Susie Garland as secretary and co-ordinator for the whole project for the next three years. This would include travelling round China to promote it.

Later Susie commented that she was reluctant to leave her work:

> After long years of ploughing and sowing with comparatively small results, the harvest was beginning, and when the work was giving us hope and gladness, I was asked to leave it and come down and prepare books in phonetic. One thing made me ready to do so, and that was the realisation that this script might sooner or later be used for literature that would help the people of China.[17]

She was determined to introduce the Bible to those who were going to start reading for the first time, before their minds were flooded with secular ideas.[18] She travelled the 1,500 miles to Shanghai once more – when the CCC recorded their appreciation in the minutes of their meeting, they described her journey as "long and dangerous". They said she had begun her new service with "promptness and energy". There were various bureaucratic hurdles to overcome, apart from the opposition of the scholars: the new script had its weak points and problems, and had never been intended for mass use. Her own script may well have been better, but this had official Chinese approval, so the churches did what they could. They endeavoured to negotiate some improvements with the National Ministry of Education without much success, so they forged ahead, undaunted. A Christian Evangelistic Fund handled costs and distribution, the Bible Society handled printing, and other societies contributed staff. It was indeed an inter-mission and interdenominational project for the whole church in China.

Producing the reading primers and biblical texts in the phonetic script was only the beginning. They had to be distributed and used, and for this a widespread programme of education and training was needed. Churches, Christian schools and universities led the way, seeing this as a major opportunity for Christians to gain access to the Word of God, and also as a means of introducing non-Christians to the Bible. They began by training literate people to teach others, on the principle that everyone who could read should teach at least one other. Secular schools were urged to use it for all children: for the many who would only ever have one or two years of education, the phonetic script would at least enable them to read and write.[19]

Most missionary women were soon teaching the local women to read. Susie herself led a two-week promotion campaign in the schools and churches of the large city of Wuhan, in 1919.[20] By the end of that year the phonetic Gospel of Mark was in its third edition, the Gospel of John in its second edition, and two catechisms and other scriptures were being processed. The whole New Testament was available by 1923, the Old Testament was under way, and they were embarking on a hymn book. In Zhili province 5,000 women and girls in the famine camp schools had learned to read.[21] The teaching schemes were so effective that uneducated women of average intelligence could learn to read in only one month.

## The poster campaign

The year 1921 marked the thirtieth anniversary of Susie's arrival in China – 30 years spent mostly not in the heart of China but on one of its furthest borders, and yet she was now at the centre of a programme that would revolutionise life in the churches and send ripples across the nation. She was 52, and tackling an entirely new kind of work with energy. As the primers and Bible material came off the presses, and the campaign was taken to the churches and schools, she was sure that still more could be done to convince people that reading was really within their reach. Susie launched out into a new sphere.

Until that point, printing in China had been very basic, in black and white, but new technology was being developed. Susie worked with the Christian literature experts to produce twelve Christian posters in colour, as well as leaflets and scrolls, with verses of scripture in the traditional ideographs with the phonetic script alongside. Elderly China missionaries still remember the impact made by those posters with two-colour printing. They were extremely popular both inside and outside churches, and also for decorating Christian homes; even non-Christians were eager to buy them. They also provided an easy way to introduce people to the simplicity of the 39 phonetic symbols. Those who could not read the characters could still demonstrate to their neighbours that they could read the phonetic script, and teach them too.[22] In the first three years, the literature business published 10 million items: there were no failures and most of her publications were noted for their success.[23]

Susie met with hostility and apathy in secular and academic circles, where the new script appeared to undermine Chinese culture, and where there was little concern for mass literacy. The churches, however, had a vision for literate congregations, and the governor of Shanxi realised the potential for his province and endorsed the use of the script in the provincial schools. The early fears that the system would undermine the traditional characters proved groundless. Once people had learned to read, they began absorbing the most common characters and moved on to the simplified "One Thousand Character" system. In fact, they could master the phonetic system with the 1,000 characters faster than the 1,000 characters on their own. [24]

In 1922, the Continuation Committee organised the National Christian Conference, the first of its kind, when half of its 1,000 delegates were Chinese; and these included no fewer than 74 of the once-despised Chinese women. They came from all walks of life. It was less than 20 years since the provincial governments had embarked on a public education programme which included women, and there were still only a couple of hundred women studying at university level. Nevertheless the conference delegates included teachers, doctors and other professional women emerging as Christian and national leaders. A revolution was taking place for educated Chinese women.[25] (See also Chapters Six and Seven.)

Across China an even more momentous revolution was taking place, as literacy came within reach of millions for the first time. That would revolutionise life for Christians, from conferences to home Bible studies, from city churches to rural preaching points, from Sunday schools to Bible colleges training women evangelists. For the first time ever, everyone could learn to read the Bible for themselves.

## The Australian Council

Her task completed, Susie returned to Australia with Annie in the autumn of 1922 for their third furlough in 30 years. They met the Australian Home Council and "gave a lengthy account of the work in which they had been engaged". Susie spoke of her work on the phonetic script, and showed them one of the "coloured printed posters which had been designed and seen through the press by herself". A letter from Shanghai was subsequently read to the Council "speaking in the highest terms of the brilliant manner in which Miss Susie Garland had organised and carried out her duties in connection with the script campaign". The Council minutes recorded their gratification on hearing of the remarkable work she had accomplished.

At the same meeting they discussed a proposal to invite two or three women to join the China Council of the CIM. This was a Council of Superintendents from the different provinces who met four times a year to advise the General Director. The mission leaders in China wanted to include people with wider gifts and experience on the Council, and the extensive work among women was unrepresented. Men were not the only people to receive spiritual gifts, and it was felt that some women also had much to contribute. Even though the China Council was advisory and not executive, the Australian Council could not agree. After four consecutive meetings, they were still divided on the role of women in the most senior council. It was pointed out that the CIM China Council had no ecclesiastical connections, so the "biblical principles" which some people stressed with regard to women in church leadership did not apply, and the Council was only advisory to the China director – it carried no authority or power. But neither the explanations of the Shanghai mission leaders, nor the example and presence of Susie Garland earlier, could persuade this minority group that women had anything to contribute at that level.[26] They even lobbied the North American Council to support their cause, though the London Council were in favour.

When the women members of the CIM were themselves consulted at the 1927 conferences, they also voted against having women on the China Council, but possibly for different reasons.[27] China was in turmoil again at the time, and in 1927 many missionaries had to withdraw to the coast. Travel to Shanghai was still very arduous, and some felt that they had more than enough to do in their local areas without travelling across China four times a year to attend a council. Others, with more limited education, had no concept of women in senior leadership. These decisions meant that the mission lost the potential contribution of some extremely gifted women for the next 70 years.

In January 1924 Annie and Susie were back in China again. Because of the time she spent in Shanghai, Susie had been out of Gansu for five years, and she noticed great changes when she returned. The roads had improved, and vehicles were replacing horses and carts, though wayside robbery was still a danger to the traveller; only the arrival of another group on the road saved them from one attack.

## Home studies

The China Continuation Committee had encouraged the different missions in each province to co-operate in holding united conferences. In Gansu the Scandinavian Alliance from the USA was already associated with the China Inland Mission, and together they formed closer links with the Christian and Missionary Alliance. In 1918 they had appointed a committee to produce home study materials which would encourage women at home to read the Bible for themselves and learn how to be effective in Christian witness and service. A course was produced with exams at different levels. Six years later, 91 women had completed the first exam, 64 had taken the second, and 31 had finished all four exams. Almost all had been illiterate when they started, but now most of them had progressed from the phonetic script to using Chinese characters.

The Committee for Home Studies was launched in 1918 just as Susie was leaving for Shanghai; Annie Garland was a member of the committee. Mrs Howard Taylor later wrote that Annie and Susie Garland "had given years to working it out. It is a thoroughly practical system for helping women, from enquirers up, to form habits of *home* Bible study." The second Gansu conference in 1924 resolved to adapt the course for men, adding two new sections, and to ask the Religious Tract Society to publish the course, study outlines, standard exam questions and diplomas, and also to appoint a committee to oversee this.[28] Annie Garland was an examiner. Susie's obituary writer later commented perceptively that she "had a mind that thought committees... Her capacity for working and getting work out of others was extraordinary. Barriers were a challenge."[29]

## More pioneering

When Susie and Annie returned to Gansu in 1924 they did not go back to Tianshui, because the churches there had their own Chinese leadership. Instead, they moved to Hui Xian (Hweihsien), a Muslim town some 70 miles south-east on the Gansu border, to pioneer Christian work there. Annie ran a small medical dispensary, and once again their circle of contacts slowly expanded. New friends included a wealthy Muslim man who had been thrown from a horse and needed medical help, his family, the two wives of the local Mandarin, and the wives of local gentry and army. Some just visited, others came to services and began to ask questions.

In 1926 Annie wrote in her annual report:

> The Chinese New Year meetings had drawn an average of 30–40 adults each night. These were followed by two tent missions, one of them in a city 20 miles away. In the spring and late summer, the local men from the church visited festivals in the surrounding towns and villages, preaching and selling literature, and found a welcome. In the autumn, J. O. Fraser, a well-known missionary to the Lisu people, visited and held a three-day Bible School for teaching, and then baptised the first Christians in the city – three men and one woman – to form the first Church in Hui Xian.[30]

It represented unusual progress in a largely Muslim area.

Afterwards Annie and three local believers went travelling again: the men went to 23 nearby villages, while the women visited a further ten. Travelling around, staying in homes or very basic local inns, was not easy for older people, but the sisters did not give up. A lot of time and effort had been given, and the results appeared meagre, but the seed had been planted and was quietly growing. Their contacts increased through their medical work and this steady, persistent visiting over a wide area. They had helped over 1,700 patients that year, and made 2,200 medical visits. As a result, Sunday services drew an average of 16 women each week, and rather fewer men, including the small nucleus of baptised believers. In the New Year the tiny church in Hui Xian hosted some special meetings and invited scattered believers and enquirers from the outlying towns and villages to join them. Some were still struggling with opium addiction.

The report describes work which was typical of that of hundreds of missionaries across China. At the grass roots, in cities, towns and villages, they worked alongside local believers in spreading the Christian message over a wide area, and then returned again and again until people began to understand that their lives did not have to be spent placating local gods, trying to earn merit through an endless cycle of fasting on certain days every month. The message of a loving God who welcomed people and forgave them was a strange one to those who were trying to "earn" forgiveness, but wonderfully liberating to those who grasped that forgiveness was a gift offered by a loving Father.

China was a turbulent country throughout this period. In 1927 civil war spread and rival factions set up three different governments in Beijing, Nanjing and Guangzhou. Nationalism and anti-foreign feeling was rife. The terrible events of the Boxer Rebellion 25 years earlier still cast a long shadow, and when the embassies evacuated their nationals to the coast, 4,000 missionaries had to leave. Susie and Annie were forced to make the long journey to the east coast once more, and were unable to return for 18 months. Susie was now 57 and Annie 66.

While some missionaries found those months of exile frustrating, Susie characteristically redeemed the time. She worked with the Bible Union of China (which linked the more conservative missionary societies), organised the Braille Literature Association, helped to prepare tracts for Muslims, and encouraged the development of "posters and handbills for visual evangelism". She was also able to proof-read the manuscript of *Pilgrim's Progress* in Braille.

The months at the coast provided plenty of time for heart-searching, reflection and prayer about the future. The first of several CIM conferences was held at Chefoo, when a hundred missionaries gathered. They decided that the time had come to extricate as many missionaries as possible from established church work, and hand over to Chinese leaders. This would set the missionaries free once more for the pioneer evangelism which was still a priority, but was too often crowded out by existing responsibilities. It was Susie "who, until her death, was always in the very front ranks of the advance" who summed up their thinking. She proposed a motion that "the Mission (CIM) be urged definitely to pray and plan for a big Forward Movement, with a view to the fulfilment of its responsibility for the evangelism of the Chinese, Mohammedans, Tribes and Tibetans, and others in the fields allotted to it."[31] She suggested that the Mission Executive should survey the areas and list the unreached cities and strategic centres which should be occupied. This motion was recognised by other conferences which followed. The needs were assessed, and in May 1929 a call went out to the sending countries for 200 new recruits to spearhead this Forward Movement. At a time when most missionaries of all societies had been evacuated to the coast indefinitely, in apparent defeat, it hardly seemed an appropriate moment to embark on anything of this kind, but Susie made it happen. She initiated what became a significant advance for the CIM. This occurred only five years after her own Home Council in Australia had vetoed women's presence on the advisory China Council of the CIM in Shanghai.

The results of the call were interesting. The tough, pioneering nature of the work on the far borders of China caused them to pray for a majority of men. Their prayer was answered within two years by the arrival of 84 men and 119 women. There was some disappointment at the failure of more men to respond, but they recognised that men tended to be slower to respond than women! Time and again when the mission received a similar response, they stressed that the need was not for fewer women – all were needed – but for more men. No one ever seems to have considered that the imbalance might represent the sovereign will of God!

# Lives less ordinary

Susie and Annie finally got home to Hui Xian in 1928, only to face a severe famine that winter. Annie died of heart failure the following year.[32] Two years later political turmoil erupted again when Communist forces from Soviet Russia infiltrated Xinjiang and encouraged the Muslim ethnic groups as far south as Gansu to rebel against the Chinese. The countryside was devastated by war, another harvest was lost, and 2,000 people in the Hui Xian area were starving. Susie once more poured herself into local relief work until she contracted typhus. She died at the age of 60.

She had arrived in China at the age of 21 and, apart from three furloughs in Australia and three years in Shanghai, she had spent her life in one of the most distant border provinces. She was never physically strong, yet she lived for weeks on end in the towns and villages, staying in ordinary inns and the homes of local people. When she was asked to move to Shanghai she was unwilling to leave them: she had a profound sense of contentment where she was.

Yet, as Frank Houghton suggested, she was "always in the very front ranks of advance", for from that isolated place she was used to shape the path of the church in China in an extraordinary way. If her location was restricted, her creativity was not. She worked for the disadvantaged, and those who were often passed over. There was the hymn book for the children, Braille for the blind, simple tracts for uneducated women, the phonetic script for the illiterate, the posters and literature, and later the home Bible studies that changed the lives of both women and men, in the churches and beyond. She used her creative energy as an individual for those around her, but she also displayed a gift both for working in a team and for mobilising others to expand her work. She moved far beyond the boundaries of her own mission and the CIM churches, to make God's written word in scripture accessible to the whole church in China.

The writer of her obituary in the *Chinese Recorder* commented:

One to whom the Lord had given five talents, gained other five talents... Her capacity for getting work out of others was extraordinary. "Learn from the ant," she would say – "Go round, or under, or over the obstacle, but get somewhere!"

And she did.

## Notes to Chapter Five

1 Broomhall, vol. 6, p. 82. Or see the new (2000) edition entitled *The Shaping of Modern China* (OMF/Paternoster/William Carey Library).

2 *China's Millions* (1883) p. 78.

3 Ibid., pp. 78–79.

4 Susie Garland, "Letter", *China's Millions* (Australian ed.) vol. 2 (September 1894).

5 Susie Garland, "Extracts from Diary", *China's Millions* (Australian ed.) vol. 3 (August 1895) p. 84.

6 Susie Garland, "Extracts from Diary", *China's Millions* (Australian ed.) vol. 3 (March 1895).

7 Ibid.

8 *China's Millions* (1906) p. 26.

9 "A Union System of Braille for Mandarin-speaking Chinese Blind", *Chinese Recorder* (April 1914) pp. 256–58.

10 Mandarin Union Braille has remained in use for the rest of the twentieth century. S. J. Garland, "Promotion of phonetic writing in China" in *China Mission Yearbook* vol. 10 (1919) pp. 176–83. The current situation was confirmed by the writer in a personal conversation with Sister Eva in Hong Kong, 1994. Other systems are in use for other Chinese dialects, and the Chinese Government is now endeavouring to unify all of them.

11 Susie Garland, "Psalms for the Blind", *China's Millions* (November 1915) p. 175.

12 Rouse and Neill, *History*, pp. 378–82.

13 S. Garland, "The Need for Women Evangelists in China" in *China Mission Yearbook*, vol. 5 (1914) pp. 221–24.

14 *China's Millions* (February 1917) p. 19.

15 S. J. Garland, "The Problem of China's Illiteracy", *China's Millions* (October 1923) pp. 154–55; Y. C. James Yen, "The Campaign against Illiteracy" in *China Mission Yearbook*, vol. 11 (1923) pp. 205–207. A. M. Cable, "The Twilight of the Gods", *China's Millions* (July 1920) p. 79.

16 C. Y. Cheng, "The Chinese Church Today", *Chinese Recorder* vol. 49 (November 1918) p. 710. Dr Karl Gutzlaff was well aware of the need to train Chinese evangelists as early as the 1840s.

17 Susie Garland, "The Problem of China's Illiteracy", *China's Millions* (October 1923) p. 155.

18 Ibid., pp. 154–56.

19 A. M. Cable, "The Twilight of the Gods", *China's Millions* (July 1920) p. 77.

20 Susie Garland, *Chinese Recorder* vol. 50 (1919) p. 861.

21 Ibid., pp. 155–56; S. J. Garland, "Promotion of Phonetic Writing in China" in *China Mission Yearbook* vol. 10 (1919) p. 181.

22 S. J. Garland, "The Problem of China's Illiteracy", *China's Millions* (October 1923) p. 156.

23 Loane, *CIM*.

24 Agnes Clarke, "A Missionary Survey", *China's Millions* (October 1935) pp. 194–95.

25 The statistics in the 1918 *China Mission Yearbook* for the previous year claim that there were 2,183 girls in the Normal and Training mission schools that year, and 312 in Union mission schools. There were 92 girls studying in the two university-level mission colleges.

26 Australasian Council Minutes, Melbourne, 19 September; 16 October; 28 November; 18 December 1922.

27 By contrast, the London Missionary Society was the first to remove all gender and race distinctions in membership as early as 1891, and men and women were treated on an equal footing on boards, committees, in leadership and at the grass roots. "Women can claim a place, not on the plea that she (*sic*) is a woman with a woman's 'right', but on the nobler basis of having the ability and the spirit to fill a needed place in service." Luella Miner, "The Place of Woman in the Protestant Missionary Movement in China" in *China Mission Yearbook* vol. 9 (1918) pp. 321–41.

28 S. J. Garland, "Home Study for Chinese Christians", *Monthly Notes* vol. 30.2 (February 1925) pp. 2–3.

29 "In Remembrance. Susie J. Garland", *Chinese Recorder* (July 1930) p. 454.

30 A. Garland, "Conflict and Victory", *China's Millions* (May 1927) pp. 74–75.

31 Houghton, *Two Hundred*, pp. 15–16.

32 Loane, *CIM*, pp. 85–86.

# Chapter Six

# A New World for Women

Jessie Gregg and Margaret King reached China within a few months of each other in 1895: their times in the women's language school may have overlapped. Both served a long apprenticeship in street and village evangelism before their wider ministries emerged, but they then moved in very different directions. From her base in north China, Jessie Gregg travelled widely across the country, leading missions and bringing many ordinary women to faith in Jesus Christ. Margaret King, on the other hand, worked with girls who were given a solid basis of Christian teaching in the course of their school years, and who often stayed on for teacher training and became leading figures in their churches and even in society. They were the first generation of new, educated leaders, and by the 1930s they were appearing alongside Margaret and others as co-workers and Bible teachers. Living in these circles, Margaret's own influence spread to Chinese church leaders at a national level. Both Jessie and Margaret had a profound influence on the Christian women of that generation.

## Jessie Gregg

Jessie Gregg was born in Britain in 1871, but little is known of her early years. Phyllis Thompson described her as a "buoyant, sometimes quite a boisterous person, with a childlike directness and an urge to get moving".[1] Once Florence Nightingale had made nursing a respectable profession, people like Jessie Gregg had been able to get training in midwifery and dispensing. She arrived in the CIM training home in London believing God had called her to China, and ready to go at once. Henrietta Soltau, who supervised the training home from 1890 to 1919, thought otherwise, and Jessie spent two years there.[2]

She found patience wasn't the only thing she needed: she noticed that other candidates had something in their lives that she lacked. They talked about the Holy Spirit filling them, changing them, guiding them, and they seemed to have a personal experience of God that she did not. It was a mystery to her until one day she saw clear water pouring out of an old rusty pipe, and remembered Jesus' words, "Out of the believer's heart shall flow rivers of living water" (John 7:38–39). All that was needed was an available channel, and she prayed that God's Spirit might pour through her life to others. It was a landmark in her spiritual life.

She sailed for China in 1895 at the age of 24, but her six months at the women's language school in Yangzhou were disrupted when she had to nurse people through a smallpox epidemic. She was then sent to join Charles Green and his wife at Huolu (Hwailu) in Hebei province, a small town of 20,000 people, a few miles east of the Shanxi border. The first missionaries had moved to the town in 1887, and the mission station was a staging post on the road from Beijing to Shanxi province. They were three or four days' journey from other Westerners in any direction.

## Struggling to communicate

Jessie was dismayed to find that her hard-won language skills were of little use here, and the women could not understand her. Would she ever be able to master the tones of Huolu? Finally an elderly Chinese woman came to her rescue. She began to pray for her daily, telling God that there was a lady who had come to help them but could not talk; that she lived in the west room of the courtyard; and would he kindly give her the oil of the Holy Spirit, for her tongue was very stiff and she could not get it round the Chinese words. And as Jessie said, he did it! Those simple prayers were answered, and three years later she passed the necessary exams.[3]

Jessie settled down to more language study, interspersed with visiting the country women, while Mrs Green visited those in the town. In Huolu and the villages around, the response to the good news was very slow, but they continued visiting, and Jessie's language skills gradually improved.

## The Boxer Rebellion

By the summer of 1900, no rain had fallen in Shanxi for eleven months. The autumn and spring crops had failed, and still the drought continued. The local people were steeped in superstition, and believed those who claimed that there would be no rain until all the foreigners were exterminated. As opposition grew to foreigners and followers of the "foreign" Christian religion, life became even harder for Chinese believers, who were often the only Christians in their families. Rumours abounded. Three days of rain brought hope that the hostility would die down but by then the movement had a life of its own. In June rioting cut Huolu off from Beijing, the coast and the outside world indefinitely: in early July the imperial edict went out to kill the foreigners, and the Boxer rebels responded. In one day, Jessie and the Greens learned of the destruction of all their nearest mission stations – north, south, east and west – and the murder of the missionaries. The Boxers were now approaching Huolu: Jessie, the Greens and their two children (aged four and two) went into hiding in the country, hidden by local friends and moving from place to place for three weeks.

In early August they were captured and dragged back to Huolu. The Chinese lined the road when they arrived, many of them watching out of sympathy. When Jessie caught sight of their house-help watching in tears, she called out, "We are not afraid, God is with us." Months later she heard how her brief words were repeated and became a source of strength to the local believers. The following day, Mrs Lin, the Bible woman who had worked with Mrs Green, managed to reach them before they were moved on.

> She took up the two children in her arms with a loving tenderness, and when leaving, embraced and kissed my wife and Miss Gregg, regardless of all onlookers, while all the time her calm, strong faith in God and loving helpful words... helped us to share St Paul's joy when glorying in his Corinthian converts... Returning home, she sent us a thick wadded Chinese coverlet to spread on the bottom of the cart, and some fruit and cakes for the children.[4]

She was only one of many Chinese who risked their lives by bringing gifts of food and clothing to missionaries abducted by the Boxers. Many Chinese Christians were also beaten, tortured and killed in the uprising. In the space of five weeks the missionary group faced imminent death no less than seven times, enduring sickness, hardship, imprisonment and public humiliation. On arrival in Hsinan the three adults had their hands and feet trussed up and were carried some 400 yards hanging from spears. Yet still they had hope: one day a man surreptitiously threw some crumpled paper into the yard where they were imprisoned. At first Charles Green ignored what seemed to be another insult, until the man signalled him to pick it up. Written on it in broken English was a message:

> Don't be afraid for Chinese robbers nearly all have been killed by both Chinese and foreign soldiers. Peking and T'ientsin belong to Europeans. Now I will go to T'ientsin [60 miles away] and tell your armies to protect you. You may tear it in pieces when you have seen.[5]

He was a Chinese businessman and kept his word (the full story has been told elsewhere).[6] Eventually the group reached comparative safety: they had been out of touch with the outside world for four months. The local officials asked how the consul in Tientsin had known they were being kept at Hsinan – how indeed! In the early stages of the uprising Charles Green had been shot at; they were given no medical help and the pellets could not be removed until they reached safety. Soon afterwards five-year-old Vera died of dysentery, and he broke down completely and was ill for weeks. Both the Greens and Jessie returned to Britain to recover from their ordeal.

Inevitably it took some time for normal life to be re-established in north China. Towns, villages and families had been torn apart, homes and businesses destroyed, and people killed. Yet as the hostility against foreigners and Christians quietened down, there was an upsurge of interest in education and the Christian faith. In the aftermath of the rebellion the Christians' behaviour was striking: Chinese religion could not explain how people could return to the very places where their homes and possessions had been destroyed, and they had suffered so much violence and abuse; nor how they could do so without resentment or bitterness, and without asking for reparation. The local people were amazed, relieved and grateful.

## Back in Huolu

In order to avoid duplicating their efforts, the various missionary societies had consulted together and shared out the responsibility for different regions. The CIM in Huolu became responsible for nine counties covering 7,000 square miles of land, and 1 million people living in 1,800 towns and villages.[7] Resources were few: only three missionaries and Mrs Liu, the Bible woman; a paid evangelist; a church with 23 members; and a village outreach centre. That was all. Humanly speaking, it was nothing.

When the Greens returned to Huolu, they resumed responsibility for the church and the general work in the town. Jessie and Mrs Liu again shouldered the laborious work of visiting the women in the villages, travelling for weeks at a time and staying in local homes.

Giving myself up to finding out all I could about the Chinese woman in her home, sleeping with her, sharing her room and living on Chinese food, I got to know her environment, and was better fitted for the next move God was calling me to. It was a long apprenticeship for the next fifteen years.[8]

In May of 1903, Jessie visited the Christian family of Mrs Five and her two sons (a day's journey of 35 miles in a springless cart) and reckoned "nearly all the women in the village came to see me and so heard the Gospel". Mrs Five's sons often went to Huolu (two days' journey on foot) and stayed for several days of Bible teaching. In July 1904, eight men and eight women were baptised in Huolu. All had been "enquirers" before the rebellion, so they had clearly counted the cost of becoming a Christian. Jessie commented that it was only the second baptismal service she had seen in ten years in Huolu; ten years of patient visiting, teaching, praying, surviving the horrors of the Boxer Rebellion, and culminating in the baptism of 16 new believers.

In an interview back in Britain many years later, Jessie revealed the moment when the size of the task utterly overwhelmed her. In spite of all her efforts, the response was so small, and she seemed so ineffective that there seemed to be no point in her continuing. She might as well pack up and go home. But as she prayed about it, she was reminded of the verse in the Bible, "one shall chase a thousand" (Joshua 23:10). Was God speaking to her through this? Would she really see a thousand people in China believe in Jesus? She could scarcely believe it, but she felt the promise had been given to her and she plodded on, wondering if the thousand would come from the Huolu district.

The next ten years were very different: the seed of the gospel was taking root and growing. Jessie's "thousand" did indeed register as enquirers who wanted to enter the Christian faith, and new churches emerged in six more towns in the area. By 1914 the full-time team had increased to two missionary couples, two single women, eight evangelists, two

Bible women, four colporteurs, and five schoolteachers. Two hundred Christians were scattered across the area in seven churches, there were 17 village outstations and some 500 to 600 enquirers.[9]

## The Huozhou school mission

Jessie also visited other areas where the CIM was operating, to see what was happening and share her vision; in 1911, one such visit was to the Huozhou school, run by Mildred Cable (see Chapter Seven). It was a visit that would open the door to a bigger field of mission than she had ever imagined.[10] When Mildred heard Jessie speak to the girls in the Huozhou school, she recognised her exceptional gift for evangelism and asked her to return for wider meetings at a later date. Three years later, when the new school buildings were opened, the opportunity arrived. Curiosity led a thousand local women to pour into the school daily. Never before had Huozhou had so many women on the streets! The church members, schoolgirls and women in training brought the Christian message to them in the courtyards all day long. This was followed by a week-long residential mission for Christian women, something that had never before been attempted, as Chinese women never left their homes. The missionaries had no idea how many women would come, but they were able to use the new premises of the church, the women's Bible training centre, and the girls' school.

> One evening, just before the mission began, we were wondering how it was going to turn out; we were drawing a bow at a venture but when we attempt great things for God, He does help us. Well, as we were going to bed that night, we heard a lot of noise at the front door. We went to the door, and what do you think we saw? Thirteen cartloads of women arrived for the women's mission... the next day... 20 donkeys came in one train... The new chapel was filled with between 400 and 500 women and girls. Not a man in the place; all women. The sight

made one's heart leap up in thanksgiving to God that we had at last got hold of the women of China, and that the women were coming into the fold of Jesus Christ.[11]

It marked a new day for the women, and a new ministry for Jessie.

## Missions for women

Jessie spent the next fifteen years taking women's missions across China, including a year in Manchuria. She kept detailed records, and over that period held 183 missions in fifteen provinces, going far beyond the CIM work. She covered 28,000 miles before the railways were built, travelling sometimes for ten days at a time and using every possible form of transport: cart, mule litter, horse, donkey, pack-mule, wheelbarrow, train, launch, and steamer. She travelled on primitive, stony roads, "in cold and heat, weariness and loneliness", and, at times, in considerable physical danger from robbers and brigands.[12]

After the Boxer Rebellion there had been many conversions to Christianity, but large numbers of these people were nominal Christians, who had received very little teaching. Jessie's missions brought many people to true faith in Christ for the first time, and those who were already believers came to a deeper spiritual understanding of what it meant to follow Christ. When questioned later, Jessie said she had not seen the waves of conviction of sin that Jonathan Goforth had witnessed in the revivals in China, but commented that he had worked among Christians with some understanding of the biblical teaching about sin; she had worked primarily among unbelievers.

Her missions were well prepared and followed up: the local people undertook all the planning and praying beforehand. If a church invited her to come, she would encourage them to co-operate with other churches and missions in the same city, and she was always willing to lead missions for other societies and other denominations. Schedules and reports of her work were included in the monthly *Chinese Recorder* that circulated among missionaries and churches throughout China. She developed a pattern of touring areas for three months in the spring and autumn; in that time she could hold some ten missions of four days each, with two or three days in between for rest and travel. It was a punishing schedule but she was ill only once, when typhoid struck.

The missions usually involved two meetings a day for four days, and childcare was provided to leave the mothers free to concentrate! The church women would meet for prayer for several months beforehand, and afterwards they would continue to instruct those who came to believe. In this way local women were trained as leaders and this too led to growth in the churches.[13] Over the years numbers attending varied from 50 to 800 women, but the average congregation was usually between 400 and 500. Jessie encouraged response and commitment on the third day of the mission, as this allowed a day for the Christians to give further explanations and help to those who needed it. By the end she had a record of over 5,000 women and girls who had responded in her meetings, and those were the ones she knew about – there must have been many others unknown to her. A friend described her work:

> The women are won by Miss Gregg's personality and manner and by the message of the cross, grand in the simplicity and clearness with which it is delivered. I have never seen in China anything like the love the women showed as they watched in the distance the very last glimpse of the sedan bearing the Lord's messenger on her way to needy Gansu.[14]

She never used picture rolls, like other mission leaders, but she did use drama. One woman remembered her binding up someone on the platform with rope, and saying that was how Satan bound people up with sin. Then she explained how Christ could untie the rope to set them free. "That afternoon

I was loosed from my sins." On another, never-to-be forgotten occasion Jessie was talking about John the Baptist and then told the women they were either wheat or chaff: one would be preserved, the other destroyed. She challenged the whole congregation to decide which they were. The country women, however uneducated, knew exactly what she was talking about. Every year they tossed the grain in the wind to separate the wheat from the chaff before the chaff was burnt. It was a powerful climax to her message.

Jessie spent eight months in Manchuria in 1924 and 1925. She found the congregations there only half the size of those she had known in China, although the women were "capable, business-like, keen and alert. I saw several of these women running foreign medicine shops, thus supporting their own families, and looked up to and respected by other business firms in the city. In China proper I have never seen this." In fact, there were four men in the Manchurian church to every woman. Jessie came to the conclusion that, in contrast with China, there were "few, so very few missionary ladies giving their whole time and strength for the evangelistic side among the women". They had been sadly neglected.[15]

In 1926 Jessie wrote to friends saying that she felt her itinerant ministry was coming to an end. She gave no reason, but when she returned to Britain the following year, it emerged that she had developed diabetes. At first it looked as if she would never return to China, and that her itinerant ministry had ended as suddenly as it began. However, with a careful diet and a promise of undertaking less stressful work, she was allowed back. Her work was continued by Marie Monsen, who led revival across China for the next five years (see Chapter Nine).

## Another door opens

Jessie returned to Huolu, which had always been her home base, just as the CIM were launching the "Forward Movement" in evangelism proposed by Susie Garland (see

Chapter Five). Many missionaries had been tied up with church work when they should have been handing over to national workers and getting back to pioneer evangelism in places where there were no churches. Of the nine counties in the Huolu area, only four had an established Christian witness, and Pingshan with its 660 villages was the largest.[16] The church in Pingshan, 20 miles west of Huolu, had an evangelist and 90 members, but the women's work was undeveloped. Jessie, now aged 57, and Maud Mower, some ten years her junior, moved there for pioneer evangelism among the women in the city and villages.

Pioneer work was physically hard, and results could be slow in an atmosphere of apathy and even hostility. Younger workers had more physical energy to give to the travelling involved; older people usually found it easier to focus on teaching and training church members in larger centres. Jessie had spent 35 years in China, and Maud, her colleague, had been there 25 years. Nevertheless these two middle-aged ladies found themselves back on the front line.

They spent seven years in "intensive evangelism", following up tent campaigns in Pingshan and the villages. They also trained three new missionaries to work in China, and their team included the pastor and a Bible woman. There were Bible study classes, short-term Bible schools, Sunday schools and further training for some women chosen as voluntary church workers. When Jessie retired in 1937, the team had taken the seed of the gospel to the whole area and fifteen small churches had been formed.[17]

A new couple had been chosen to replace Jessie and Maud, but the Japanese invaded in that same year, and the missionary help they anticipated never came.[18] However, the Pingshan church was now self-supporting. They had appointed four deaconesses to continue the work among women in the city and the villages, and they were about to call another evangelist. When the political crisis came, the church was prepared.

Jessie's lifetime of work in China involved hardship, danger and extensive travel: her life and message affected the lives of thousands of women, who were brought to faith and new life in Jesus through her ministry.

At the 1922 CIM Conference Jessie had been described as a "delegate from Zhili (Hebei) and representative of a wider field" – which could be regarded as something of an under-statement.[19] Before the conference she sent a letter to the CIM directors, endorsed by other women. It asked that senior women should be appointed, to whom the CIM women could refer. There was a real need for better representation of the women's work at headquarters, and much would have been gained if the missionary women had had a forum where their work could be discussed and planned. Jessie herself had been an effective evangelist and teacher over a very wide area; she had extraordinarily wide experience as a result of working with different missions across China. She could have made a significant contribution to the China Council, but the oppor-tunity was lost.[20] Jessie Gregg died in 1942, five years after her retirement.

## Margaret King

Margaret King was born to a Scottish family in Montreal in 1866; she had four brothers and was the eldest of four daugh-ters. At the age of eight she went to live with her wealthy grandmother, who later took her on a European tour to broaden her education. She was 21 when Hudson Taylor crossed Canada for the first time in 1887, and she heard him speaking of the lives of women in China; she was deeply moved. When he returned to China at the end of his tour, fourteen young people sailed with him from Vancouver. It was the beginning of the North American branch of the China Inland Mission.

Two years later Margaret and her grandmother visited the Keswick Convention in Britain, and both were challenged to a deeper commitment to following Jesus Christ. Back in Montreal, Margaret withdrew from her social round and gave herself to working in the poorest areas of the city for the next seven years, helping the Salvation Army and others. She was particularly concerned for the street girls; she faced hostility and danger, but her courage grew as she saw their lives transformed, and she won their friendship and love. Yet the call to China did not go away. She reluctantly gave up a relationship that could have led to marriage, and instead she undertook medical studies and qualified as a nurse before applying to the China Inland Mission.[21]

## Yangzhou

Yangzhou was an ancient city of 350,000 people, situated near the Grand Canal that once linked the Huanghe (Yellow River) in the north with the Yangtze River in the south, making it the longest canal in the world at that time (1,100 miles). Hudson Taylor and Maria were the first Protestant missionaries to live there in 1868 and survived a dangerous riot that year (see Chapter Two). In 1886, as the CIM prayed in faith for 100 new workers (and got them), the mission recognised the need for proper language and training schools for both men and women, with a more structured course of study. As Chinese etiquette required that the two groups of single people should not meet, the men's language school was established in Anking, 200 miles away! Mariamne Murray, an older woman who had reached China two years earlier, established the other CIM language centre for women in Yangzhou.

Margaret was 30 when she joined the community in the Yangzhou home in 1896. Her fashionable dresses had been abandoned in Shanghai for the loose-fitting jackets and trousers worn by the local women: to the Chinese, the fitted bodices of Victorian dresses appeared indecent and offensive. She found language study to be hard work, but she made good progress and went on to cover all the six courses required of the men. At the same time, she revealed her ability for friendship and she mixed easily with local women, giving considerable medical help when local remedies failed.

She was equally at home with both the rich and the poor in the city, but one particular friend, Mrs Fang, took her under her wing. She went out of her way to help her with the language, training her in the etiquette of the upper classes, and insisting on giving her better quality Chinese clothing, and a sedan chair of her own so that she need not hire one. One day that training would prove valuable: the upper classes were hard to approach. Meanwhile, when time permitted, she began visiting the villages with Mrs Sie, a local Bible woman "over 40 years of age and one of the holiest people I ever knew". They became fellow-workers for the next 20 years. It was Mrs Sie who taught Margaret how to understand and communicate with the village women.[22]

When her studies were complete, Margaret was asked to stay on the staff of the women's training home in Yangzhou, and she was able to pass on her growing knowledge of daily life and culture to new arrivals. The years passed, and the Boxer Rebellion reached Yangzhou. Margaret, Mrs Sie and another CIM couple were besieged one night by a mob that planned to return the following day to kill them. They planned an escape route over the wall to neighbours, but in the end it was not needed. An official received the orders to kill the missionaries, but before posting it up around the city, he changed the word "kill" to "protect". His action saved their lives, though when the Empress discovered what he had done, she had him executed.

Margaret returned to Yangzhou in 1902 after her first year of furlough, and joined two other women working near a large temple that attracted crowds of people. She found the work frustrating: after the Boxer Rebellion there was widespread interest in the Christian faith, but the three of them were the only women in the city who could devote their whole time to evangelism.

## Grounded in Montreal

The next few years must have been even harder to understand. She was settled in Yangzhou, overwhelmed by all the opportunities, when her father suddenly died, and within six months her mother asked her to return to Montreal to care for her sick grandmother. She spent eight months at home before returning to China in the spring of 1904, only to learn of her mother's illness and death four weeks later. Both her grandmother and her sister were now unwell, and Margaret returned home reluctantly to care for both of them. It seems strange that, in a family of eight children, Margaret should have had to carry this burden, but it was not unusual for families to expect single women, and especially missionaries, to give up their own work in such circumstances. It was four years before she saw China again, but by that time her home ties were all gone and she was completely free.

A great deal had happened in those four years. By 1908, Japan had defeated Russia and was flexing her muscles. Reform was the key word in China and for the first time in centuries China was looking not backwards to the past, but forwards to the future and change. People were eager to study science and explore Western culture; education for girls was on the increase; railways were being built, and newspapers were proliferating.

## The Yangzhou girls' school

Back in Yangzhou, Margaret's close friend Emmie Clough had started a girls' boarding school in premises next door to the new language school. Margaret was delighted to be asked to live at the school as a companion for Emmie. Her own focus would still be on local evangelism and medical work for women, which included frequent emergencies with attempted suicides and opium overdoses. Opium still brought destitution and tragedy to millions of families, and her heart ached at the human misery she found on the streets. She could do so little to help.

In these circumstances, Emmie's friendship and the cheerful routines of the schoolgirls were good antidotes to days of sorrow. She loved the contact she had with the girls. Most staff would have lived in a separate house, but for Emmie and Margaret education went beyond acquiring knowledge. It included self-control, mental and moral training, and the development of Christian character. The girls came from several provinces including distant Gansu, and many of them were from first-generation Christian homes; usually their mothers were completely uneducated. At the cost of their own privacy, both women chose to have their own rooms near the girls' dormitories, and their study/living room was next to the classroom. Margaret's room was closest to the younger girls, with a balcony outside for sleeping in summer. In this way they would be closely involved in the daily lives of the girls, and they endeavoured to live out before them what it meant to be a Christian.[23]

There was a daily half-hour assembly for prayer and Bible teaching. Chinese teachers helped with a curriculum that covered all the normal primary and elementary school subjects up to high-school level, including physical education, needlework, Chinese sewing and embroidery. Later they were able to train their own senior girls as monitor teachers, and Emmie hoped these girls could take charge of the school under Margaret's guidance when she went on leave.[24]

## The Goforth revival

Soon after Margaret returned from Canada, Jonathan Goforth (also from Canada) held special meetings to describe the revival that had recently broken out in Korea. Margaret and Mrs Sie attended the meetings and both of them received a new experience of the power of the Holy Spirit, which had a profound influence on their future ministry. Some people were so overwhelmed by their sin that they were weeping as they confessed it. The leaders were aware of the dangers of emotional responses: it would have been easy to manipulate them, and some apparent responses faded out. One of the pastors involved began asking people to report the results that were still evident a year later – that was the sort of change that counted in people's lives.

When Margaret returned to the school, she shared what they had experienced informally one evening and she was amazed at the unexpected response from the girls. She later commented that the senior girls who were not yet Christians became Christians that night, and the whole spiritual life of the school was raised to a new level.

## Future leaders

This marked a turning point in Margaret's ministry. She had a new vision of the potential of these girls. The teachers had always hoped and prayed that the girls would commit themselves as followers of Jesus Christ, and become significant in the churches as Christian wives and mothers. In fact, however few they appeared to be, within a few years they would emerge strategically as the educated women leaders of the future. The earliest schools had all been Christian. The provincial governors were beginning to recognise the importance of girls' education, but they could not have schools without teachers – and for the moment, only the Christian schools were producing teachers. Margaret continued to reach out to ordinary women in the towns and villages, but her daily life at the school gave her a good rapport with schoolgirls, and she began to accept requests to hold missions in various girls' schools, even if this impinged on her local evangelism. The Yangzhou girls prayed for her as she visited these other schools where sometimes as many as 80 girls might profess conversion.

In the winter of 1910–11, not for the first time, Margaret was critically ill with pneumonia. The following summer, to avoid the heat, she went to the Guling mountain resort above

Lake Poyang, where many missionaries used to retreat. She found a common concern among the varied people gathered there: young people in China were on the move, leaving the past behind and reaching out to the future. The girls were unbinding their feet, cutting their hair and adopting Western dress. They were searching for meaning in life and questioning the old ways, and Western literature was flooding the country. There was a growing need for Christian leaders who could guide the young people both within the church and outside. People on vacation in Guling that summer began to pray for such leaders.

Dr White, an American seminary president, was speaking at the Guling Summer Conference. In 1911 the North China Union College was providing the first university education for women in Beijing. Ginling College would follow in 1915. Dr White challenged the missionaries to think ahead and develop theological training for educated women Bible teachers as well as men. Such Bible training as existed tended to be at a low level, and illiteracy among women was still a major hindrance in education. The normal Bible women were humble people who served faithfully, but who would reach the middle-school and high-school graduates who were now emerging? Margaret's own priority was evangelism rather than teaching, but she recognised the wisdom of his plea and was ready to support others who took up the challenge. Before anyone could act, there was more political upheaval in 1911. Revolution brought down the remains of the Manchu imperial rule, and Dr Sun Yat-sen became president of the Chinese Republic.

## Theological training for women

In 1912, seven mission boards co-operated to establish the Nanking Union Bible College for Women, where Christian middle-school and high-school graduates could be trained for Christian service in the new Republic.[25] Other mission boards were co-opted. There were many difficulties: mission boards were slow to catch the vision and provide the finance; students were slow to take up this new opportunity, and no sooner had they organised a faculty of four women than the principal became ill and had to return home. They filled the gaps and broadened the scope of the faculty by inviting visiting teachers – Margaret King was one of those invited.

After Margaret's first course of lectures to the 20 or so students, the new principal, Mary Culler White, could not speak too highly of her. She was impressed by her fluency, as she communicated in excellent Chinese. She was also impressed by her down-to-earth practicality after 20 years of experience as a missionary. Her careful explanation of the Bible and her ability to draw out the fundamental truths underlying the text were unusual. Her approach was not dry and intellectual: all she said and did brought the students closer to God and ever more deeply committed to serving him. In spite of considerable pressure later to join the faculty, and even to become principal of the college, Margaret firmly adhered to her prior call to evangelism, but she did continue to give several courses of lectures each year, and in 1916 she joined the board.[26]

In 1915 Ella Shaw wrote the annual report on the college in the *Chinese Recorder*.[27] The first three girls had graduated the previous June, and "Miss King of Yangzhou" had been the speaker. They had fourteen students left (they lacked space for many more) and they included high-school graduates, teachers and some more elderly, Chinese-educated Bible women who would benefit from more training. The students came from four of the coastal provinces and three just inland, from various denominations.[28] Singing and organ playing were significant in the curriculum for their future work. They studied the Bible, had a course in "physical culture" (one of the results of bound feet was the impossibility of any physical exercise, with disastrous consequences for health), advanced English for those who had studied it already, homiletics and church history. Students also had weekend assignments in the churches. In addition, they provided part-

time training for local Bible women and Sunday school teachers, but they needed more lecturers and more space.

In 1914 a large conference in Nanjing (Nanking) was
attended by 500 women teachers, high-school students, and
Bible women from Jiangsu and the adjacent provinces.
Margaret was the only foreigner there. Already, committed
Chinese women were emerging as gifted Bible teachers and
evangelists. As Margaret continued to lead school missions
over a wide area, she told the girls about the Union Bible
College and the opportunities it offered for training in
Christian service. One day in 1926 she was walking through
the college and the principal was astonished to see girls running up to greet "this China Inland Missionary" –
Presbyterians, Baptists and Methodists to name but a few.
How on earth did such a wide range of students know her?
Most people lived within their own denominational circles –
but not Margaret. She had an open door to the new generation of educated Chinese girls through the missions she was
leading in the various mission schools, and many girls from
different schools and churches were entering the college
because of the impact she had had on their lives.

Meanwhile Margaret's work among the local Yangzhou
women continued. Railways and better roads were being
built, but the village work was still hard. The missionaries
either walked up to 20 miles a day, or they were wheeled in
the traditional wheelbarrows with their wadded bedding
softening the rough ride, or they used springless carts with
crude wooden wheels. At least around Yangzhou they could
use boats on the canals.

After 20 years of working alongside Margaret, Mrs Sie
was forced by failing health to retire at the age of 60. On her
birthday, her friends presented her with the traditional gift
of grave clothes – except that she requested them to be white,
rather than the usual red, because white was the colour of
heaven! In her place, some of the new graduates like Miss Nyi
of Nanjing Bible School began to work with Margaret. On one
occasion she had to reassure some anxious mothers that

arithmetic would not in any way damage their daughters – she had studied it herself without ill effects! The incident gives a glimpse of the huge change taking place for women in this generation.

The third decade of the twentieth century opened with the Union Bible College celebrating its tenth anniversary with new premises, 100 students and courses for both high-school and university graduates.[29] There were still only two university colleges with a total of 78 women students for the whole of China, and yet a start had been made. In 1922 the landmark National Christian Conference was held in Shanghai, when more than 1,000 male and female represen-tatives from the churches and the missions gathered; half the delegates were Chinese (see also Chapters Five and Seven). Margaret King had represented the CIM in the evangelism section of the China Continuation Committee that had organ-ised this large conference, and later she was one of four who represented the CIM on the National Christian Council. She always spoke Chinese, unlike many missionaries. Someone commented that she was "one of the few women to make an important contribution" there. She was also described as "the best-known missionary in central China". This breadth in her ministry meant that she contributed at national level to the Chinese church, and came to know many of China's signifi-cant Christian leaders, in addition to influencing some of the younger men and women emerging as future leaders.[30]

Her senior status and experience made her a valuable resource for newly arrived missionaries, and she could give helpful advice on behaviour and dress. She also contributed to a debate in the *Chinese Recorder* on "The Present Problems of Country Work":

> I believe the real problem to be the point of contact, and solv-ing it in part lies in the centre from which we do our work... I have found it a great advantage to live as one of the family in a Christian or enquirer's home if possible. This has its disad-vantages in the comfort and quiet the guest enjoys, but for get-

ting into heart-touch with the women and children, it is far ahead of the plans before tried. Regular teaching may be given the one who has invited you... morning or evening worship may be used as an evangelistic meeting, relatives invite you to other centres etc. Much of this contact cannot be obtained on a boat or in a rented place.[31]

It was a costly policy to live without privacy, sharing the *kang* (sleeping platform) with the other village women in the family. (Another missionary staying at an inn once had the chickens put in her bedroom for safety, while her hostess took the ducks, and the pigs had to stay outside the bedroom door!)[32] Her grandmother's wealthy, upper-class home in Montreal must have seemed like something from another planet! This degree of identification enabled her to get close to the women, and was the foundation for a ministry that spanned 34 years.

In 1927 Margaret spent a year in Canada, when political turmoil had led to most missionaries evacuating to the coast. China had been simmering with anger ever since the Western allies took Shandong province from the Germans after the First World War and, instead of returning it to China, gave it to Japan. Communist sympathisers stirred up the people and Nanjing, the southern capital, was the first place to be attacked. Many Christian buildings were damaged. The Bible college and the Yangzhou school were looted and one of the school buildings was burned. The college closed for the next 18 months.

The college was already facing other difficulties of a different nature. It was a Union college answerable to seven mission boards, and as board members changed, so did the policy; eventually the board was out of step with many of the faculty and students. Some of those on the board had more liberal views and wanted a broader-based religious education. Co-operation became increasingly difficult, until finally they decided to separate by mutual agreement. Most of the faculty and students were committed to keeping the Bible central to the curriculum, and concentrating on the essential skills the students needed for their future work. Mary Culler White, the principal, others on the faculty including Margaret King, and most of the students withdrew to form the Bible Seminary for Women. They established a conservative doctrinal basis, but had no mission boards behind them and no financial resources. They took a major step of faith, believing that if the work was of God, he would provide the buildings and equipment they needed. They agreed, on principle, never to go into debt or spend money they did not have.

## The Bible Seminary for Women

In the summer of 1930, the new board and faculty were preparing for the new academic year, with applications coming in from new students, but the leaders were still searching for premises. There was not enough money to buy a building, and in Shanghai, where they were searching, nothing suitable to rent or lease. Then, in July, Dr Dora Yü offered to lease her premises in Kiangwan in the Shanghai suburbs. Dora was one of the early Chinese women leaders. She had spent eight years as a missionary doctor in Korea and then operated a retreat centre in Shanghai for prayer and Bible teaching. However, she really wanted to be free for a wider Bible teaching ministry across China, and if the Bible seminary used the premises, the other ministries at Kiangwan could continue. The seminary board, staff and students were overjoyed at what they received as the Lord's answer to their prayers and Dora Yü was delighted that the buildings would be used in this way.

The autumn term opened smoothly with 53 students from seven provinces. The senior students who transferred brought with them the ethos of the previous college. When the board began to discuss the possibility of buying the premises, Dora Yü unexpectedly and most generously gave them the deeds of the property as a love gift. As more money was given, they were able to purchase more land and even erect a faculty residence just before the winter set in (the teachers had been sleeping on camp beds on the verandas outside their studies!). Other buildings followed later.

At the end of the first autumn term, Margaret, as vice-president of the seminary, braved the cold weather to travel 200 miles from Yangzhou to Shanghai. She had been very ill earlier in the year – probably pneumonia yet again – and spent October recuperating at the CIM headquarters in Shanghai. She loved it there as she met so many people, known and unknown, travelling to and from remote parts of China to the coast. She was back in Shanghai at the seminary in early December for a board meeting, took the students through Peter's first epistle, and was present at the end of term when the deeds of the property were handed over. She also officially opened the new faculty residence. Miss Brittain introduced her as the "Mother" of the seminary, and reported on the joy of the students at having her there. "She was wearing a long Chinese gown, as she often did in cold weather, and it became her well."[33]

She hurried straight back to Yangzhou for another mission, and celebrated Christmas with her adopted daughters, Jean and Katie, and their families. It had been a busy month and Margaret was tired. She caught a cold, which deteriorated into pneumonia yet again. She died nine days later on 6 January 1931, at the age of 65. Three days later, the local evangelist led her funeral service. A Chinese general attended and provided a military band to lead the procession, and representatives, both Chinese and Western, of several missions and Bible schools attended. Many of them spoke about her life, spent in constant work for the Chinese church and especially the evangelisation and education of its women.

Jessie and Margaret arrived in China within months of each other and both began with the local women; women who were regarded as incapable of learning, many of them crippled and unable to move far from their homes, spending most of their lives behind the walls of their courtyards, shut in from the streets; women dominated by their mothers-in-law and husbands, bearing innumerable children year after year, with little to alleviate the monotony.

Jessie Gregg, with her lively, down-to-earth style, managed to get through to hundreds of them, telling them of a God who loved them and died for them, affirming their value in his sight, whatever other people said, and challenging them with different ways of thinking and believing.

Margaret King kept in touch with these local women, but she also caught a vision for the newly emerging young women of the next generation, spending their teenage years not shut up at home doing nothing, but studying at school, gaining in knowledge and maturity, training as teachers and going to university-level colleges. Many had come through the larger mission schools with a Christian background. They were the new generation of future leading women who would have a significant impact on China as she moved through the twentieth century.

## Notes to Chapter Six

1   Thompson, *Each to Her Post*, p. 83.
2   By 1919, Henrietta Soltau was 76 and unable to keep up with the post-war generation. Even so, it was a most reluctant retirement! Cable and French, *Woman*.
3   Jessie Gregg, "These Forty Years", *China's Millions* (December 1937) p. 224.
4   Marshall Broomhall, *Martyred*, p. 169.
5   Ibid., pp. 178–79.
6   Ibid.
7   C. H. S. Green, "Sowing and Reaping in Hwailu", *China's Millions* (July 1912) p. 110.
8   Jessie Gregg, "These Forty Years", *China's Millions* (December 1937) p. 224.
9   C. H. S. Green, "Sowing and Reaping in Hwailu", *China's Millions* (July 1912) p. 110.
10  Jessie Gregg, "An Interview with Miss Jessie Gregg", *China's Millions* (November 1920) pp. 124–28.

11 Jessie Gregg, "Revival Work Among Chinese Women", *China's Millions* (July 1913) p. 107.

12 Jessie Gregg, "These Forty Years", *China's Millions* (December 1937) p. 224.

13 Jessie Gregg, "An Interview with Miss Jessie Gregg", *China's Millions* (November 1920) p. 125.

14 Mrs C. H. Stevens, *China's Millions* (September 1917).

15 Jessie Gregg, "Miss Gregg's Mission in Manchuria", *China's Millions* (September 1925) pp. 138–39.

16 *China's Millions* (September 1926) pp. 138–39; (September 1928) pp. 140–41; (November 1931) pp. 205–206.

17 *China's Millions* (January 1938) p. 8.

18 Jessie Gregg, "These Forty Years", *China's Millions* (December 1937) p. 225.

19 CIM Conference Report 1922, p. 133.

20 Thompson, *Each to Her Post*, pp. 98–100.

21 Geraldine Howard Taylor, *Margaret King*, pp. 1–20.

22 Ibid., pp. 24–46.

23 Ibid., pp. 48–52.

24 Boarding was necessary since the girls could not walk alone through the streets. Some people have asked whether this education alienated the girls from their Chinese families and nation. Inevitably education changed their lives, and removed them from the narrow secluded life in the family, but the girls in many schools bonded very strongly with each other and left school with a deep commitment as potential leaders in the future, to do all they could to help China. Hunter, *Gentility*, pp. 244–45.

25 Also known as "The Bible Teachers' Training School for Women". *Chinese Recorder* vol. 46 (March 1915) p. 199.

26 Geraldine Howard Taylor, *Margaret King*, pp. 59–60, 66–71, 103–104, 112–13.

27 *Chinese Recorder* vol. 46 (March 1915) p. 199.

28 Ibid., p. 200. Shandong, Fujian, Hunan, Jiangsu, Anhui, Zhejiang, and Jiangxi. Anglican, Calvinist, Arminian, Presbyterian.

29 Ibid., pp. 112–13

30 Geraldine Howard Taylor, *Margaret King*, pp. 90–93, 116.

31 Margaret King, "Present Problems of Country Work – a Symposium", *Chinese Recorder* (March 1918) p. 169.

32 "Women's Work", *China Mission Yearbook 1915*, vol. 6, p. 369.

33 Geraldine Howard Taylor, *Margaret King*, p. 145.

*Chapter Seven*　　**A Passion for Education**

## Eva French

Born in St Omer in 1869, Evangeline (known as Eva) French grew up in a comfortable Anglo-Irish home. On her first day at school the lively, headstrong, rebellious little six-year-old scaled a high wall – and then negotiated with the nuns over her descent in return for a bar of chocolate and no punishment! Other dangerous escapades punctuated her childhood and teenage years, until the family decreed that no one should endanger their own lives in trying to rescue her. When the family moved to Geneva in her teens, the strict routine and discipline of her Swiss secondary school redirected her energies and she buried herself in study. At that time Geneva was a lively centre for European culture and politics, and she thrived on intellectual debate and a busy social life. Her literary mother attracted many visitors to their home, which was later described as "a cross between a restaurant and a dormitory". The social round in her home left little time for developing domestic skills or forming close friendships.

In her teens several things happened which in retrospect gained in significance. During a period of personal doubt and confusion, she asked a chaplain how she could find satisfaction. He suggested church services, with their intellectual sermons and arguments, as the solution, but she was already attending those. She was living in Geneva when the *Maréchal*[1] and the Salvation Army brought a breath of fresh air to the intellectual climate, challenging the local bye-laws against open-air meetings and blazing a trail through the streets with much zeal but very little French language, to the amusement of many, including Eva. She also heard an American woman who had taught in China describing the deprivation and exploitation of the women there; Eva had encountered Bolshevik and revolutionary thinking, and she was already concerned about widespread poverty in the cities of Europe.

When her parents finally returned to England, Eva and her sister Francesca found themselves in an unfamiliar world; Eva particularly felt herself a misfit in the rigid roles of Victorian society. She was sophisticated, well-educated and bilingual, and Portsmouth was a far cry from the cultured world of Geneva. She was now confronted with suffering on her doorstep, and she rebelled against a society that discriminated against women, exploited them in sweatshops, and tolerated extreme poverty. Her family were formal churchgoers, but it was a chance visit to a church in a poor district that finally changed her life. After all the theological discussions and debates, suddenly the basic simplicity of the gospel came home to her: at last she understood the reality of personal sin, Jesus' death on the cross for the sin of the whole world, and his readiness to forgive each person who recognised their sin before God and turned to him for forgiveness. Her family were not impressed by this personal commitment, but for Eva her whole life was reorientated. Before long she sensed that God was calling her to serve him in China.

The rebel clothed herself with the meekness and quietness popularly associated with Christian women, but they sat unnaturally on her and her family knew it. For a long time she hid herself behind this mask: it would be ten years before she was able to relax and be herself, using her natural gifts in Christian service. Meanwhile she began to prepare for China. The China Inland Mission sent her to the Liverpool Deaconess Home for Training – noted for its rigour – and after a year of biblical studies, she was sent out visiting the Liverpool slums. She was also directed to begin training as a nurse, but medical work did not suit her, and after a month on the wards she collapsed. When the doctors forbade her to return to nursing, she went back to the poorest areas of Liverpool, where she developed her gift for personal evangelism, and thrived.

The episode in the hospital had raised questions about her health, and the principal of the Deaconess Home felt strongly that she should serve in Britain, and not in China. It was Hudson Taylor who finally overruled this advice and in 1893, at the age of 22, she left for China. After six months of Chinese study in the Yangzhou training home, where she would have overlapped with both Jessie Gregg and Margaret King, she fell ill again. Once more Taylor intervened, this time to ensure that she went to the hot, dry climate of Shanxi province in north China, where her health improved and she never looked back. Because of the Sino-Japanese War, the journey there took three months by boat and cart.

With a Chinese woman for company, Eva was soon travelling extensively by donkey, staying in private homes when invited and sharing the Christian message with village women over a wide area; her fluency in the language increased steadily. Pingyao soon became "the place where she kept her boxes". Later she visited the opium refuges developed by Pastor Hsi to support opium addicts through detoxification. Nights spent in village homes could be disrupted by women waking for more opium at midnight, and the bedding might be verminous, but as she lay wrapped in her quilt on the sleeping platform with the other women, she learned a great deal about their daily lives within the confines of the courtyards.

In the seven years she spent in Shanxi province she became widely known and made many friends, but finally the atmosphere began to change. The anti-foreign Boxer rebels were making their presence felt, threatening not only the foreigners but also the Christian Chinese. Eva realised she had to try to prepare these simple believers for possible persecution of a kind they had never before faced. They knew that trouble was coming, but even so, when the storm broke in the hot summer of 1900, the suddenness and the violence were greater than anyone could possibly have anticipated. (See also Jessie Gregg, Chapter Six.)

Eva was evacuated together with two couples, seven other single women and two pre-school children. As they fled from town to town, the means of travel steadily worsened until, sick and weak, they were spending ten hours a day in spring-less wooden carts crashing over the stony roads. The two children did not survive. "Fifty days," as the missionaries said later, "of heat, misery, unutterable fatigue, hunger, thirst and rioting, conveyed as prisoners from city to city, sleeping in prisons, temples, or verminous holes." Yet on two occasions, Eva's childhood courage and defiance came to the fore when, to the astonishment of the rioting crowds, she quietly walked through them to the *yamen* (city office) to plead for protection from the city rulers.

The missionaries owed their lives to Christian Chinese who endured the same suffering and danger to help them reach safety.[2] She returned to Britain shocked, not surprisingly, by the prolonged physical and mental suffering she had endured, and mourning the deaths of many friends, both Chinese and missionary.

One year later she was back in China. The rebellion had been fiercest in Shanxi province and many Chinese believers had also suffered persecution and even martyrdom for their faith. It was a sombre homecoming to find houses and possessions gone, and churches and schools destroyed. Eva made it her first task to visit all the believers in the Huozhou (Hwochow) area, and listen to their stories of suffering and death. She took with her Mildred Cable, a new worker fresh out of language school. For Mildred, it must have been a daunting introduction to her future life in China.

## Mildred Cable

Alice Mildred Cable was born in 1878 and grew up with her three brothers and two sisters in Guildford. Their rigid nursery routine was dominated by a nurse who did all she could to keep the children on "the narrow way" with threats and warnings about the judgement of God. Even as an adult,

Mildred recalled the "sleepless, tearful nights" of her child-hood, spent worrying about waking up in hell before the next morning. Her escape was to invent her own fantasy world where such horrors did not exist; unfortunately, when her parents became aware of this, they removed all the more imaginative books from the nursery shelves. She was then left to protect herself by retreating into her own world.

Nursery life was followed by a series of strict governesses, and after that the academic rigour of Guildford High School, then in its second year of operation. The town's mayor had insisted that the new school must provide an academic edu-cation – not merely the traditional female accomplishments – so inadvertently he had a profound influence not only on Mildred but also on the schoolgirls in Shanxi province in China![3]

The curriculum at Guildford was so crowded that there was no room for games or gymnastics or any creative or friv-olous activities. Even in the school holidays Mildred's life was regimented by a governess at home who "spoilt every minute by her mere presence". Mildred was steadily pushed academ-ically until she had no time for leisure or relaxation. In ret-rospect, she said she "was in danger of becoming a learning-machine". Her innate capacity for joy burst out at intervals, but those moments were so rare and brief that the joy "tipped the balance of pleasure till it touched the index of pain".

As a child she had once had a significant dream: she dreamed that she was in the Jerusalem Temple and saw Jesus playing with the children. He beckoned her to join in and she did, recognising his love for her for the first time. She said nothing about this dream, but she felt it had a profound effect on her – though it was years before she linked it with her understanding of the fatherhood of God. Later, on the family beach holidays on the Isle of Wight, she enjoyed the informality of the children's beach missions run by Scripture Union. Eventually she had the opportunity to attend a chil-dren's mission in Guildford. After the first meeting, some parents felt it was too emotional and withdrew their children, but Mildred's pastor asked for permission to take her to the final meeting. On the way home she committed her life to Christ: she was twelve years old. As usual, she kept her decision to herself, but she began attending the weekly children's meetings that followed.

At the time the denominational walls separating the Guildford churches were still high, but a few years later a small group organised a local version of the well-known Keswick Convention, and invited well-known speakers including D. L. Moody. These meetings attracted many people from different churches and broadened Mildred's horizons. Finally, in 1893, at the age of fifteen, Mildred met Emily Whitchurch of the China Inland Mission and realised that God was calling her to serve him in China. She was rather reluctant at first: she would rather have gone to India. While still at school, she got in touch with the CIM, and stayed at the training home on several occasions.

This was not the life her parents had in mind for their academic daughter. When she left school, her mother allowed her to spend six months at the CIM training home, hoping the spartan regime would get China out of her daughter's system, but it did not. Then her father took her on a luxury European tour for three months and that also failed to have the desired effect. She moved to London, where she studied privately under one of the early women scientists (very few women studied science then). She did not want a medical degree, which might have restricted her to hospital work, so a course was put together which would give her a more general training for the future. She qualified in pharmacy, and also studied advanced physics and chemistry, anatomy, surgery and midwifery. Her weeks were packed full of lectures.

Spiritually she thrived in a Friday-evening Bible school started in North London by a young minister, the Revd G. Campbell Morgan, and he and his wife became her lifelong friends and mentors.[4] When he recommended her to the CIM, he wrote: "I have never recommended anyone for missionary work with more heartiness or stronger conviction of her fitness."[5] At a time when Bible colleges were few, many of those who were about to serve overseas attended this school on Friday evenings. Later their work took them across the world to teach what they had learned, so the influence of this young minister was far-reaching. In addition, his church members were encouraged to vacate the church for visitors on Sunday evenings and take the gospel on to the streets. They began to hold an alternative Sunday evening service in the Variety Hall: a lantern projected hymns on to a screen, and the services were cheerful, informal and lively, with personal testimonies and a short but relevant message. It proved popular, and many people responded to the gospel.

In 1900, seven years after Mildred had first sensed a call to China, she was ready to move forward, but the Boxer Rebellion broke out. There had been signs of unrest beforehand, but no one had foreseen the terrible extent of the violence against foreigners and Chinese Christians. Emily Whitchurch, who had been so influential in her life, was the first CIM missionary to be killed. It looked as if the door to China might be closed for years. Mildred's plans for China had not been made alone: there was a young man in her life who also intended to be a missionary, and they planned to marry. Now she received a disappointing letter from him: he was no longer heading for China. She could marry him and remain in Britain, or face China alone. It was a bitter blow, but she kept her eyes firmly fixed on China (though it was years before she really got over that loss). In the end she was able to sail in the autumn of 1901, much earlier than she had expected. She could begin language study on the coast until it was safe to move to inland China.


## To China

A year later Eva French became her senior missionary. Eva was seven years older than Mildred, but it was the beginning of a partnership that would last for the rest of their lives.

They moved into the wrecked mission home in Huozhou to work with the church community. A Chinese pastor led the church, and there were two opium refuges. Huozhou had been spared the worst of the Boxer attack, but believers in the surrounding towns and villages had been through great suffering. Eva and Mildred were to focus on the women.

The first two women missionaries to reach Huozhou, fourteen years earlier, had been the first Norwegian missionaries ever to go to China. Sophie Reuter had been a governess in a wealthy home: on her arrival she started a girls' school, beginning with three pupils. Anna Jakobsen, her partner, had been a housemaid. Mildred later described Anna as

> enthusiastic and independent in thought and action... [and] she soon acquired the spoken language to a remarkable degree... She studied the classical works of the Chinese, and at the same time could vie with most of the women in all branches of their domestic activities.[6]

The local people had taken the two lively, outgoing Scandinavians to their hearts. The missionaries organised a meal on Sundays for the believers who walked in from the country areas – until they found that all and sundry were turning up for a free meal, and the owners of the local eating-places were not amused. After some years, both girls married and were replaced by two more CIM ladies who were determined to re-establish some boundaries and be less familiar. The church members had drawn unfavourable comparisons. Those two women died with 44 others in the massacre in Taiyuan: Eva and Mildred took their place. The church members were cautious. They had met Eva before and knew that her Chinese was "as good as Miss Jakobsen's"! Mildred, on the other hand, was young, not known to them, and she had not been through the recent trauma. Even before she opened her mouth, they told her they could not understand her.

I had only one asset, and that was the fact that this being my first station I should belong to them, and when the day dawned that would release my stammering tongue, the honour of having taught and trained me would be theirs![7]

Eva loved the village work and Mildred was eager to be involved: it was an exciting business. The Chinese women were illiterate, and rarely left their homes: they knew and heard little of the world outside. Sometimes the men had become Christians, but their wives and children remained deep in ignorance and superstition. They would only hear the Christian message if women visited them at home. There was a growing movement against binding the feet of small girls, but mothers who wanted to protect their daughters from a life of hard labour bound their feet out of kindness. Bound feet ensured a genteel life sitting at home: unbound feet would lead them to a life of heavy labour on the farms. Eva had shared their lives for seven years and understood the culture. In 1903 she wrote of a large gathering when some 40 women were baptised, including some women who had been in the first Huozhou school in childhood. She followed this up by visiting the 19 villages from which they came, to give them further teaching. She found many open doors and commented that hundreds wanted more teaching.[8] All the newly baptised women had unbound their feet. Nothing could repair the physical damage done to them in childhood, but choosing the Christian way led them into a new freedom. They left behind their fear and superstition and the burden of trying to earn merit, and entered into a life where there was a God who loved them and welcomed them into his family. Unbinding their feet became symbolic of a much greater inner freedom.

## Training women for the future

In spite of their love for village work, as Eva and Mildred prayed and planned for the future, one question dominated their thinking: what does the Chinese church need now? And two urgent things surfaced. Firstly, they needed more help in evangelism. After the horrors of the Boxer Rebellion and the courageous witness, even to death, of the Chinese believers, crowds of non-Christian Chinese began visiting the churches in the towns and villages, wanting to know more about the Christian faith. The missionaries were far too few to handle what was almost a mass movement, and it was clear that the task of evangelism must fall on the church members. The time had come for missionaries to step back from the "front line" and train Chinese Christians to take their place. That was another reason for discouraging foot-binding: they needed to train older, mobile Christian women as Bible women and evangelists who were able to travel on foot and visit women in their homes.

The second great need was for educated Christian wives and mothers in the next generation. Far more men than women attended church services, because women could not go out, and the few who did try to go to church had to endure verbal abuse in the streets. Ever since foreign women had been allowed to live in China some 40 years earlier, missionary women had run small schools for a dozen or so children in an effort to contact girls and their mothers and teach them to read the Bible. Most girls from eleven years of age were still confined in their homes until they married, but school could now provide a much more interesting alternative for teenagers! Learning to read was the key to education, but the task of memorising 4,000 ideographs presented a colossal barrier: the Chinese script took years to master. The churches were using a romanised alphabet to help the Christians to read, but even this was not ideal.

Education was a controversial subject among the missionaries. At one extreme, some felt that they had a duty to provide the supposedly superior Western-type education: this would prepare China to take her place in the modern world, and also prepare the way for the Chinese to grasp Christian concepts, which were so different from Buddhist teaching.

Others, including many CIM missionaries, saw advanced education as a diversion from the supreme call to evangelise. However, there were other considerations. The missionaries were few and China was vast: the population of Shanxi province alone reached 10 million by 1908. Also, time might be short: the Chinese, with their long history and ancient culture, had an independent spirit. Western countries might scramble for spheres of influence, but China never became any other nation's colony. They would not tolerate churches led by Westerners indefinitely. Consequently most people focused on encouraging Chinese leaders to take over in the churches as soon as possible, and they needed to train both men and women to that end.

Eva and Mildred put their own love for village work to one side in order to tackle this greater need in the church. In 1904 Mildred opened a new girls' school in Huozhou with 24 girls, all of them with unbound feet. The Christian parents were prepared to make a stand. The following year she reported that a friend, unaware of any specific need, had sent a gift which enabled them to build a new courtyard for the girls' school. This gave them accommodation and classrooms for training the young wives of Christian workers, in addition to the schoolgirls aged from nine to 16. With the addition of the women who helped at the opium refuge, they had no fewer than 70 women and girls there – a most unusual arrangement in China. The wives of Christian workers came for short courses of a week or two to study the Old and New Testaments, to teach some of the school classes, and to learn how to work with women and children and how to help opium patients. They also learned to read the Chinese Bible in the romanised script.

The missionaries paid the teachers' wages and provided food for those who came in from the villages for teaching, since when they visited the villages, they lived as the guests of local Christians. The rest of the work was largely self-supporting: the children brought flour and basic food for themselves (wheat noodles were more common than rice in north

China). The opium addicts paid to come, as did the young women. The girls represented a challenge: in their homes, the girls had been rejected one moment and then spoilt the next. Now they had to learn obedience and the discipline of living by a timetable. The following year there was a conference for 40 young women, when such topics as "foot-binding", "wine-drinking" and "the value of child life" (with special reference to female infanticide) were on the agenda. The churches were pioneering a new way of life for women. They had a long way to go.[9]

## A year in Britain

Eva and Mildred returned to Britain in 1908 after an absence of seven years; Mildred was now 30 and Eva 37. Eva's sister, Francesca, had cared for their failing parents until they died, but now she was free to join Eva in China. It is never easy to open up a close friendship to a third person, even if she is a sister. Mildred was determined to make her welcome, and as Francesca had considerable literary gifts, they worked together on several books which were later published under both their names. The books have scarcely dated in 70 years. Mildred assembled the main material and Francesca did the detailed editorial work, but she may have made a greater literary contribution to the enormous success of their books than is normally recognised. Mildred's first book, *The Fulfilment of a Dream*, seemed stilted in places. Either she grew in skill, or Francesca's handiwork improved her style. Francesca was much quieter and more sensitive than the older two women, though she had quite strong views of her own. The plan was for her to help Mildred in the school, and keep the daily domestic routine running for the "Trio", as they came to be called. They were to work together for the rest of their lives.

It was on this furlough that Mildred transferred her church membership to Westminster Chapel, where the Revd Campbell Morgan now served; she remained a member there for the rest of her life. Other members of the congregation were enthusiastic supporters of her work. When the time came to return to China, the Trio were praying that God would give them the money they needed to put up adequate buildings for the expanding women's Bible school. They never asked for money and they never went into debt, but trusted God to give them what they needed if this was his will. They reckoned they would need a minimum of £500. Before they left, the Chapel took up a collection and was able to give them £450 – a large amount of money in 1909. The Trio were grateful, though they were a little disappointed that it fell short of their need. They returned to China by train across Russia and Siberia with the £450. Soon after their arrival they visited a bank in Beijing; when the bank clerk overheard Eva's name he looked startled. Apparently a gift had been sent to the bank for her three years earlier and they had been unable to trace her. It was for £50 and had now accumulated interest! Mildred commented; "A strange coincidence you say! Yes… unless we take our courage in both hands and call it God."

Back in Huozhou, the number of schoolgirls had risen to 86, and an extensive building programme began. In addition to the new Bible school (which carried a plaque acknowledging the generous contribution from Westminster Chapel), the girls' school was expanded and a new church building for 600 people was also erected for the rapidly growing congregation. Strict economies, like buying up disused houses and reusing the building materials, enabled them to achieve all this using that gift of £500.

## The first women's mission

In the spring of 1910, after the new church had been dedicated, a new step was taken. First the compound was opened to the public, which created enormous local interest. This was followed by a six-day mission for Christian women, publicised widely in the towns and villages, some up to 50 miles away. Mildred had already identified Jessie Gregg's special gift for communicating with women, and she was invited to come and speak. In a culture where women rarely left their homes, let alone their villages, for several days, and anyone with bound feet needed transport, no one knew what the response would be. They could only wait and see.

The first guests arrived one evening from Chaocheng in thirteen unsprung carts with solid wooden wheels. They must have travelled 30 miles. The following day more arrived on trains of donkeys with their babies, others in barrows or sedan chairs. The guests finally numbered 350, and together with the church women, the student teachers, Bible women and schoolgirls, there were 500 people. The church men had bought the food since the women could not appear in the market, and the courtyards looked like campsites as they all cooked their meals. There was even a crèche provided for the babies. At the end of six days, 250 women courageously stood up at the final meeting to share publicly what they had learned. It was another momentous step forward in their lives and in outreach to women.

The following year the school numbers reached 100, and in 1913, the first class of teachers graduated.[10] The pupils travelled from the Shanxi province mission stations and the adjacent provinces by cart, donkey or litter or on foot, some for several days. They lived on the premises, where a shop and a bank were provided for them. If parents travelled in for church services on Sundays, they were able to spend time with their children.

Mildred was trying to give them an education that would combine Christian teaching with Chinese classics and at the same time keep them in touch with their family lives. The school summer holidays were timed to set them free to go home and help with the crops and wheat harvest. They had to make their own traditional cloth shoes and look after their Chinese garments. They demonstrated an incredible capacity for learning by rote: a ten-year-old could learn to recognise and write 500 characters in three months. Most children could memorise five chapters of the New Testament a day, and began learning whole books of the Bible by heart.

Mildred also encouraged them to think for themselves. Alongside the Confucian ethics of their own culture she introduced science, and encouraged them to explore the natural world around them. Astronomy was taught in order to break the obsession with astrology and fortune-telling which determined every decision. In a period when a broad education in the West focused on accumulating facts, the graduating teachers had to be able to explain the advantages and disadvantages of feudalism, the Spartan methods of disciplining children, and the causes of the French Revolution. As the Manchu dynasty crumbled, the budding teachers learned how democracy replaced feudalism in the West. The medieval history Mildred had studied at Guildford High School took on a new life in China, as this great nation began to move towards more democratic government.[11]

In 1911 the old Manchu imperial dynasty collapsed and Sun Yat-sen established the Chinese Republic. In the political turmoil that followed, hundreds poured into the churches and Christian education expanded rapidly, but the CIM continued to focus on the children from Christian families and the need for future church leaders, since it did not have the resources for widespread public education. The Trio's work was part of this church-focused expansion. The First World War came and went. Through Susie Garland's efforts, the new phonetic script was making the Bible and literacy accessible for all, and it was not a coincidence that Huozhou claimed to have the first fully literate church in Shanxi (see Chapter Five). An average woman, regardless of age, could now learn to read in a month. This alone would transform the women's work in villages, towns and Bible schools.

In 1921, when the Trio spent another year in Britain, the CIM experimented with a five-day winter school at Swanwick Conference Centre. Most of the guests arrived at dusk on the same train! Some had "conveyances" from the station but "the more adventurous spirits enjoyed a tramp along the footpaths across the fields with nothing more than the glow of a distant smelting furnace to warn them from the... mire left by heavy rain". There were meetings for the younger people "seated in free and informal fashion on the floor, in the friendly light of the fire", and the report referred to a session by Miss Cable, "to whom the work of Christian education has become a passion". Did anyone have an inkling that within two years the Trio would be heading into the unknown?

## The Shanghai conferences

In 1922 they were back in Shanghai for two major conferences, one with the CIM and the other representing the CIM at a National Christian Conference for the whole Protestant Church in China. In the course of the CIM Conference, both Eva and Mildred were involved in committee work, discussion and giving papers. Eva was asked to report specifically on her work in the Huozhou women's Bible school. The original local classes for women had led to requests for longer courses. These were run for three months at a time, and after eight years they had linked up with the Huntung Bible Institute, some ten miles down the river, and developed a two-year course. Correspondence courses were not feasible until the phonetic script brought literacy within reach of all. The Bible school was flexible, beginning with literacy for those who had no education, and allowing those with some education to gain more at the adjacent girls' school during their stay at the Bible school.

Eva could no longer be involved with village evangelism, but she still spent time every week praying with and encouraging the local male evangelists and Bible women. The older Bible women travelled and visited homes; the younger ones worked with the women in the local churches. By 1923, between 800 and 900 women had been in residence for periods varying from a few weeks to the full two years. Some became full-time Bible women, while others returned to their village homes committed to sharing what they had learned.

In the same year, Mildred contributed an article to the

*Chinese Recorder*, commenting on the work done in the women's Bible schools. She pointed out that women as well as men received spiritual gifts for the upbuilding of the church, and these should be recognised, and not restricted to work with women and children:

> The church will suffer loss if [a woman's] sphere were limited to the schoolroom. In the circle of the church... a totally different atmosphere to that found in a non-Christian audience exists, and the woman teacher has her place on the platform of such assemblies.[12]

She was not afraid to be controversial, and her views were sometimes well ahead of those of the evangelical world of that time. Women missionaries had usually devoted themselves to the "women's world" in China, but they found that many Chinese men were eager to attend the more informal women's meetings. Increasingly, where women had the gift of teaching, there was such a hunger to learn more that men gathered as well, and churches were blessed through their teaching. However, where Chinese women were concerned, patriarchal culture tended to reassert itself, and they were slower to acknowledge the gifts of their own women; hence Mildred's appeal.

At the 1922 CIM Conference Mildred spoke of the importance of training Christian leaders, and commented that "from the Huozhou girls' school there are over 50 now teaching in mission schools, and over 70 in government and other schools". She stressed the need for an overall mission educational policy, under which missionary staff should first have had grass-roots experience in village evangelism in order to understand their pupils. The teachers should be Christian, and a minimum of 75% of the children should come from Christian homes in order to preserve the ethos. In the past, schools had opened and closed as missionaries moved to and fro, leaving local teachers with no livelihood and children with no further education.

By this time, the CIM was responsible for educating 10,000 children of church members in 484 schools.[13] It was suggested that an education officer should be appointed with a brief for co-ordinating all the mission's educational work, and that a woman might undertake this task.[14] Mildred would have been the obvious choice, but within a year her future would be leading in a very different direction, and new government regulations would soon have a serious impact on Christian schools.

When the Chinese government laid down their own policies for public schools, they prevented Christian schools from teaching the Christian faith, and did not recognise their pupils' qualifications unless they were registered with the national schools. Some Christian schools continued regardless, but others, which saw evangelism as a priority, were not prepared to invest money and energy in education when they could not share their faith as well. Mildred faced an even greater problem when she returned to Huozhou after the conferences. The excellent Governor of Shanxi (a province with a population of 10 million people) had decided to open 70 new provincial schools for girls, using the phonetic script material. The only problem was that he had no teachers with which to staff them.

Mildred's school had 150 girls from Christian homes on the roll, aged from five to 20. Over the previous 20 years, 1,000 girls had passed through her school, 60 of her trained teachers were teaching in mission schools across five Chinese provinces, and 70 more were teaching in lower-grade government schools. Overall, she estimated that her graduates were teaching 5,000 girls. Now the Shanxi Governor was desperate for teachers; he needed her student teachers in training immediately, and also those with *any* secondary education.[15] In Huozhou the Chinese staff were quite competent to run the primary school, but the rest were mobilised throughout the province. Mildred realised this might be only a temporary problem for a few years, but meanwhile, what were they to do?

## What does China need now?

The Trio's 20 years in Shanxi had had an impact on the churches both in that province and in the five adjacent provinces, and Huozhou was now the centre for Christian women's work. Their foresight had put the schools 20 years ahead of any public policies for women's education, and Christian women were emerging as significant leaders for the future. The Trio had given their lives to this. In mid-life, they might well have retired or moved to less demanding work, but instead they began asking once more, "What does China need now?" They prayed for guidance, researched the current situation in China, and talked to those who knew more. The answer, when it came, stunned the people who knew them.

### Notes to Chapter Seven

1   The young Kate Booth, the controversial and gifted daughter of William and Catherine Booth, was nicknamed the *Maréchal*, or Field Marshal, as she led the Salvation Army teams preaching through the streets of the leading cities throughout Europe.
2   Cable and French, *Something Happened*, pp. 42–54.
3   Norma Denny, "From Guildford to the Gobi Desert – Mildred Cable (1878–1962)" (*sic*), *Surrey History* vol. v. no.1 (1994) pp. 46–59.
4   Morgan, *Man*, pp. 324–25, 350–62.
5   Platt, *Three Women*, p. 32.
6   Cable, *Dream*, p. 20.
7   Ibid., p. 34.
8   *China's Millions* (April 1903) p. 54; (May 1903) p. 64.
9   *China's Millions* (April 1905) p. 47; (May 1906) p. 78.
10  Mildred Cable, "School Work at Huochow, Shansi", *China's Millions* (April 1905) p. 47.
11  Cable, *Dream*, p. 267. From the 1915 Final Examination Paper of the China Inland Mission Normal Training College for Training Teachers.
12  *Chinese Recorder* (February 1922) pp. 118–20.
13  *China and the Gospel* (1922) pp. 46–47.
14  CIM Conference Report 1922, pp. 99–101.
15  Eva French, Mildred Cable, and Francesca French, "Twenty-one Years' Work in Hwochow", *China's Millions* (September 1923) pp. 136–38.

*Chapter Eight*     The Silk Road

"Our bodies are hardened like tempered steel through exposure to such extreme temperatures." The words conjure up a picture of young, energetic sportsmen, engaged in mountain-climbing, ocean-sailing, or arctic exploration. They scarcely bring to mind three middle-aged women, who had spent the first 20 years of their adult lives working in the structured, orderly activity of the girls' school and women's Bible college in Shanxi province. For only after that did Mildred Cable, with her two colleagues, Eva and Francesca French, embark on years of travelling the main trade route of Central Asia. There they faced extremes of heat and cold as they crossed and recrossed the Gobi desert and Tibetan foothills where the mountain passes (and some roads) rose to 10,000 feet and more. When international politics finally forced them to retire to Britain, they were honoured with national and royal recognition for their journeys, and today are included among great British women travellers of the twentieth century, although the travelling was entirely incidental to their main objectives.

## What does China need now?

Some 20 years earlier, after the Boxer Rebellion, Eva and Mildred had asked that question and prayed for an answer. As they prayed, they came to the conclusion that the major need at that time for the churches was the training of their women and girls: virtually all were illiterate and entirely uneducated.

So Eva and Mildred devoted their energies to education, putting on one side their love for evangelism. Now, after 20 years, the sudden government demand for provincial teachers had emptied their senior classes – for the moment at least – and the three women found themselves asking the same question once again. What does China need *now*?

Mildred had commented at the CIM Conference in 1922 that "we purpose moving from our settled stations to unevangelised regions; but in practice the time never seems to come". Now, with the unexpected closure of the senior school, they were free to return to the evangelism which had always been so close to their hearts. The three women had already been challenged by the maps and reports prepared for the National Christian Conference of China in 1922, which revealed the absence of any Christian witness for 1,000 miles along the Silk Road from northern Gansu to Ürümqi, in Xinjiang province. In 1921, Gansu province had a population of 12 million people and only 50 missionaries to help the new churches – one missionary for every 240,000 people.

Even when they lived in Huozhou, they had been aware of the distant provinces so different from the land of the Han Chinese. Tibetan pilgrims travelled the Big Road through Xi'an and Huozhou for a thousand miles to the sacred Wutai Mountain, prostrating themselves every few steps, hoping to see the famous lotus open. Travellers from the far west and the south – caravans of camels, laden donkeys, officials' wives swinging in litters hung between mules and families in carts – all converged on the same road to Beijing, just as Marco Polo had done centuries before. Life in the far north-west was hard: bitterly cold winters, blazing hot summers, and living conditions as primitive as any in China. In 1921, the three women, aged from 43 to 50, wrote for advice to Geraldine Howard Taylor (herself aged 60), who had just spent five winter months there. She wrote back encouragingly: enthusiasm and experience were more important than youthful fitness.

The mission leadership was less happy about their decision. Apart from George Parker and his wife in the early days of the mission, only three CIM men had ever ventured across the Gobi desert to Ürümqi in Xinjiang. (Two of them, George Hunter and Percy Mather, still lived there, some 51 days' journey from their nearest fellow-missionaries.) The Trio were highly respected senior women in the CIM, but some people accused them of restlessness after spending 20 years in one place. Others were concerned about the nature of the challenge: quite apart from their age, the primitive conditions and the extremes of climate and terrain that they would meet, they were moving from working among the Buddhist/Taoist Chinese to the Central Asian Muslim ethnic minorities. The Trio's local Chinese church was deeply distressed, and their pastor wept. He was planning to buy a plot of land for a church cemetery in Huozhou, where their beloved teachers might one day be laid to rest!

Undeterred, they left behind their personal belongings, and simply packed necessities, only to discover they could manage with even less when they lost several boxes to robbers within weeks (including their passports – even these proved dispensable and they managed with Chinese documents for the next four years). They commented, "from this time forward the higher estimate of our real needs steadily diminished."

## Journey to Gansu

The journey began on 11 June 1923, when they climbed into rickshaws and took the main road south from Huozhou. They knew very little of where they were going, except that it was 50 days' travel to Jiuquan, near the end of the Great Wall and the beginning of the Gobi desert. One day's journey was about 20 miles, and the speed, whether on foot, by donkey or cart (it made no difference which), was three miles per hour. They took their time, visiting mission stations and taking meetings for women as they went.

The province of Shanxi was orderly and well-governed, but Henan and Shaanxi were both overrun with robbers, and two women missionaries had just been abducted. It was far from reassuring to have a military escort forced on them, and anyway, the men disappeared at the first sign of trouble, "watching from a point of vantage" as they helpfully explained afterwards! The main road was almost empty, and the inns barely surviving, but the Trio were grateful for a roof over their heads, and slept to the music of the mules munching outside the door. The centuries-old road led westwards to the beautiful city of Xi'an where the terracotta army still lay buried, and where evidence had recently been unearthed suggesting that the first Christian missionaries had reached China as early as the eighth century.

There they changed to litters slung between two mules. The heavy boxes were put in the bottom, covered with bedding, and the passengers perched on top, using what they could for a back rest. In places the mud was six inches deep, and as autumn approached and they moved into the Tibetan foothills, the hooves of the animals would break through the thin ice into water below. They passed through an area devastated by earthquake two years earlier, when 200,000 people had died. They crossed the 9,000-foot pass over Lupan Mountain and made the risky descent before reaching Lanzhou, the capital of Gansu province, with its CIM mission hospital and schools. After a further seven days' journey north they passed through the last CIM outpost before Ürümqi, over 1,000 miles away.

The panhandle of Gansu, known today as the Hexi Corridor, stretches 600 miles north-west of Lanzhou, through a wide valley between the mountains of Mongolia and the high Tibetan plateau, up to the border with Xinjiang (an area technically beyond China's borders, but traditionally under her control). Their first target was Zhangye (Kanchow), where Marco Polo had stayed some 650 years earlier. A new, independent church had sprung up there, and they wanted to visit it.

In 1918 a young Chinese couple, Dr and Mrs Kao, had been called to pioneer evangelism in the area. Dr Kao's views

Teachers of the girls' school at Huozhou in 1923, the year the Trio return to England

The girls' school courtyard at Huozhou. Pastor Wang, pastor of the Huozhou church, stands in the foreground

On the road: the Trio and Topsy take a rest during their journey

Trio and Topsy at tea: (from left to right) Eva French, Topsy (the Trio's adopted daughter), Mildred Cable and Francesca French

The Trio: a world away from travelling across the Gobi desert by donkey and cart (Victoria Station, 1928)

The Trio in Chinese dress: (from left to right) Eva French, Francesca French and Mildred Cable

Many Chinese attend a meeting conducted by Anna Christensen (seated second row, fifth from the left)

**Left:**
Marie Monsen with Mrs Hsi,
Pastor Hsi's widow

**Below:**
Phyllis Thompson

on church government led him to support himself while he evangelised the area, and as people became Christians they were encouraged to do the same. In consequence there were no paid pastors, and as churches spread, they were led by the believers. Dr Kao was a gifted evangelist who gathered his small band of converts into a self-supporting Christian community, financed by a small farm owned by the church and his income from his medical work. After five years the church now had 40 members, and all were deeply committed to local evangelism. Together they systematically visited villages around Zhangye, but the doctor lacked the gift of teaching them the broader foundations of their faith. Even before Dr Kao met the Trio, he had encouraged the church to pray for two older women teachers who could survive the local conditions and provide deeper Bible teaching for them – Dr Kao found it hard to get on with Western men![1] Now at last Dr Kao's wife and two children travelled for two days down the road to meet them. By the time the Trio finally reached Zhangye, they had travelled 800 miles from Huozhou in nine months, and it was now March 1924. They had anticipated stopping briefly in the town, as they had done in so many other places, but something very different unfolded.

## The Zhangye church

Around 150 people crowded into that first Sunday service. The congregation included the 40 baptised believers, many more who were seeking the truth, and also the curious who had never seen foreign women before. All were welcome! Dr Kao reminded the church that they had been praying for two experienced Christian women to come to their aid, and in consequence they warmly welcomed them as God's gracious answer to their prayers. God had actually sent *three* of them (not just two, as requested); they were indeed experienced, for their hair was grey; and they could endure hardship, for they had survived the long journey across north China. These women had come to teach them. The Trio heard his words with some consternation – the church clearly expected them to settle there as teachers, when their intention was to move on to the unevangelised areas beyond.

Dr Kao reassured them.[2] He proposed that the Trio should spend the summer months that year in Zhangye, in concentrated teaching, and then go out with the church's evangelistic teams to the autumn fairs in the area. The church would then send a team further north-west to Jiuquan (Suzhou) to work with the ladies for the winter, when the farms were quiet. As it turned out, this partnership was to form the basis of their relationship and work for the next ten years.

The Trio began with a four-week Bible school in Zhangye for 25 men and women, undertaking six hours of instruction daily for a month. After a two-week break for evangelism, 50 more men and women studied for three weeks. Those who were illiterate learned to read the new phonetic script. It was a heavy teaching load, and it involved a great sacrifice of time for adult students, but at the end of the summer 90 more people were added to the official list of enquirers – those who were prepared to burn their idols and receive further teaching before baptism. This would identify them publicly with the Christian church there. Before the Trio left Zhangye in the autumn of 1924, 50 men and women were baptised, doubling the size of the church since the spring.

The church members spent several days sewing a tent big enough to hold 300 people at the autumn fairs, which attracted people from villages for miles around. Towns were few and most people lived in farmsteads scattered up the long valley: every farm would try to send at least one person to the fairs to buy necessities and get the latest news. Visiting the tent to hear the Christians became part of the day's entertainment, and crowds came to listen and buy Gospels. Any literature the Christians could offer was valued, read and passed around, and was sure to reach people over a wide area.

That year the teams made numerous trips with the Trio; such journeys involved carrying all the necessities from bedding to cooking pots, and sleeping in inns or rented houses in very primitive conditions. The extreme heat and the constant crowds were exhausting, but the work was rewarding. They would travel for two or three days to reach other towns in the valley, or the Tibetan lamaseries in the mountains, and always they had the opportunity to preach and discuss their message. The priests, too, came to the tent, eager to buy literature. People were searching for the truth, trying to gain merit and to obtain forgiveness of sin, a major concern in Tibetan Buddhism. A Buddhist visited the tent one day and sat listening spellbound to the story of the prodigal son. Afterwards he commented,

> "The forgiveness of that young man by his father is a thing I can understand, but what of the burden of sin of previous lives, which binds us to the wheel of life?"

> "The Lord Jesus Christ is the Door *out* from all of the past, as well as being the Entrance *into* a new and Eternal Life" was our answer.[3]

In the autumn when the fairs were over, they held teaching missions in the villages where churches were already emerging as a result of the witness of the Zhangye church. In one place 83 enquirers gathered for several days of teaching: most of them were illiterate and teaching them to read was a priority, to enable them to read the Bible. Before long there were groups in seven towns needing such help. Over the next three years, 523 people learned to read in the course of Bible study. Mildred commented that all these people called themselves Christians, even though as yet they knew so little. Dr Kao might lack the gift of teaching, but with the Trio's help some of his members were developing that gift. As the gospel spread across the countryside, so did the need for teaching: since the missionaries themselves hoped to move on, they were anxious to train as many of these men and women as possible, to provide the teachers and evangelists that were needed. As always, they were training their replacements; Eva once said she would never do anything if someone else could do it.

## Jiuquan (Suzhou), the city of prodigals

As winter approached it was time for the Trio to move on, and more than one person recommended the city of Jiuquan as their future home base. Six days' journey beyond Zhangye, Jiuquan was known as "the last town in China" before the Gobi desert and the frontier. Every traveller about to cross the desert had to pause there for two or three days to collect supplies for the next three weeks. Everyone arriving from the desert needed to replenish their supplies. Jiuquan was a busy place of constant coming and going.

The city also stood near the junction of two great trade routes. On the one hand, there was the southern desert route from Pakistan via Kashgar to southern Mongolia. On the other was the northern route from Kazakhstan and Russia through Ürümqi to China. Literature was scarce and valued, and anything bought or received was likely to be treasured or passed on along the trade routes of Central Asia. With such vast distances and scattered populations around them, the Trio were maximising their few resources and planning their future work.

In the late autumn of 1924, they moved up the Silk Road and settled in Jiuquan for the winter, accompanied by the "Pioneer Band", an itinerant Bible school team of 30 men and women from Zhangye. They were able to rent premises for the Bible school, and the Trio made their permanent Jiuquan home in a beautiful one-roomed garden pavilion; the sun poured in and they looked out on the Tibetan mountains rising to 13,000 feet. However, Jiuquan offered no protection from the Gobi desert to the west or the Mongolian sands to the north, and the roaring winter gales were horrendous, covering the rooms with sand or dust. The women's Chinese gowns were already padded for the winter, but as their apprehension grew, they added a further layer of camel hair.

They searched the carpenters' shops for a table and chairs and found only black and red lacquered coffins! The landlord lent them a table and three stools, and they concocted a dresser, bookcase, desk and beds from planks, bricks and packing cases. The main room became their living and guest-receiving room. At each end there were recesses with sleeping *kangs* – platforms which they curtained off for their only privacy as bed-sitting rooms. They were unable to build their kitchen stove, put in a proper floor, plaster a wall or fill the crevices against the howling winter winds for several months, because *feng-shui* forbade it, and to upset the gods of wind, water and earth could lead to disaster. They assured the landlord that, as Christians, the demons had no power over them. He agreed:

> I know that none of these things can harm *you*, because *you* are under the complete protection of your God. I, on the other hand, am under the power of these influences, and it would be highly dangerous for me, or for you, to take a midway position, for then we would be removed from protection, and consequently exposed to the assaults of both forces.[4]

Out of courtesy to the landlord, if not to the god who controlled the earth and forbade it to be disturbed at this point, they spent the autumn months with a loosely trampled earth floor so dusty that the first storm left the floor rippled, like a beach after a retreating tide. It was a reminder that the lives of the people around them were dominated by superstition and fear, and they had brought the message that could set those people free.

They enjoyed a good diet in Jiuquan: rice and macaroni were the staple foods. Mutton, yak beef and pork were available, though of poor quality, and milk could be bought until the cows became sick and died. Vegetables and eggs were plentiful, and there was lots of fruit from the oases in the summer. Often linseed oil was the only fat available for cooking. "In spite of every effort, we were never able to accustom ourselves to the strong taste nor eat it without revulsion." They ground their own wheat on a millstone, turned by their own mule, and used the bran as insulation to prevent the eggs from freezing in the winter.

The team put up posters all over the town, and every afternoon, after six hours of study, the men preached in the streets, and sold Bible portions. The most tactful and experienced men went to the Muslim settlement in the eastern suburb: anyone doing this work must be prepared to receive insults without retaliation, and keep his temper when his books were bought, only to be torn up before his eyes. The women students embarked on the vital work of breaking down the barriers of fear with friendship, systematically visiting women in their homes, sharing the message as often as possible. When the local women found that the foreigners spoke Chinese, they willingly invited them to their homes.

In this way, the Zhangye Christians were able to put into practice what they were learning, and the inhabitants of Jiuquan could scarcely fail to become aware of the Christian presence and message. J. O. Fraser, well known for his pioneer work in south-west China among the Lisu people, reached Jiuquan while undertaking a survey of Gansu. He reported:

> I don't suppose we have in the whole of the CIM a more capable teacher of any subject than Miss Cable. She was recently offered a position at the Shanting Christian University. The thoroughness with which she teaches the Scriptures to Dr Kao's young men is almost appalling! She makes them go through the whole Bible – no skipping – Minor Prophets, Revelation, everything. You should see their voluminous notebooks and the questions Miss Cable sets them to puzzle out for themselves. It is remarkable that whereas so many of us common missionaries have been more or less satisfied with a superficial knowledge of the Bible in our Chinese Christians, here – right up in one of the remotest corners of China – you have a band of young men who are being grounded in the word of God as very few others are in any part of the country... Miss Cable asks you what book you are

reading and if you aren't reading anything wants to know why you aren't.[5]

The seed sown in Guildford High School and Campbell Morgan's Friday-evening Bible school in London over 25 years earlier was still bearing fruit!

With the coming of spring, most of the students returned home to Zhangye, but a few remained to accompany the Trio as they began to visit more widely. They explored the road north to the city of Kinta, for the spring festivals at the temples, taking their huge tent with them. When they returned to Jiuquan, the children absorbed their attention. Their parents had warned them of the dangerous foreigners who would put out their eyes and kidnap them, but the children, undaunted, stalked the Trio all day long. They trailed them everywhere they went, and found an excuse to haunt the garden by picking sticks. They decided that the "evil foreigners" seemed harmless.

Finally the infinitely adaptable Trio began a children's service every evening. The little organ was accompanied by "tambourines, mouth-organs, jingles, pipes, when hymns were sung to the accompaniment of bangings, clangings, clapping of hands and stamping of feet, all in excellent rhythm, forming part of the service". The children's band proved irresistible to the adult population, and soldiers, businessmen, officials and even the country people thronged in night after night for the music, followed by a brief message. The children had broken the ice, and half the seats were reserved for them. Later on, when the Trio visited homes in the town, they found that everyone already knew them and welcomed them. Mothers they had never before met had learned texts, hymns and prayers from their children. Many years later they would often receive a welcome from some of those children, grown to be adults, living hundreds of miles away across the desert.

In May they were back in Zhangye where, in spite of persecution, 98 more people had been baptised. They held a Bible school for them. In July they travelled 40 miles south to another lamasery high in a Tibetan pass. Then, at the end of August, they turned their faces to the desert and embarked on a two-month journey, visiting all the towns in Gansu between Jiuquan and the border.

## The oases of the Hexi Corridor

The missionaries' purpose was to evangelise, so they took their time over journeys, talking to travellers along the road and in the inns, and turning aside to visit towns, villages and monasteries off their main route. Mildred always had her eye on strategy, endeavouring to survey the whole area as they travelled, establishing objectives and planning the future, as the early CIM pioneers had done across China.

They passed through the big fort of Jiayuguan (Kiayükwan), standing at the end of the Great Wall of China, and now guarding only a crumbling village and an army out-post. The city gate was inscribed with poems written by exiles as they left China forever. The Trio contributed a poster with a message of hope for a people who spent their lives trying to earn forgiveness: *Christ Jesus came into the world to save sinners.*

Three days further along the road was Yumen, the old city of Jade Gate, which had been a guard post on the trade routes for 2,000 years, and survived now in this dry landscape by means of careful irrigation. All along the road were deserted towns and villages, overwhelmed by the sands blow-ing in from the Gobi desert. Further on again was Ansi, the last town before the border. Here the wind turned to hurri-cane proportions every afternoon, hurling grit and stones in people's faces. In winter the cold was so bad that the town closed down, its people huddled at home in a haze of opium.

Now the Trio turned south-west to visit Dunhuang (Tunhwang), the City of Sand – four days' rough travel away. This was another crossroads town, where, over the centuries, India, China and Tibet had met. They found a prosperous oasis surrounded by orchards of apples, grapes, nectarines and pears. However, opium was taking over, and as the Chinese succumbed to its effects, the Muslim Uighurs, who were forbidden to use alcohol or drugs, were prospering and taking over the commerce. Here other cultures prevailed. When two gracious Kashgar women visited the inn and carefully removed their shoes before ascending the *kang*, a Chinese woman was horrified. (Because of their deformed, bound feet, Chinese women never uncovered their feet in public.) When the women invited the Trio to their home for a meal they put a plate of lamb chops on the table, explaining gently, "You know it is not our custom to use chop-sticks." They solemnly sat and gnawed the meat off the bones. Most cross-cultural missionaries have to identify with one culture. The Trio were now living in at least six very different cultures simultaneously, and ultimately became at home in all of them.

At Dunhuang the Trio found two places where they could escape from the crowds. Centuries earlier, Buddhist shrines had been placed in caves along the southern trade route, and some of these were situated a short distance from the town, with the ancient paintings still beautifully preserved in the dry desert air a thousand years later. Wong Tao-sï, a priest, lived there and ran a guest house for travellers. Single-handed he was trying to rescue and restore the paintings. He welcomed the women, and they spent many hours talking to him about the way of Jesus. He read the books they offered him and was fascinated by John Bunyan's *Pilgrim's Progress*.

The other treasure in their desert was the Lake of the Crescent Moon, just three miles from the town. The turquoise crescent of water lay quiet and remote, concealed in the high sand dunes. The only resident there was the priest who cared for a small temple and a rest-house which gave shelter to the occasional traveller. The women could retreat there whenever they wanted rest and quiet, and it became one of their favourite haunts. As they were about to leave, a travel-stained and weary lama from north China arrived on his way to

Lhasa. They gave him a copy of John's Gospel and began telling him the story of Jesus. His face lit up. "I know about this," he said, "This Jesus of whom you speak has been troubling me lately in my dreams. I know I shall *have* to believe in him." And he went on his way.

## Journey to Ürümqi

When the missionaries returned to Jiuquan for the usual winter Bible school, they found the church growing. There was considerable goodwill towards the Christians in the town, but other groups were emerging who were intent on causing trouble for them. The Christians were prepared to protest when the innocent were attacked and beaten, and this made them many enemies. A riot was contrived when a beggar was killed and the Christians were blamed; Dr Kao was falsely accused, imprisoned, and taken to Lanzhou. When he was released, the army forced him to give them medical help, so it was months before he was home again. Life was not easy for the new Christians.

There was a further development that winter. There were many beggars on the streets of Jiuquan, but the naked and hungry children were the most vulnerable and pitiful of all, huddled in doorways in the bitter cold. "Our helplessness in view of such suffering is the hardest thing to bear," commented Mildred, "A little money distributed, or a few meals bestowed, afford but temporary relief to some individual, while the main problem remains unsolved." Missionaries often found themselves helpless to act when surrounded by terrible overwhelming social evils. In this case, they did their best for the homeless street children by opening a barn on their property and providing shelter and clean straw, and a daily hot meal.

In 1926, several matters made it desirable for the women to return to Britain again on leave. North China was deep in civil war, so they could not return the way they had come. They questioned travellers about the conditions, and finally decided to continue along the Silk Road for 800 miles to Ürümqi, where their CIM "neighbours" George Hunter and Percy Mather lived. The journey across the Gobi desert would take six weeks. From there, travelling on a better road and using a Russian four-wheeled *tarantass*, they could reach the Russian border in two weeks. If they could cross Lake Zaisan in September, before it froze, they would be able to get the steamer down the Irtish river to pick up the Siberian railway at Omsk.

In June, a party of eleven (the Trio, five church members, two carters to care for the animals, and a cook) left Jiuquan to follow the Silk Road north-west across the Gobi desert to Ürümqi. Because it was summer, they had to travel in the comparative cool of the night. One of their three carts carried nothing but literature; Bible Society had kept them well supplied with this in the eight languages in use.[6] Mostly they gave away their literature, but selling it also provided them with some ready cash: in the absence of banks, and the presence of robbers, carrying money was always a problem. Paper money could only be used in the town where it was printed, and travellers on remote roads were easy targets for thieves.

Primitive inns marked each day's journey along the great road: if there were settlements, these were generally small and struggling. There was usually well-water of a sort, often brackish – not as dangerous as salt water, but never thirst-quenching. They carried a tent for emergencies, but they preferred to stay in the inns wherever possible, regardless of the vermin (they armed themselves with Keating's anti-flea powder). They were there to meet people and share the message, and this was easier to do in sociable inns than in secluded private tents. The inns provided rooms round a courtyard, with *kang* platforms for sleeping. Travellers carried their own grain and borrowed the inn millstones to grind the grain each night. They could share the communal camp fires, one person bringing wood, another a little food, and then sit round the fire talking.

The border between Gansu and Xinjiang came at the

Valley of Baboons, a two-mile-long narrow pass. By carefully monitoring everyone who travelled, whether from the West or from China, the Governor in Ürümqi did his best to keep control of the province: after the Bolshevik Revolution, he had every reason for doing so. Many Communist sympathisers had seen the imperial regime overthrown in Russia, and planned to encourage a similar revolution in China. If they could undermine Chinese influence in Xinjiang by persuading the Muslim ethnic groups to rise against the Chinese, so much the better. So everyone needed a permit to proceed across the border, and permission from Ürümqi could take several days.

Even with their passes, the Trio found themselves held up indefinitely in an ill-assorted crowd of restless people who whiled away the hours with gambling, fighting and cursing. The Jiuquan team brightened up their days by getting the organ out and breaking the monotony with morning and evening services of singing and preaching, and this proved to be a popular attraction. A motley crowd gathered, glad of the diversion, and curious to see the first foreign women to pass that way. Some of them stayed on afterwards to talk at a much deeper level.

After several days, they were relieved to be allowed to continue their journey, and covered the 150 miles to Hami in six days. There had been few people to visit at the desert stages, and they had maintained a steady pace on the road as far as the surface allowed, anxious to get clear of the desert as soon as possible: the route from Jiuquan to Hami was known as one of "unmitigated bitterness". Now they found the settlements getting bigger and more prosperous. Just outside Hami, a light Russian horse-drawn cart appeared, and they were greeted by George Hunter, at first sight almost indistinguishable from the local Uighurs. He had travelled for three weeks from Ürümqi to meet them. The comfortable inn he found for them in Hami provided the first hot water they had seen since leaving Jiuquan.

The oasis at Hami had a diameter of twelve miles: it was

the first large centre after the desert, and the gateway to central Xinjiang. As they moved onward towards Ürümqi they found that the towns on the main road were flourishing oases, supplied with meltwater from the snow-covered mountains above. The population was increasingly multicultural, as Chinese, Mongols, Tibetans, Kazakhs, Tungans, Turki (Uighur), Kalmuk, Nogai, Kyrghyz, Manchurian and Russian exiles left their scattered homes to visit the bazaars in the towns. Each group preserved its own culture, family structure, language and way of life: Xinjiang was truly a focus for the Central Asian trade routes and peoples, and had been such for over two thousand years. The Gobi sands shifted, the armies and empires came and went, but life went on.

The Trio seized every opportunity to visit, accepted invitations into people's homes, and explained why they were there. They were trying to learn Turki, although it was a complex language and quite different from Chinese. But if they could not speak, they could leave literature, and as they became familiar with the culture and customs of each group, they learned to adapt their behaviour appropriately. The heat was still extreme, but now it was possible to travel by day, leaving at 2.30 a.m. At Kucheng they skirted the foot of the Bogdo-Ola, "the Mount of God", which rose to 20,000 feet, and felt the journey's end was approaching.

## Ürümqi – the cross-roads of Central Asia

As they neared Ürümqi, George Hunter went on ahead to prepare for their reception, and Percy Mather came to meet them. When they arrived, they found that George had replaced his native costume with an immaculate black suit, soft felt hat, a turn-down collar and tie, and leather shoes instead of local boots, "transformed into a Scottish divine". The ladies were clearly impressed by this gracious, old-world welcome so far from home!

They found the mission compound quite different from any others they had visited. There were three small two-storey houses, two of them occupied by Hunter and Mather, and the third newly built for the women. In spite of working together for 18 years, the men lived in separate houses and always addressed each other formally as "Mr". The flat mud roofs gave good views over the city, and the living was austere but adequate – indeed, after the Gobi inns, it was downright luxurious. The ladies' house boasted a table instead of the floor for meals, bedroom doors, a bed, an oil lamp, a jug and basin for washing, and a cup and saucer instead of a bowl for tea. Netted windows excluded mosquitoes and flies, and the distant stables and hay lofts kept the animals out of hearing, instead of outside their inn door. Four-star accommodation indeed!

The five missionaries must have enjoyed each other's company: all of them had active minds, and were intensely interested in the many cultures, languages and peoples around them, so conversation and discussion flowed as they asked and answered questions over the following days. Both men had done hours of linguistic work, collecting material and translating books and literature, and even a Mongolian dictionary. Mather had learned Mongolian, but as the only informant he could find was a prisoner, he had his daily lessons inside the prison, to the amusement of the town!

Ürümqi itself was a crossroads of trade routes, a cosmopolitan city with a huge variety of goods available, though in the heat of summer it was plagued with flies and the smell of rotting rubbish. As the first British women ever to visit, they were granted an extended meeting with the Governor. The political situation was increasingly fragile. Historically, the area was constantly under dispute and had been the site of many battles. Many ethnic groups claimed it as their home, and now there was the added complication of the Bolshevik Revolution. Governor Yang was desperately trying to keep control of his people by isolating them from the fermenting politics on the borders, hence the strict border permits, the ban on newspapers, the censorship of mail, and his personal control of the telegraph and wireless offices. At least this meant that the Xinjiang roads were free of bandits where the Chinese roads were not.

When they left Ürümqi they still had an epic journey ahead of them. It was 700 miles to the Russian border, but, once across, their hearts were warmed to find church buildings in the villages. They abandoned the Chinese gowns they had lived in for the last five years, and each acquired a skirt, jumper, headscarf and sandals for the next part of the journey. At Lake Zaisan, their hearts rejoiced at the first electric light they had seen for years, and they travelled the length of the lake by boat to pick up the Siberian railway at Omsk. In Brussels they acquired hats and leather shoes, and slowly prepared themselves for a return to their own country. As they had been unable to warn anyone of their arrival, there was no one to meet them in London. They hunted for a private hotel, but inns in England charged more than tuppence a night. The landlady sized up the three quaint women and took pity on them: "See 'ere, you can 'ave the beds for six shillings a 'ead, and in the morning I'll throw in a pot of tea." It was 27 October 1926 and they were home!

## Furlough in Britain

After a period of rest and adjustment, they were launched into an extensive speaking programme visiting churches. CIM supporters knew much about China, but almost nothing about Central Asia and its peoples. The quarterly prayer letters and articles in *China's Millions* had prepared the way but little was known of other lands and cultures. In that year, 1927, the BBC got its Royal Charter: Mildred, the communicator, was not one to pass up an opportunity. On 4 March 1927 she "broadcast a missionary talk from 2LO during the Missionary Hour". It was typical of her ability to switch from a mule-cart culture to the latest scientific advance.

In the summer she addressed the CIM Annual General Meeting in the Queen's Hall in London. She talked about Tibetans, Uighurs, Mongols and Kazakhs, whose countries were closed to Christian messengers, but whose people could be contacted along the Central Asian trade routes, and she pleaded for more people to go to that area while it was possible. Civil war had closed the door to China in 1927, and most missionaries had been evacuated to the coast. The door to Xinjiang was still open – but for how long? Communism was already on the advance there, and the Western churches seemed oblivious.

As the Trio prepared to return to Asia, Mildred wrote a final message for the readers of *China's Millions*: people had taken the Trio to their hearts and there was enormous interest in what they were doing. They had always kept their feet on the ground, and they endeavoured to keep others as well as themselves grounded in reality. Mildred added one such paragraph here:

> We need scarcely remind you that many incidents which are romantic and faith-inspiring when viewed from a distance, are wrought out in circumstances when loyalty is tested to the uttermost, and guidance sought through the cross-lights which but accentuate the confusion of the dimly-discerned way – when the servant of God has no light, and must stay his (*sic*) heart upon Jehovah.[7]

In the light of later events, the words were prophetic. They left Britain on 22 March 1928: Eva was 57, Francesca 55 and Mildred 50.

## Return to Gansu

The door to Xinjiang was still open, but getting there was another matter. China was closed by civil war and Russia refused them permission to travel the Siberian railway, so they sailed to Bombay and travelled by rail to north India, planning to enter Xinjiang from the south-west. As it happened, the snows were late in melting and they found that the Himalayan route was impassable – but by then the Chinese ports were open once again. So they retraced their steps across India and sailed from Ceylon to Shanghai, then made their way across China to Gansu, arriving in November 1928. Maps indicate the vast distances they had covered: they had been travelling for eight months.

As they passed through Zhangye they were asked to hold another short-term Bible school for 40 young, enthusiastic men and women. At the end, four people confessed that Jesus Christ was the Son of God and were baptised by one of the elders. As the women approached Jiuquan, some of the believers went out to meet them with a hymn of welcome, and soon they were back in their one-roomed garden pavilion with its surrounding courtyards, which the Zhangye church had now bought as a base in Jiuquan for the use of the church and Bible school.

A great deal had happened in their two-year absence: widespread civil war between Nationalist and Communist armies had swept across China, and almost the entire missionary population had evacuated to the coast to avoid a repetition of the Boxer massacres nearly 30 years earlier. The national church leaders were left to function on their own and in consequence they had grown in spiritual understanding and stature. Gansu had been ravaged by another earthquake, followed by fever, and then there was yet more fighting between Muslims and Chinese. An estimated 200,000 people had been murdered, and the situation continued to worsen. That winter was bitterly cold, and bandits, fighting and famine made life a misery for many. The political situation was falling apart.

The compound was still a haven for naked, starving street children, and while the Trio were away, the believers had gathered up waifs from the streets daily. The Buddhist system of belief offered little sympathy for those who had nothing: it held that people received what they deserved. The Christians themselves had little enough, but they saved many lives by their offering of daily meals of porridge, the shelter of a barn at night, and clean straw to sleep on. It sounds primitive, but some of the inns probably did not offer much more.

Two of the youngest children received special care: Grace had been sold into slavery at the age of eight, and her foot had to be amputated because of neglected frostbite. She was sent to a Christian school, and later married a church worker. The other child, Topsy, was a seven-year-old deaf mute. The Trio adopted her and eventually brought her home with them to Britain.

In their letters home, the Trio said little about the companions who worked with them, because all their correspondence was censored, and they did not want to cause trouble for the believers in the future. Nevertheless, the work in Jiuquan was evidently a partnership, with missionaries and Chinese working closely together, with daily meetings for children and adults, extensive home-visiting, Sunday services and a constant stream of visitors at the door.

## Travels to the borders

The following months saw the women making another journey to the borders of Tibet and Mongolia, reaching new areas with the gospel. They set out in the spring of 1929, travelling first south-west from Jiuquan to a lamasery in the Tibetan foothills. It was situated on one of the most ancient routes from Hindustan to China, and crowds passed through from distant places. It was the time for the spring fairs when people gathered to buy and sell before the farming year began, and again they received a warm welcome and curious crowds filled the tent to listen. Then they followed the actors and stallholders as they moved back two days' journey across the valley to the sands of the Gobi desert on the Mongolian border.

Here both language and culture were very different: each clan lived independently on its own walled farm in the centre of its land. Still, the crowds gathered from farms scattered far and wide, and again people packed the tent to hear about a God who loved them and was willing to forgive their sins and receive them.

Back in the Hexi Corridor, they found that every city

along the Silk Road had its gates locked and guarded against the encroaching Muslim forces; some cities had already been devastated. The Tibetan and Mongolian tribes were retreating to mountains and desert, and trade along the road was severely reduced. The main road had been paved for vehicles for the first time, to facilitate army movements. The Trio had planned to leave for Ürümqi immediately, but were delayed when the army in Jiuquan mutinied, sacking the town and making travel impossible.

It was July before they were able to set out for Ürümqi: the Trio and Topsy, Elder Liu and his wife, and Brother Chen the cook. At times they were forced to dodge the hazards of the main road and take side tracks for safety, but that led them through new areas as yet unvisited, and they made the most of every opportunity, finding a welcome and shelter in various homesteads. When they finally reached the border their papers were rejected. The inns were filled with soldiers, and the Christian party were told to pitch their tent on a piece of waste land, among the tethered camels and mules. They faced "flies, litter, and noise on that absolutely shadeless, sun-baked rock which made the six days of delay a nightmare".[8] Nevertheless they held daily services which once more provided a welcome diversion for the men marooned there. The Trio wrote to their friends:

> This letter has been written under great difficulties... None of the party has escaped the ill-effects of the acrid waters and dirty conditions. We live without privacy, and it is impossible to secure the quiet which is essential for the compilation of a consecutive record.[9]

Eventually they reached Hami once again and spent several weeks there. When they attempted to escape for a day from the hundreds who visited them, the local folk cheerfully brought picnics and joined them! The Tibetan *lama* at the temple served them tea and stayed to talk. They asked him what the crowds were looking for when they came to the temple:

"The remission of their sins."

"Do you know of any way by which sin may be remitted?"

"No, I do not. Men must do good actions and thus acquire merit."

"Forgiveness is free, Lama, and eternal life is a gift. It is not to be won by good works or fastings, for all have sinned. Jesus Christ, the Son of God, is Saviour of the world and all who trust in Him have life – eternal life."[10]

Their approach was gentle, courteous, friendly. They sat and listened and shared their own faith quietly, and here and there the seed took root in the hearts of the listeners.

From Hami they made a detour over difficult mountains to reach the town of Barkul (of James Hilton's *Lost Horizon* fame) for the first time, and once again met someone who had attended the children's meetings in Jiuquan. War had scattered people far and wide across Xinjiang and even in new places they came across people who knew them. As they left the desert behind them, the towns became increasingly prosperous, compared with war-torn Gansu. The Muslim inn where they had stayed before welcomed them again (in Muslim areas they conformed to Muslim food restrictions so that food was not a barrier to friendship). They were also hailed with delight in the market. "The Teachers of Righteousness" had come back. (They were, after all, the only Western women for hundreds of miles in any direction!) Some people were confused – they had disappeared to the west two years earlier and now reappeared from the east. How could that be? The postmaster produced a sack of papers and 122 letters. It was several months since they had seen any mail or heard news from outside so there was a great deal to catch up with.

Another six days' journey took them to Ürümqi at last. The city in autumn was less welcoming.

The large and crowded town is entirely without drainage. The autumn refuse from mounds of rotting melon rinds and house-

hold dumps, is covered for a time by the first mantle of snow,
then the ceaseless traffic churns snow, mud and refuse into a
loathsome mass of greasy sewage... Men... wear high leather
boots and wade through the slush, crossing the street by leap-
ing from one stepping stone to another... Twice a year, at
spring and early winter, Urumchi wallows in her mire. By early
December the heavy winter snow has filled every crevice and
the streets are frozen hard until March... [B]efore the spring
thaw sets in, we shall be on tramp once more. If delayed, the
carts must wait until the sun has... turned mud to dust.[11]

The spartan house built for them earlier on the compound
was "comfortable", with a stove and "a thousand small luxuries unnoticed in times of ease". Mildred retained her childhood gift of maximising joy in the midst of prolonged
hardship. The versatile Muslim teacher who had built their
house now gave them daily lessons in the Uighur language,
started making their padded clothes for the winter, and
cleared their snow daily. When the temperature fell to -24°
Fahrenheit (-31° Centigrade) they remained warm and snug.

The Trio spent the next two months visiting homes daily,
starting with the Provincial Governor and his wife. As
women, they were welcomed into the private quarters to
meet the officials' wives and relatives, something prohibited
to the two bachelors. Hunter had felt life was so primitive in
Ürümqi that he could never ask a wife to share it with him.
Consequently the church had been deprived of the Christian
wives and mothers it might have had as role models, and now
three single women had braved the conditions to reach the
women. In addition to systematic visiting in the town, the
Trio also included the Muslim and foreign quarter stretching
over a mile south of the city gate, where the Kazakhs arrived
on camels to shop, and the call from the mosque attracted
many to pray at noon each day. As a result, although Hunter's
official figures for the church in 1930 stood at twelve men
and five women, in fact they were reaching many more who
were passing through. As officials were appointed and

brought their wives and families, these also included women. Numbers at the Sunday services grew steadily, and the Trio organised a women's mission for a week. Percy Mather wrote to his sister:

> It was fine to see the Church crowded every midday and to watch some three hundred women listening to the gospel message, Our Sunday services are now a great sight and at last the women's side of the Church is filled as well as the men's.[12]

Chinese New Year passed, and late February found them packed up and driving out of the city for the homeward journey to Jiuquan before the spring thaw made the road impassable. They had several days of monotonous, hard travel with violent winds and snow before they dropped down to a green oasis in the midst of a barren wilderness.

Turfan is the deepest inhabited town on earth, nearly 1,000 feet below sea level. In winter the temperature drops to 0°F; in summer it rises to 130°F. The people lived in their basements and ventured out to shop only in the cool, dark evenings. The markets were roofed with matting to protect them from the heat of the sun. Everyone slept on beds in the courtyards because in the summer the underground areas also became a retreat for all kinds of insects (including scorpions) and vermin. The local well-water was only fit for the streets (and encouraged mosquitoes, which added to the misery), but clean water could be carried from the *karez* – tunnels at the foot of the mountains containing meltwater. The Turfan area was prosperous and famous for its grapes, which were dried into sultanas in this unusual climate.

On the Sunday their room at the inn was crowded with Muslim men ready to debate questions about the Bible, and Jesus as the Son of God. The Muslims usually despised the Chinese but they found Elder Liu well able to defend his faith. The Trio watched with a sense of a job well done as their former Bible-school student held his ground and explained the gospel. They were well aware that Christianity had first reached this area some thousand years earlier, yet now there was no witness and Islam had taken over. Mildred commented:

> Let those who can, triumphantly sing together of lifting up His royal banner which "must not suffer loss". For ourselves, we are silenced, save to witness afresh.[13]

They spent a month there, visiting homes and holding public meetings, and by the end they were well known and were greeted warmly. Then as the temperature (and the insect population!) began to rise, they were off again, slowly climbing up from the Turfan depression. After an eventful journey (which included a broken cart axle, some hostility and stone-throwing, and even a whirlwind that half destroyed the inn where they were staying), they found themselves back in Hami for the third time. Here they paused for another month, building on previous friendships and contacts, based in a comfortable Muslim inn.

They wanted to get home to Jiuquan, but the worst part of the journey across the desert still lay ahead, and bandits had closed the main road. Their kindly landlord arranged for them to stay at the summer palace of the King of the Gobi – a cool, shady oasis with water, trees and gardens. To start with they were somewhat alarmed by the unrelenting attention of his servants, but managed to escape this by pitching their tent in the garden and living there! It was a welcome break from the crowds where they could relax and read and be quiet.

By the end of June, the road was safe again and they returned to Hami to find the town now rife with "pestilence and fever". They moved on but Eva went down with cholera, so they made a hasty overnight journey to camp in a safe oasis while she slowly recovered. Finally they tackled the ten days across the desert, but they found changes at the border. The whole atmosphere was different: the soldiers were cheerful; no longer were people delayed for days and weeks; the gambling and opium had gone. The cause seemed to be the new Commandant, who had been in contact with the YMCA and owned some Christian books. He wanted to buy a complete Bible but they had sold out, so Mildred gave him her own, personal, leather-bound one. When they reached the towers of the Jiayuguan fortress they paused to give thanks to God for a journey safely undertaken, and soon found themselves back in Jiuquan after 16 months away.

What had they achieved in those 16 months? Mildred was always reluctant to give figures. The enduring harvest was still unknown. Mildred commented, "That concerns our Leader." For their part, they had sown the seed. They had

> witnessed to every place to which they came. Prolonged visits were made to Golden Tower, the Tibetan foothills, Jade Gate, Hami, Barkul, Muhlei-ho, Kucheng, Ürümqi, Turfan, Lucheng and Shan. We visited 2,700 homes, and conducted 665 meetings. As far as possible, a present of Christian literature was made to the priest in each Temple, hoardings were posted with Scripture texts, and about 40,000 portions of Scriptures were sold, apart from the larger number of books and tracts distributed free. As we passed over that portion of the field we had sown previously, we were able to see the blade, the ear, and signs of the ripening corn in the ear. From the Richtofen hills to the sands of Mongolia, from Jiuquan to Ürümqi, from Hami to Barkul, and Turfan, the heralds proclaimed the Coming King and in every hamlet on the route and in many an isolated farmstead and nomad's tent, the Name of the Lord Jesus has been made known, and His offer of salvation proclaimed.[14]

## The chaos of war

That autumn they rested in the comparative luxury of their Jiuquan home while Eva regained her strength, but life on the Silk Road was dominated by the seasons, and they knew they could go nowhere from December to March. In October they made a circular journey, travelling first north to the

Mongolian border and then south again through new towns to Zhangye. There they found the Muslim army dominating the area, living off the peasants, kidnapping young boys for army training and massacring some settlements. Villages had been abandoned. The Zhangye church had endured severe persecution; some had recanted and others had fled. No country folk travelled the roads or even left their homes, so the planned Bible school never took place, but they met with old students for Bible study and took them through Paul's letters to the troubled Corinthian church.

In Jiuquan that winter, typhus and diphtheria ran rife, destroying whole families, and meetings and house-visiting were curtailed. The new Christian community was becoming known for its charity, helping the poor and needy as far as it could. Christians also spoke out against injustice and ill-treatment, unusual in a Buddhist culture where people were assumed to deserve their *karma*, the fate allotted to them in this life. One of the old inhabitants commented:

> "The spirit of the town is quite changed and things once done openly are now viewed with shame."
> "How is that?"
> "Public opinion. Since Christianity has been declared here and especially since the Ten Commandments of God have become known to all, a sense of sin has been created which formerly did not exist."[15]

In spring they retraced the journey of the previous autumn, heading north along the Edzin-gol river towards the Mongolian border, moving between the Mongol *gers* (tents), small settlements and Tibetan lamaseries. One woman they had met before reappeared, saying, "I have been praying to God... and I don't know if I am praying aright... I say: 'I pray you, Lord Jesus, to pity me and forgive my sin, to cleanse my heart and to save me.'" As they said earlier, the seed had been sown, and the first shoots were appearing.

However, war was never far away, and that summer it

overtook Jiuquan. The town was overrun by soldiers, the civilian leaders were terrorised, and ordinary civilians were executed. A brief, private letter from Mildred to a friend revealed a little of what they could not say publicly:

> Life is of no value and last night in our court we were held up by firearms and ordered to pay up. The sleepless nights, the weary morning when the firing persists, the impossibility of doing anything because of the perpetual interruptions – soldiers all over the place, news that one's animals have gone, people in trouble... Pray for us and for all who are in peril by robbers, it is a tremendous strain. I shall look forward to reading the book on Daniel that you mention. There are so few good books on the Bible for advanced study.[16]

Finally, in the autumn, the Trio decided to get away and revisit the oases along the Silk Road and then go back to Dunhuang. The Muslim army under General Ma had moved up the Silk Road to take over Hami, and destroyed the desert wells behind it so that no one could follow, but as Dunhuang was several days' journey from the main road, they hoped to be able to work and visit there in peace.

They found the great Jiayuguan fortress left derelict in the wake of the army, but happily the roads were empty. They spent time at Yumen (Jade Gate), and when they finally reached Dunhuang they were surprised at the crowds of people who came out to welcome them, after their absence of five years. They were able to have sole possession of a Muslim inn for their team, and immediately began working out a programme of Sunday and weekday services, including a children's band, and prepared for the daily stream of visitors, including those who sought medical help.

On the first Sunday, the small team of Jiuquan evangelists gathered for Bible study and prayer before the public service began. They hoped that a few people would gather for public worship, but to their amazement more and more quietly slipped in until the inn room was crowded to the doors.

After the service was over, first one and then another stood and asked to have his name enrolled on a list of enquirers: the team were surprised to see so many believers.

"Where did you hear the Gospel? When did you believe?" they asked.
"How should we not believe when five years ago you came and preached to us? You left us the Scriptures, we read them and know they are true."[17]

They included the police inspector, one of his officers, a businessman, a young farmer, and two boys from a Christian school elsewhere. The Trio had faithfully sowed the seed, believing that the Lord of the harvest would cause it to bear fruit, and they were not mistaken. Jesus had said he would build his church, and a new church was already emerging in Dunhuang.

They continued to visit locally until the brigand army arrived. General Ma and his Muslim army had risen against the Chinese and devastated Gansu, before crossing the Gobi to Hami to join up with the Muslim uprising in Xinjiang. He was finally forced back to Gansu with gunshot wounds in both legs, and took over the entire area from the Gobi to Zhangye: 600 miles of the Silk Road were under his control. The terrified city of Dunhuang surrendered immediately to avoid bloodshed, and refugees fleeing across the Gobi desert from Hami also poured into the city.

The Trio's spacious inn became home to over a hundred refugees and their animals, and the wounded needed medical help: within weeks, food supplies were dwindling and typhus was beginning to spread. Suddenly the general summoned two of the Trio to travel to Ansi, the army headquarters 80 miles away, with medical supplies. They were in no position to decline, but they flatly refused to be separated. They left under military escort after the Christians had prayed and sung, "I am weak, but Thou art mighty, Hold me with Thy powerful hand." As the captain of the guard explained to the waiting escort, "These women can't travel without that."[18]

After four days' travel the army found them a school room as a home and they began daily visits to the young general to dress his wounds. He was arrogant, unpredictable and brutal, ordering executions without a second thought, but anxious lest the disinfectant on his wound might sting! The army were supposed to feed the women, but food was running out. They were in a dangerous situation, held indefinitely in a place where there was no communication with the outside world. They feared they might be held for a long time to give medical help in the war, or as hostages to give the general bargaining power.

Once his wounds were healed, they decided they must try to get back to Dunhuang at least; eventually they obtained the necessary permit to leave. Wherever the Trio went, they endeavoured to leave something meaningful behind and this delicate situation was no exception. On the last occasion when they spoke to the unpredictable general, his bodyguard stared in amazement as Mildred handed him a copy of the New Testament and the Ten Commandments of God, and urged him to reflect on his own life.[19]

Back in Dunhuang that winter there was plenty to do. The Muslim Turki women, accustomed to the privacy of the harem, found public life in the inns hard, and they were glad to be able to talk to the Trio in Turki. Conditions were deteriorating as supplies vanished from the shops, and the Trio, praying earnestly about the future, began to hoard what food they could for a journey. Flight was dangerous, and Mildred in particular was worried about disobeying those in command: the guards on the few tracks across the desert had orders to ensure the Trio did not leave. To be caught defying the general was extremely dangerous – people had been executed for much less than that. Did Mildred recall her words as they were leaving Britain four years earlier, about their need for "guidance... when the servant of God has no light, and must stay his heart upon Jehovah"?

In early April, they packed up their essential goods and left as though setting off on a local visit: they concealed their extra food and left the house looking occupied. When they enquired about the guards at a farm on the outskirts of the town, they were told they had gone off for the day. The "prison doors" had opened: for them it was a sign from God, and they hurried off across the desert. Some hours further on two soldiers accosted them. They were looking for deserters and travelling was forbidden. Had they a permit from the general? Shaking in her shoes, Mildred prayed and produced her impressive-looking but irrelevant Chinese Central Government passport, the only paper she possessed. The illiterate guards scrutinised the document, were duly impressed, and were none the wiser. They waved them on.

It was a hazardous journey: pursuit was a real possibility and they could easily have been overtaken by horsemen following their tracks across the sand. The roads were empty except for occasional deserters; the wells were destroyed and inns abandoned; they depended entirely on their own dwindling supplies of food and water; and they were vulnerable to any robbers in the area. Just before they reached the Turpan oasis, they found Mildred unconscious one night, face down on the filthy stable floor where she had gone to check on their mules – another mule had kicked her and she had a serious head wound. As soon as possible, they left the dirt and noise of the inn and were given shelter and care by Muslim friends while she made a slow recovery. They were relieved when they reached the comparative safety of Turpan, where old friends welcomed them. It took them eight weeks to travel from Dunhuang to Ürümqi, where some of the Christian women travelled out in small carts to meet them and escort them home. Percy Mather welcomed them, but George Hunter was away paying his first visit to Shanghai for 26 years. The British Vice Consul from Kashgar was visiting Ürümqi at the time, and was greatly relieved to know of their safe arrival.

They found many changes. The fearful events of the Muslim rebellion dominated everyone's thinking and the Governor in his panic was resorting to similar brutality. Percy Mather was "a wreck of his former self. The old spirit was still alert, but the body was worn and weary." He had exhausted himself the previous winter completing dictionaries and grammars in Manchu, Mongolian, Tartar and Kalmyk, and in the new political climate he found himself under suspicion and attack. At this time the CIM was initiating the "Forward Movement" proposed by Susie Garland, and intended to send six young men back with Hunter to Ürümqi. However, it was clear to the Trio and Percy, who were on the spot, that the political situation was worsening and that war was inevitable. The reinforcements would be arriving too late.

Even while organising their journey home to Britain, the Trio made the most of their time, continuing to train their successors and running a final three-day mission. "The response was beyond our expectations." One message during the mission was given by a young woman schoolteacher who had been converted and baptised back in Jiuquan a thousand miles away. The ripples of their work were spreading across Central Asia, as they had hoped and prayed.

Percy Mather saw them off at the Russian border and they promised to write from Berlin to the CIM directors in Shanghai asking them not to send the new recruits to Ürümqi (everything in Xinjiang was censored). Sadly, their letter came too late and the party of new workers had already left with Hunter for Ürümqi. Within a few months of their arrival the city was under siege. The young Emil Fischbacher (the only doctor) and Percy Mather worked themselves to exhaustion caring for the wounded, until both contracted typhus and died during the same week in May 1933.[20]

## The final visit

After three years back in Britain, the Trio returned to Ürümqi via the Siberian railway in 1935. Eva was now 64, Francesca 62 and Mildred 57. Rapid changes were taking place. Literacy was increasing, and better roads were being constructed; Ürümqi now had electricity and telephones. The political situation was still poor: the USSR was trying to extend its influence south, and Japan had started encroaching on China from the north.

No one could move without permits and the Trio had to wait all winter before they could start back down the Silk Road. They received a warm welcome from all who recognised them, but war had devastated the countryside. Homes and villages had been destroyed, and their friends killed or scattered. The use of opium was on the increase. In one place Christian posters still fluttered on the ruined walls of their friend's house. They spent time in Dunhuang once again, when more people were baptised. A bystander remarked:

> "I saw you in Barkul and you visited my mother in Turfan... yet you turn up looking just the same as ever. I suppose in your country you are not even old at 100. Look at us, at 70 we're done for."
>
> Another replied: "You don't know what you're talking about. These venerable ladies eat no pork, neither do they smoke opium or tobacco. They don't drink wine: they don't even wear ear-rings. Besides they have neither husbands nor children, and all that keeps them young. They have an undivided heart for good works."[21]

In Gansu there was famine again, and it was having its usual effects: food was scarce and expensive, and people resorted to selling their children. They met a group of over-dressed girls in one inn: it was possible to buy girls for $1 each in Gansu and sell them for $10 each in Hami. Their future was bleak.

Finally they reached Jiuquan, where they were able to stay for six months. They received a great welcome though many faces were absent – after the terror of the rebel occupation, typhus had also taken its toll. Now for a few months the children's service was resumed, and the class for literacy, and another for Bible study. They could visit again, and even travel in the region, but they knew their time would be limited. Communist pressure was growing, tensions increasing, and Mildred was struggling with asthma. Finally, in August

1936, the order came for foreigners to leave. They bade their friends a sorrowful farewell and climbed into a lorry for Lanzhou, 400 miles away.

Remarkably, the lorry broke down in Zhangye and they had to spend the night there: what others might have seen as a strange coincidence, the believers undoubtedly saw as the hand of God! By early morning the word had passed around the church, and by 6 a.m. people were arriving to spend the day with the Trio. Further down the new tarmac road, they also spent a night in Wuwei (Liangzhou) and met the Christians there. From Lanzhou the road was closed and they flew to Xi'an to get the train to Beijing, where they paid £25 each to travel across the continent on hard 4th-class seats on the Siberian railway to London.

## The last stage

When they returned home in 1937, Mildred and Francesca rented a flat in London, but retreated occasionally to the cottage in Dorset which they shared with Eva and Topsy. Mildred was asked to build up Bible Society's women's support groups, and she continued to do this right through the war. The Trio had caught the imagination of the Christian public over the years, and they were in great demand for speaking at meetings. Between them they kept in touch with China Inland Mission, the Salvation Army, Bible Society, Girl Crusaders, Zenana Bible and Medical Mission, and Ludhiana College and Hospital.

In 1943, Mildred and Francesca produced their superb book on the Gobi desert, unsurpassed even today and still recommended in guidebooks. It covers the peoples, cultures, resources, geology, history, botany and wildlife of the area. They were awarded the Livingstone Medal and the Lawrence of Arabia Memorial Medal for their travels, and Mildred lectured to the Royal Geographical Society. In 1943 Queen Elizabeth invited them to Buckingham Palace for tea – and wanted to see their photographs.

During the war, Mildred also worked for the Women's Voluntary Service (which later became the WRVS). The Trio were not daunted by the thought of Hitler – he paled into insignificance compared with General Ma of the Muslim revolt! Their flat took a direct hit from a bomb but they emerged without major injury. When the war finally ended, Mildred and Francesca visited Australia and New Zealand, then India and later Latin America, on speaking tours.

Mildred continued to have problems with her health; she died unexpectedly in April 1952, after a bout of shingles, at the age of 74. Evangeline and Francesca lived on with Topsy at Willow Cottage: when a friend protested because Francesca, aged 88, was sleeping on the floor to be near Eva, who was ill, she retorted, "I've been sleeping on the floor all my life!"[22] They died within three weeks of each other in 1961. Topsy lived on until the year 2000.

The three women shared a ministry for so long that it is hard to disentangle them, and yet they each made their individual contribution to the partnership. Eva was the first to reach China; she was described as "puckish", frank, unpredictable, sometimes mischievous, and unsentimental. Mildred was the writer and communicator, "our star" as the other two referred to her; intense, sometimes withdrawn, analysing, planning, targeting. Francesca was much quieter, practical, gifted in writing and poetry, keeping the daily routines going for all three of them.

Over 35 years in the CIM, their influence spread across the four northern provinces of China and beyond, through the women they trained. When they moved across to Gansu province, they were known and respected along a thousand miles and more of the Silk Road. As they explained:

> [B]eing the first Western women missionaries who had ever travelled by this road, our presence created quite a sensation, far more from the fact of our being women missionaries and unmarried, than by reason of our foreign nationality.[23]

When Sir Ivor Beauchamp and his wife (CIM) visited Jiuquan in 1934, the church gave them a warm welcome, and accommodated them on the church property. When they were able to travel the Silk Road, they were astonished at the number of people who knew the Trio and spoke very warmly of them. In an area where Christians were comparatively few, they were very widely known.

The Trio had resolutely set out to make Jesus known along the main trade route; they achieved this, selling relevant books and distributing literature in several languages which would then be carried throughout Asia. They visited and revisited, building relationships and winning confidence and respect, repeating the message until people began to understand. It speaks volumes that the Muslims referred to them as "the Teachers of Righteousness". Certainly they incurred anger and hostility in some circles, but they also generated respect and affection; as women they seemed less threatening than men, and thus they were able to do much more. They travelled five times along the 1,000 miles of the Silk Road from Jiuquan to Ürümqi, and over the years systematically visited the towns and oases of the Hexi Corridor six times.

Nothing can detract from these women's achievements in spreading the gospel, but the civil war, which subsequently destroyed whole areas and killed thousands of people, did affect the growth of the infant churches. The church in Xinjiang today is made up of Chinese immigrants, and even today only a very few believers are found among the 11 million (largely Muslim) ethnic peoples. Yet Mildred's comments in 1933 remain true:

> During the more than 30 years of my missionary life I have seen the seed spring up in such unexpected places that I have done with questionings and fears as to whether there will be results. Statistics in things spiritual mean nothing to me now. It is ours unstintingly to sow the seed whose life is in itself. It is God's husbandry and He will give the increase.[24]

## Notes to Chapter Eight

1 *China and the Gospel* (1924) pp. 126–28. Crossman, *Mountain Rain*, pp. 149–50.
2 Mildred Cable and Francesca French, "The Call of China's Great North-west", *China's Millions* (August 1924) pp. 126–28.
3 Cable and French, *Jade Gate*, p. 58.
4 Ibid., pp 86–87.
5 Crossman, *Mountain Rain*, pp. 149–50.
6 In the nineteenth century a Russian missionary society had circulated literature in 30 languages along their Asian border, and in 1834 George Burrows had urged the British and Foreign Bible Society to make a base in Kiakta to reach the Central Asian peoples, but it was considered too risky. Platt, *Three Women*, pp. 71–72; Marshall Broomhall, *Bible*, pp. 122–33.
7 *China's Millions* (May 1928) p. 70.
8 Cable and French, *Desert*, p. 75.
9 Ibid., p. 76.
10 Ibid., p. 79.
11 Ibid., p. 94.
12 Cable and French, *Hunter*, p. 86.
13 Cable and French, *Desert*, p. 112.
14 Ibid., pp. 143–44.
15 Ibid., pp. 173–74.
16 Addressed to Miss Watney and dated 3 June 1931, in the possession of Peter Conlan.
17 Cable and French, *Something Happened*, p. 226.
18 Ibid., p. 230.
19 Platt, *Three Women*, p. 167.
20 See Cable and French, *Hunter*, and Cable and French, *Pioneer*.
21 Platt, Three Women.
22 Ibid., p. 210.
23 The Misses French and Cable, "A Dispatch from Turkestan", *China's Millions* (February 1927) p. 22.
24 *China's Millions* (July 1933).

# Chapter Nine

# Revival in China

The early women who went to China gave their time and energy to the "women's world" which could not be reached by men, and this remained their focus for many decades afterwards. However, the turmoil of war, civil unrest and the social and economic changes of the twentieth century combined to bring down the barriers between the two worlds of men and women. Even in the early years of missionary endeavour, people were surprised at the willingness of Chinese men to attend some of the women's meetings: they had such hunger for Christian teaching that they did not mind who gave it. Increasingly the women were asked to include men in their meetings. When revival came, people were meeting God through what they heard, and whether the speakers were male or female no longer mattered: they were mere channels for the message.

Two Scandinavian women in particular played an important part in the revival movements of the 1930s and 1940s: Marie Monsen from Norway and Anna Christensen from Denmark.

## Marie Monsen

At the turn of the century the Norwegian churches were deeply concerned that so many of their young people were emigrating to North America; Marie Monsen was determined that she was not going to be one of them. She had trained as a teacher, and spent a further year gaining some experience in hospital work, followed by some time in England, but she felt a strong call to China. She was feeling torn between this call to mission and her desire to remain in Norway, when a pastor reminded her of how Jonah had heard God's call and refused to go. "At first he was allowed to go his own way, but God didn't go with him... *Don't be a Jonah!*"[1] Those words haunted her and she finally joined the Norwegian Lutheran China Mission. In 1900 the Boxer Rebellion prevented her departure for China, but she finally reached Shanghai in 1902, just as the shattered churches and missionaries of north China were beginning to rebuild their lives.

Marie's mission was never officially associated with the CIM, but in her later years she worked closely with the CIM members and churches, and the CIM published two of her books in English. Her ministry ultimately spread far across China, but in her early years there was little indication of what lay ahead. There was nothing remarkable in the arrival of a young Norwegian girl whose heart was set on teaching in a mission school.

## Disappointments

At first everything seemed to go wrong. First there had been the delay in leaving for China, because of the Boxers. Then, a month after her arrival, she fell down an iron staircase and lay unconscious for several days. The headaches that followed persisted for the next six years, and ended only after special prayer and anointing. For the first two years she was forbidden both language study and teaching on health grounds, and she was left trying to learn Chinese by listening – no easy task at the best of times, and even harder with a difficult language like Chinese.

Several months after her arrival she contracted malaria, and a high temperature brought her to death's door and close to despair. Had God called her to China only to let her die within a few months? The spiritual anguish and rebellion she endured were worse than the physical illness, but eventually she reached a point of acceptance where she was able to say, "Lord, if it was only this that was your will, Your will be done." That day, her temperature fell. "I knew from that time onward that the call was all of grace," she said, a gift received from God. The attacks recurred, as malaria does, and, together with dysentery, they left her chronically weak and debilitated for years. She was so fearful of being invalided back to Norway that she drove herself to continue working. Her first seven years were miserable and frustrating: from childhood she had always wanted to teach but every time she was about to begin work, she fell ill again.[2] Ten years passed before she was delivered from these chronic conditions in her second term of service in China, again in answer to special prayer.

Instead of teaching, she was designated to pioneer evangelism in Henan, one of the last provinces to admit missionaries. It had always been hostile, and only three or four years earlier, Jonathan and Rosalind Goforth and their party had been attacked as they fled south from the Boxers through Nanyang. Now Marie and her co-worker found themselves living in Nanyang, trying to make friends with the women, though "ignorance, superstition, suspicion and hatred of foreigners built a thick wall around their hearts and it seemed impossible to break through these fortifications".[3] The situation seemed hopeless, and only her strong sense of call from God kept her there. She began to ask why their experience was so different from the days of the early church, and would not accept it when some missionaries shrugged it off, saying that the times were different, or the Chinese were different. Why did God not act in the same way today? Had he changed?

At the same time, she was challenged by the faith of a simple but devout elderly Chinese Bible woman who had been sent to help them. She always prayed aloud, even in private, about everything. Since the lower walls of her room were made of mud, and the upper of paper, everything was audible in Marie's room next door. Marie could hear her confident, childlike prayers, and knew they were answered, even the "impossible" ones, whereas she herself was so overwhelmed by the problems she faced that there was more doubt than faith in her own prayers.[4]

After the Boxer Rebellion in 1901 there had been a surge of interest in the Christian faith across China, and the churches grew. Now, with larger numbers and less persecution, it was easier for people to become Christians, and there was a lack of solid teaching: they were told to "believe in Jesus" without any real explanation of what this involved. Consequently many of the new converts had little genuine spiritual life, and they showed little desire to share their faith with others. Orthodox mental assent could easily be substituted for true faith in second- and third-generation Christians, unless the Holy Spirit brought new life in response to prayer.[5] There was spiritual weakness in many areas of church life.

In 1907, Marie attended the Centenary Conference in China, and three years later, at home for her first leave, she attended the famous 1910 World Missionary Conference in Edinburgh. She returned to China knowing that she could never achieve anything through trusting in her own gifts and training, but only through God's power. She came to the conclusion that, all too often, missionaries who focused on evangelism talked in general terms about "repenting of sin" without explaining exactly what this meant. They only realised years later that people had agreed to a faith they did not really understand, and in consequence they had not experienced true Christian forgiveness and new life.

Marie began to find out all she could about revival: news was spreading of the revival in Korea which had begun under Jonathan Goforth in 1907. Goforth had seen many people turning to the Christian faith in Korea and Manchuria, and claimed that when people were really taught the Word of God, new spiritual life would inevitably follow, whether through people becoming Christians for the first time, nominal Christians coming to understand what they professed to believe, or true Christians learning to live in the light of what they already believed.[6] In 1911 the ministry of Margaret King and Mrs Sie had been transformed as a result of Goforth's meetings in China.

Marie longed to visit Korea and see for herself, but as she prayed about it she felt God telling her that she did not need to travel: she could receive what she was looking for right where she was. This conviction was followed by a deep experience of the power of Jesus, which served both as an anchor in her own sea of doubt and to encourage her to continue praying for renewal and new life in the churches. As she continued studying, she realised she needed a "long-term" view, to lay the foundations for future blessing in prayer and teaching. There were no quick solutions, no short cuts. She engaged in less evangelism and focused her efforts instead on giving Bible teaching to illiterate Christian women, and praying for the church. She withdrew from other work and relationships to such an extent that she marvelled that she was not sent home; she was to persevere for 20 years before she saw her prayers fulfilled.

## Literacy and spiritual growth

Her second term of service was extended for various reasons and coincided with the launching of the phonetic script in 1918. This had a radical impact: instead of spending years learning the thousands of characters needed to read the classical Bible, people could learn to read the phonetic-script version in a matter of weeks. The teachers used chalk to write on the mud walls, and for the women and children "the earthen floor was their slate, a nail their pencil". The four- and five-year-olds joined in and learned faster than their mothers! Bible study courses were developed and Marie set out to give these women, converted from paganism, as much Bible knowledge as she had absorbed over her years in her home church in Norway. When her second furlough came, she turned down an opportunity to teach Norwegian young people (which at one time she would have loved to do). Now her priority was to keep on praying for revival in China, and gather others into groups committed to doing the same.

She returned to a China struggling with change, nationally and internationally. The previous 20 years had seen the end of the imperial Manchu dynasty and the establishing of the Republican government under Sun Yat-sen. The Chinese Communist party was formed in 1921, and the subsequent civil war spread across the country. As communications improved, China was grappling not only with her own problems but also with the problems of the wider modern world: materialism, social change and secularism. The railways and roads that were transforming travel also proved useful to bandits and private armies. Nationalism was on the increase and China was becoming disillusioned with the West. For many Chinese, Christianity represented Western interference, and the organised church became the scapegoat for anti-foreign feeling.

C. Y. Cheng, an outstanding Christian leader and chairman of the National Christian Council, contrasted the situation in the 1920s with that of 1900. (The memory of the Boxer Uprising still haunted both missionaries and Chinese.) He suggested that the Boxer Rebellion was based on ignorance, hatred and prejudice, because most people knew almost nothing about Christianity and the West. Now people knew much more, and their opposition was based on a clearer understanding of some of the issues involved.[7] If science had disproved religion and the Bible, why were missionaries still there? Some criticisms were unjustified, some were due to misunderstanding, and others were valid because Christians were not perfect. Some Chinese rejected Western denominational churches, but were ready to follow Jesus as a great teacher.

Marie's third term of service in the mid-1920s coincided with the increasing political turmoil of that period and the resulting social change. The secluded world of women was fast disappearing.

They grew accustomed to flee at a moment's notice, accustomed to walking about in the open and being seen. Men grew used to seeing them at all hours, which was not the least significant result of the upheaval. Christian women had marvellous opportunities of meeting heathen women fleeing from their ravaged homes and were able to be the Lord's witnesses to them in time of trouble... The first time I saw how the unrest was turning into a fulfilment of the word given to us... was in one of our out-stations... The congregation was five times as large as we had ever seen it, and three out of every five among them were women. I began to wonder if the time would ever come when we would have to pray that more men would come to our meetings as we had prayed for more women.[8]

The use of the phonetic script was already having a profound influence in enabling Christian women to become literate, read the Bible for themselves, and be more outgoing and confident in their witness. Marie began asking Christians what it was in the Christian message that led them to respond and believe.[9] She tried to identify why some had spiritual life and understanding and others did not, even though they were known as Christians and might even be Christian workers. She found that some talked easily of "believing", but if asked whether they had been born again, were blank. They had "believed" without a real understanding of the Christian faith and what was involved. She spent a year or more talking with Christians about their faith, and learned a lot about the state of the church, which would be invaluable to her in later years.[10]

The first signs of change came with a two-week residential Bible school for Bible women. This should have been a time of solid teaching and spiritual growth, but there were problems. First, she was asked to include 30 unsympathetic wives of Christian evangelists and mission workers. (Many Christian leaders and workers had wives who were not Christians, and who made life very difficult for them.) It was hoped that these women would be helped by contact with

Christian women, but it would clearly alter the group dynamics of the school. Then she was also asked to include 16 women from a mountain district, to whom a Christian doctor had witnessed once or twice. Humanly speaking, it was an impossible task to handle a group with such diverse needs: each day, as the women cooked their meals, the two missionaries spent an hour praying that the Holy Spirit would work in their lives.

After three days of teaching, there was a remarkable change. The first to respond were the women from the mountain district: thirteen of them confessed to taking the lives of several of their own babies. One had taken the lives of thirteen babies, "but they were all girls". Another asked: "Do you mean we can't do what we want with our own children?" It was a common practice to destroy unwanted babies (especially if they were girls, since they were a financial burden on poor families until they married), but Marie had never heard anyone admit to this in public before. Later, when she came to talk to them individually, she was unsure where to start with women who had so little understanding of God. She was amazed and humbled when one woman, after confessing, said with a radiant face,

> It is just as if I were a great bandit and... the soldiers dragged me before the Mandarin; and instead of denying everything, I confessed everything, and the Mandarin did not say, "Take her away and execute her," but he said, "She has confessed, it is no longer held to her account. Go home in peace."[11]

It was a remarkable description by a peasant woman of what theologians would call "justification by faith". She had grasped what it meant. Someone was working in her life, enabling her to understand, and Marie was conscious that she herself was simply a spectator as the Holy Spirit opened people's eyes to the truth.

# The 1927 evacuation

Just as they were beginning to see these encouraging signs, the political situation became critical and anti-foreign feelings peaked. In the spring of 1927, the consuls ordered the evacuation of all foreigners to the coast: they did not want to risk a repeat of the horrors of the Boxer Rebellion 27 years earlier.[12] It was another of those occasions when everything seemed to go wrong. How long would they be away, and what would happen to the congregations? Leaving the work at this juncture felt like entering a dark valley for Marie, though she was able to accept it as God's will for her. It was a time of severe testing: in their absence the destruction of Christian schools, hospitals, churches and other property was extensive. As pressure was also brought to bear on Chinese Christians, many of whose commitment was nominal, some of them withdrew from the churches, and some even recanted. The Western press was quick to proclaim the end of mission work in China.

Exiled from their home areas, some of the missionaries found other avenues of service for the moment. With her early experience of inner-city Toronto, Margaret King moved readily from her ministry among the most educated girls in the mission schools and colleges to the prostitutes on the streets of Shanghai. Others (and there were 1,500 missionaries gathered in Shanghai alone) faced an indefinite stay in overcrowded conditions, prevented from working. With normal pressures removed, they had time to search their own hearts and reflect on their own lives and service, the state of the national church, and the providence of God in that situation. They prayed for the present and the future.

Marie seized the opportunity to visit some veteran Danish missionaries in Manchuria. On arrival, she found that a regional conference was planned, but then, the evening before they were due to start, news came that the Chinese speaker could not arrive until the final day. The missionaries were bitterly disappointed. For years they had given all they could to the church, and felt they could do no more. To her dismay, they turned to Marie and said, "Now you must take the meetings." She had 24 hours' notice to tackle what was a far cry from informal meetings with country women. But, after praying, she felt she should do it, and her messages touched people's hearts in a way they had never done before.

Afterwards she made her way to Yantai (Chefoo) on the north China coast for the summer months, where other evacuated missionaries were still waiting, and she found that many of them shared her concerns for the church in China, and longed to see more life and effectiveness, both in the churches and in themselves. More and more people were praying for new life and power. Marie prayed with them, and the new friends she made there (like Sofie Romcke, a fellow Norwegian, and Anna Christensen from Denmark – both CIM members) continued to pray for her ministry and invited her to visit their areas in the coming years.[13] Circumstances were beginning to move Marie out of the "women's world" in China, and even beyond her own mission and church boundaries.

## Opening doors

In September 1927 she left Chefoo with Sofie Romcke. They had hoped to make their way back to Sofie's home province of Shanxi, but they found their way blocked by continued fighting.[14] Instead, they spent the next ten months responding to requests from various friends to speak at meetings in Beijing and the north of Hebei province. Finally, in August 1928, they were able to return to Sofie's home in Chaocheng, and Sofie and her two Norwegian colleagues were able to introduce Marie to the churches in Shanxi. After seeing so many churches bursting with new life and enthusiasm elsewhere, it was a special joy for Sofie to see the same things happening in Chaocheng. Meetings were held in the boys' and girls' schools, and in November, at the request of the church leaders, Marie returned for two weeks of meetings for women and one week of meetings for about 100 men. It was still difficult to communicate with both groups together.

Sofie Romcke settled into local work in the heavily populated area around Chaocheng, but as the wave of new life moved through the churches, increasing numbers of people wanted to hear the Christian message. Marie was invited to church after church, as those who had newly come to faith, or been restored to it, took the message to other areas.[15]

Marie's meetings at the Huntung Bible Institute in November 1928 were typical of her approach. She talked individually with each student and teacher beforehand, asking them directly if they had been born again. Some were offended by such a direct question to people who claimed to be Christians; some admitted they had not received the new birth; others were not sure. While normal classes continued the next day, Marie spent the time praying for each one that the Holy Spirit would work in their lives.

Three days of morning and afternoon meetings followed. Marie stressed that unconfessed sin was a barrier to new life. She spoke about a different sin at each meeting, such as hatred, stealing, lying, jealousy, or impurity; she showed how many people, including leaders in the church, had acquired peace, forgiveness and new life by recognising and confessing their sin before God.

Reports said that she spoke quietly, slowly and impressively, and many people came under deep conviction of sin. She did not encourage public confession, but in between meetings and in the evenings people were free to talk to her and other leaders in private, and many did so. Some wanted to confess their sins in these private conversations. By the end, almost all of the 31 students were rejoicing in a new experience of forgiveness and freedom from guilt.[16]

In April 1929 Marie was invited to Shandong by a group of American Southern Baptists, but she failed to arrive. Her ship was boarded by pirates and she was held for three dangerous weeks before being put ashore in Manchuria.[17] After a few weeks with the Danish missionaries there, she went on to

Peitaiho, a resort in north China, hoping for a summer break, but rest never came. Instead, she found herself in demand, ministering to the many other missionaries who were vacationing there. For the first time she realised why the door to schoolteaching had closed for her 25 years earlier. As a schoolteacher, she would never have understood the struggles and frustrations of evangelism and church-planting, but now, after years of discouragement in similar situations, she could identify with her colleagues. The wave of revival was touching the missionaries as well as the Chinese.[18]

## The Shandong (Shantung) revival

It was autumn before Marie finally reached the Southern Baptists in Shandong. The story of the Shantung revival has been recorded elsewhere: its beginnings can be traced to Marie's visit in the autumn of 1929, and it continued through the 1930s.[19] Mary Crawford described it as being born in prayer groups, some of which had begun as early as 1925. And then, when Marie came,

> it was a work of deep faith, relying on the convicting power of the Holy Spirit. In the first revival meetings in Shantung there was very poor singing, no altar calls, no chance given for public confession, but only the pressing home of the quiet question, "Have you been born again?"

Marie had spent many months questioning believers about their faith, and realised that nominal belief had become all too common. She asked this simple question wherever she went, speaking to Christians or seekers, and she did not go on to pressurise them. When people saw the response that Marie evoked, they knew it was nothing she had done, but the Spirit of God at work. That is why, even after she left each place, the work continued: ultimately it was God who was at work.[20] Many years later she wrote:

I never had any power stored up which I could use as I liked. Each time I began to count with myself and my own unfitness, I was poorer than anyone... I found rest in realising that I was walking in the works the Lord had "prepared beforehand", and could by faith rely on the power given for the task awaiting, the power was always there.[21]

Marie was not a "one-person band". Others could take her place. Sometimes other Scandinavian friends like Sofie Romcke, Laura Moller and Anna Christensen accompanied her, and she teamed up with Chinese leaders and local missionaries wherever she was. Many people were involved in the personal counselling afterwards. She would have been the first to recognise that she had been chosen to reap where many others had spent hard years in ploughing and sowing.

Blessing came to large numbers of Christian leaders, both Chinese and missionary. Those who had seen little response to the Christian message had been discouraged by apathy, feeling God had abandoned them. Some had lapsed into doubt; others had tolerated sin in their attitudes and relationships. Now they had a new experience of the power of God. The message was as old as the New Testament, but as Marie talked to individuals, she found that many "Christians" had failed to have a real understanding of the work of Jesus. For over 20 years, large numbers had been entering the churches, but too often the preaching had been vague, calling people to "believe" without explaining what and why. One missionary was converted: she had assumed that she became a Christian as a child when she raised her hand at a meeting, without understanding what it signified.[22] Others had become Christians without an inward understanding of what God had done for them. When people realised in their hearts what they had believed theoretically with their heads, their love for God deepened and led to great joy.[23]

Many people in the Shandong revival also experienced what was known as the fullness or baptism of the Holy Spirit, a second specific stage after conversion. This was not usually taught among Southern Baptists, but nevertheless it became a hallmark of this movement. It was widely promulgated in the second half of the nineteenth century in both North America (by Robert and Hannah Pearsall Smith) and Britain, where it became the focus of the new Keswick Convention. It extended the teaching on salvation by faith to receiving sanctification, or holiness by faith, in a second experience.[24] Marie herself did not appear to stress this, though she described having such an experience herself. In her joy she said she had praised God in every language she knew! But she also commented that she did not "speak in tongues". (In the early days of the Pentecostal movement some thought the gift of tongues would enable them to preach the gospel in different languages.) Other revival groups in Shandong stressed the seeking of spiritual gifts. Marie focused on conversion and repentance.

Marie's ministry continued for the next two and a half years. She made return visits to the Hongtong (Huntung) Seminary and also to Shandong province, where the revival continued to spread. In the spring of 1932 a wave of new life came to the churches in western Henan. R. W. Frame, an American CIM missionary, reported on her "spirit-fired ministry", which continued long after she had left, as many Christians came under conviction for different sins and restitution was made. He also commented on the way so much of what was happening confronted normal Chinese culture and practices.

> [The Chinese] are... a most proud and self-righteous people. They strive above all else to hold up a good face for the world to see – whatever they do in the dark. There is only one way whereby a person may... sin and yet appear innocent and respectable... and that is to keep his sin covered up. "Nothing is sin unless it be found out" seems to be the principle on which... life is run in China; so woe betide the person who exposes his neighbour's sin.[25]

In the spring of 1932, Marie paid a final visit to Sofie Romcke and the church in Chaocheng, before returning to her native Norway.

## Revival movements

One view of the period 1927–1940 suggests that there were waves of revival across China throughout the 1930s.[26] Some were influenced by international speakers such as Stanley Jones; others came through the work of national Chinese leaders such as John Sung, Wang Ming-dao, Watchman Nee, Andrew Gih and Miss Wang Pei-chen. These were well-educated pastors and Christian leaders with experience, and though their methods varied considerably they preached a similar message of repentance and faith. Some were quiet, others noisy and dramatic; one rarely invited people to believe, others "strained to get results"; some emphasised public confession, others confined this (if it was done at all) to private interviews. However it began, the new life and zeal that emerged found expression in a deep desire for evangelism. One characteristic was the development of "preaching bands" who came from all walks of life and became a powerful force in the life of the churches. These Christians had a deep desire to share what they had received, and formed evangelistic teams to visit the villages and share the Christian gospel with others. Apathy and lethargy had gone, and this change of spirit was not a brief phase. People's lives had changed, and even their non-Christian neighbours recognised it.[27]

There were also spontaneous movements in local churches. First there were the American and Swedish Baptists in Shandong, who emphasised sin, repentance and restitution, followed by the baptism of the Holy Spirit as a second experience. They also saw people healed, but the emphasis was on God, not the phenomena. The missionaries found themselves on some unfamiliar ground, but there was blessing, the churches came alive, people were converted, relationships in the family and community were healed, restitution was made, and homes and families were transformed, not for a week or two, but for years.

Secondly, there were unofficial leaders who laid much greater stress on spiritual gifts so that these became the main focus. Some of these groups indulged in various extremes, and the meetings were noisy and even disorderly: here the Bible was less central, and the way was thus left open for elements that were not Christian. (Eventually regulations were imposed which led to greater moderation and order.) Marie was not connected with these groups: in her meetings occasional excesses occurred, but they were always restrained.[28]

## The critics

Naturally, this ministry attracted some criticism from both the liberal and the more conservative wings of the Christian community in China. It is surprising that Marie's name was not mentioned in Paul Abbott's article written on the subject, but she was neither internationally known nor a national Chinese leader.[29] She was also a woman, and some men struggled with that: male missionaries and pastors had prayed for revival for years – why was she chosen to lead this movement? Why indeed. She said herself that she was not a speaker; there were missionaries far more eloquent in Chinese than she, and some particularly gifted male leaders. There were Chinese pastors and evangelists who understood the culture far better. Someone at a large missionary conference in Scandinavia dismissed the revival as "a women's movement", although this was quite untrue.[30] Marie quietly insisted that it was the work of God, and as time passed, more men, both Chinese and missionary, were involved.

Daniel Bays, Professor of Modern Chinese History in Kansas, writing about her in the *Biographical Dictionary of Christian Missions*, was somewhat contradictory. He described her as "quasi Pentecostal... and her meetings were emotional if not disorderly. She was by all accounts softly-spoken, and it is not altogether clear why she prompted such a strong response."[31] Marie would surely have pointed him gently to the Holy Spirit. Other eyewitnesses deny that the meetings were unduly emotional. Marie belonged to a Lutheran mission, and the Southern Baptists, Methodists and CIM missionaries with whom she worked were not Pentecostal. Those who witnessed the extraordinary things that were happening in people's lives could discern only the hand of God at work. In 1930, Mary Crawford wrote of the meetings in Tsinan:

> Right here I want to say that none of these "Born Again" revivals had the least taint of sensationalism about them. The singing was the usual mediocre singing of the congregation... Miss M. (*sic*) herself is one of the quietest speakers I have ever heard, but anyone with any discernment at all could see and feel that she was depending upon the promises of God in a remarkable way.[32]

Marie was careful not to pressurise people, and constantly warned others against "picking unripe fruit". That could only produce spurious results, which were not the work of the Holy Spirit.[33] But when people became aware of their sins, their responses would inevitably be accompanied by emotion, and sometimes by tears for what they had done. Then, as they appreciated God's love, mercy and forgiveness, and his welcome to those who trusted in what Jesus had done for them, many also experienced overwhelming relief and joy. In the old Chinese religions many people spent years obsessively fasting, making long pilgrimages and doing penances. They had lived their lives in bondage trying to earn forgiveness, and now the good news of Jesus had set them free. They had something to rejoice about.

## The results

The results of this ministry were practical and enduring. Once sin was acknowledged, restitution followed: what had been stolen was returned, or compensation given – one person filled a wheelbarrow with things he needed to give back. Long-standing hostility between individuals was confessed and forgiven, even though this involved "loss of face" in front of others. This particularly ran against Chinese culture, and non-Christians were astonished at what they saw. In some cases, leading men apologised to women for their behaviour. Women admitted infanticide and ill-treating their daughters-in-law. Husbands admitted treating their wives harshly, to the point of physical violence. The witness of changed lives spread blessing: ordinary church members formed evangelistic teams and went out to country villages with the message of forgiveness for those who repented. Whole churches were transformed. Two years later it was reported:

> Almost all our stations have been affected. God has found both men and women, Chinese and missionaries, whose voices He has used to awaken sleeping souls... Very few of the newly saved seem to fall away.[34]

The word "revival" is used in various ways today. Literally it means a return to life. Though it is sometimes used for evangelism, it more correctly refers to those who have had their spiritual life renewed. For over a decade after 1927, in spite of, or perhaps because of, increasing political turmoil, there was a remarkable response from both Christians and non-Christians. Jonathan Goforth had seen such a revival in Korea, Manchuria and China before the Great War, and in the 1930s, other people such as Stanley Jones, John Sung, Andrew Gih and Wang Ming-dao were involved in the waves of renewal that came to the Chinese churches. Leslie Lyall, who arrived in China himself in 1929, stated that in 1927,

the pioneer of the spiritual "new life movement", the hand-
maiden upon whom the Spirit was first poured out, was Marie
Monsen of Norway. Her surgical skill in exposing the sins hidden within the Church and lurking behind the smiling exterior
of many a trusted Christian – even many a trusted Christian
leader – and her quiet insistence on a clear-cut experience of
the new birth, set the pattern for others to follow.[35]

Marie left China for the last time in 1932 and returned to
Norway, where she remained to care for her mother. The
renewed life which had come to so many churches through
her ministry would prove to be vital preparation for the suffering and persecution they had to endure when Japan
invaded China in 1937.[36] In Marie's place, Anna Christensen,
a younger Danish woman who had also been one of her associates, took up the ministry she had laid down. For the next
18 years, until missionaries were forced to leave China, Anna
was used in a remarkable ministry of evangelism and teaching across 19 of China's 24 provinces. Marie Monsen died in
1961.

## Anna Christensen

Anna Christensen had spent thirteen months at the CIM
training home in London before sailing for China in
September 1914, just as the First World War was starting. Her
work in her first term of service included Bible teaching and
evangelism in Huozhou, taking over from Mildred Cable
when the Trio left for north-west China in 1923.

After ten years' service Anna spent a two-year furlough in
Denmark; when she returned to China in the autumn of 1926
she revisited Huozhou to help the local evangelist with special village meetings. After three weeks in the first village, no
fewer than 19 families had burned their idols, and they set
apart a place for regular Sunday services. Then the political
situation deteriorated and the missionaries had to be evacuated to the coast. Anna found herself with Sofie Romcke and

Marie Monsen at Chefoo, involved in the prayer for revival movement which began there.[37]

Anna managed to return to Huozhou in September 1927, to find that the pastor had died and the church had been split by false teaching. A few months later, she responded to a request from a small church in the mountain city of Chinuen. Missionaries had visited, but never lived there, and their evangelist had just left. A number of men had come to faith, and they asked for someone to come and teach the women. Anna travelled for five days (some 80 miles) into the mountains to reach them, and found that the group included 16 village women who had come into town specially. She reported that "more than 30 women were born again... even the neighbours were commenting on the great change in their lives. Several men were convicted of sin, and twelve homes took down their idols." Husbands were overjoyed that their wives were now united with them in the faith. She was invited to visit several more villages, and in one place services were held again after a lapse of two years. When she left after seven weeks, she was urged to return.[38] While political turmoil and anti-foreign feeling were causing havoc elsewhere, she had been received with warmth and kindness, and was surprised at the people's eager response and hunger to learn.

When Marie Monsen and Sofie Romcke finally got back to Chaocheng in the summer of 1928, and arranged special meetings for November of that year, Anna went downriver from Huozhou to join them and shared in the tide of blessing that followed.[39] This seems to have been a critical point in her service. For fifteen years she had had a fairly settled ministry in Shanxi province, working out from central towns to the women in the surrounding villages. Now all that was about to change.

In August 1929 she wrote to her friends:

We are having a very encouraging time here in Shanxi. The Lord has begun to show us a new thing in answer to the prayers of many years and it has meant the re-making of some of us missionaries. Souls are being saved in many places, such as I have never witnessed before here in China. It has been my privilege to go round to a number of stations conducting revival meetings, and in each place there has been such a conviction of sin, that people found no peace night or day until all was confessed and put away. I have experienced more this last year in China than in all the other years put together – truly an answer to many prayers. To Him be the glory.[40]

In September 1929 Anna embarked on an eleven-day journey by mule, to spend six weeks with the Norwegian Mission to China in the north-west of Shanxi. She spent two weeks each in Linhsien, Kolan and Hsinghsien, leading two sessions each day for Bible women.[41] The Torjesen family from Norway lived in the remote city of Hequ (Hoku), near the borders with Shaanxi and Inner Mongolia.[42] Valborg Torjesen took her baby son and four local women from Hequ, four days' journey by mule (some 70 miles), to a two-week women's conference where a "dynamic preacher from Denmark was used of God to meet these women's deepest spiritual needs". The women had never ridden mules or been outside Hequ before. Because their feet had been bound in childhood they were permanently crippled, and could not dismount on rough mountain paths. After four days, they must have been saddle-sore as well! It was the journey of a lifetime to reach Anna's meetings in Kolan.

This experience must have been shared by hundreds and even thousands of women. The country churches in China emerged because the believers wanted to learn, even when it involved hardship and radical changes in their lives. Anna moved on to lead more meetings in the extreme south of the province. By 1930 she had travelled "in the north, south, east and south-west".[43] Given the primitive methods of travel in Shanxi at that time, it is not surprising that Huozhou saw little of her for 18 months.

A period of expansion followed the evacuation in 1927. The hostility against Western influence made it clear that the churches must become independent of foreign control as soon as possible, and also be financially self-supporting under their own leadership, but it was a difficult step to take. The country people were poor, and accustomed to Chinese workers being supported by foreign funds – they were not used to contributing much themselves. Yet the evacuation had shown that a capable national leadership was developing, and this would free missionaries to move to areas without Christian witness.

## The "Forward Movement"

The CIM decided that, in addition to redeploying many missionaries, they could place 200 more in the next two years, and the call went out for "the two hundred", as they came to be known. As civil war broke out again eleven foreigners were killed and others abducted or robbed, so it was hardly an auspicious time to advance. Nevertheless, by 1930 eight new stations had been opened in Shanxi alone, and two years later Anna and a colleague were appointed to start work in a new town thirteen miles away.

In the autumn of 1932, Anna went east over the border to the province of Hebei. The church at Shunteh, praying for revival, approached the Chinese evangelistic Bethel Band, as well as Anna, and in the event got both! One of the Bethel Band teams held meetings a few weeks before Anna arrived. The CIM and the American Presbyterians worked together to erect a simple tent of straw mats, heated by stoves for the cold November evenings. The meetings were no longer segregated, but included both men and women. The Revd H. S. Cliff reported:

> there was a marked quietness in the tent, and those present seemed to drink in every word... There was no undue excitement or mere emotionalism, but hearts were just broken with grief for sin.

Almost all who confessed mentioned adultery. One woman had drowned a baby girl; another had killed a girl as old as six; a third had disposed of several babies of both sexes. One man suddenly realised it was his abuse of his wife that had led to her death. Hearing these people bare their souls was traumatic.

Baptisms in the CIM churches were now increasing to over 6,000 annually, and many people who said they believed were only just beginning to face the enormity of their past actions. It was not only new Christians, but even church leaders who were convicted of their sins. Yet as sin was acknowledged and confessed, they entered into a deeper understanding of the meaning of the cross, and the depth of God's love and forgiveness, and they were often overwhelmed by the joy and peace that followed.[44]

After Marie Monsen retired in 1932, Anna Christensen's ministry expanded in ever-widening circles; by the time of her own retirement in 1950 it had effects across most of China. There were others with a similar ministry, both male and female, Chinese and missionary, but few continued the work as long and as persistently as she did.[45] She benefited from the rapid social changes in China over this period, not the least of which was a transport revolution. From 1927 onwards, as Chiang Kai-shek endeavoured to control rival factions and unify the country, modern roads and railways were introduced, and journey times between major cities were rapidly reduced from days to hours, though where smaller towns and villages were concerned, travel could remain as difficult as ever.[46]

## Teaching and preaching tours

The Henan spring tour south of Shanxi province in 1933 was carefully planned. There were six days of meetings in each of twelve different towns, with a further four weeks of teaching for church leaders and voluntary workers, both male and female, based on a Bible school. In the autumn Anna had a similar schedule in seven more centres in Henan, when six-day missions were held in each. In some places 400 or 500 people travelled in from rural areas.[47] She spoke to churches and schools, men and women, and taught in Bible schools, and the pages of *China's Millions* preserve reports from other missionaries describing the lasting impact of these meetings. In July 1933, the monthly headquarters letter also quoted some of these reports. "There has been no emotion on the part of the speaker – just a simple, faithful presentation of the Word of God in the power of the Spirit." One deacon walked 60 miles to attend. Elsewhere, teams of lay Christians formed to spend their Sunday afternoons visiting and preaching in the villages.[48] The churches were already taking responsibility for their own evangelism, and lay preaching bands became a marked feature of the Chinese churches in this period.

It was a heavy schedule, and in 1934 Anna took a well-earned furlough in the UK and Denmark. In her absence the Shanxi railway line was opened from Taiyuan south to the Yellow River. Meanwhile the Japanese consolidated their position in Manchuria and tried to extend their influence over China's northern provinces, including the Shanxi and Hebei provinces where Anna had been working. Chiang Kai-shek drove the Communist forces out of the southern province of Jiangxi and they began the 6,000-mile "Long March": soldiers, many still in their teens, were forced to march in cruel conditions, and of the 85,000 who took part, only 8,000 reached their destination. The Red Army took two CIM men as hostages, forcing them to march with them for nearly 18 months. Within days of their capture, John and Betty Stam, a young CIM couple in their twenties, were beheaded.

It was a terrible time for conscripts and townspeople alike, as the soldiers left a trail of devastation and death among the local population.[49] Chiang Kai-shek's sphere of control was limited to southern China, but there he initiated the New Life movement which led to real material progress.

The local currency was stabilised; towns were planned and organised; road and rail travel were established and air flights developed. However, conditions elsewhere were so bad that CIM women on leave were not allowed to return to China in 1935; Anna seems to have been an exception.

Early in 1936, Anna travelled beyond the Great Wall of China to Suiyuan in Inner Mongolia, on the southern edge of the Gobi desert. The Swedish Alliance Mission, a CIM associate mission, had established ten stations there in the main cities, with some 30 outstations. There were 19 missionaries, 100 paid and voluntary Chinese workers, and some 2,000 other believers in a population of 2 million.

The early months of 1937 were peaceful until the Communists abducted Chiang Kai-shek for two weeks and forced him to co-operate with them and confront Japan. They did this by invading Shanxi province, which then became a battleground between Chinese and Japanese troops. The missionaries were technically neutral and avoided political involvement, but attacks and counter-attacks on the towns seriously disrupted the lives of everyone, both Chinese and foreigner.

In the spring of 1937 Anna accepted an invitation from the CIM churches in Sichuan, so she was far away when the Japanese invaded Shanxi later in the year. She remained in the south-west for the next four years. The churches there were poorer and simpler, and the people much less educated than those in the east. They were overwhelmed by the arrival of many sophisticated, educated Chinese who were fleeing west from the Japanese. The new arrivals were eager to help the local churches, but the gulf between them and the local Christians was not easy to cross.[50]

Anna travelled extensively, leading a series of meetings on "Deepening the Spiritual Life" in different centres, for periods varying from five to eight days each. At first it was not easy. The country folk who came in from the outstations had lost their harvest through drought the previous year: a week of meetings included meals for the starving, and so food naturally came to dominate the week for them. The people from the city dashed in and out of meetings when they could, and were unable to withdraw from the daily pressures of work to focus on what they were hearing. An average of 100 gathered daily. They would begin with 25 minutes of singing, following which Anna spoke for an hour each morning and afternoon, and then came a period of open prayer when all could take part. Others took the early-morning prayer meeting and the evening meeting. It was a full programme, but people were eager to learn. Victory over sin in daily life was preached, not as an unattainable ideal, but as a reality through the power of the Holy Spirit. A fellow missionary gave a vivid glimpse of her simple methods when he described her using a picture of three hearts,

> each under the dominion of a different lord – "Sin", "I", "the Lord". These were filled with small cards on which were written the sort of characteristics appropriate to the rule of each of the "lords". The reaction was naturally varied, though the attention to what was said was as a whole very good. It is not easy for those who have been church members many years to discover in the Light of the Spirit that they have a "name" without the reality, or that many things in their lives which they slurred over and took no notice of are Sin in God's sight and must be faced as such. [51]

The response varied, but many men and women were deeply touched. In every place the emphasis was on the need for repentance, new birth, and victory over sin. One woman burned her opium crop, and an army officer confessed to stealing $8,000 from public funds, which he intended to pay back.

In January 1938, Anna moved south to the tribal churches in Yunnan, and embarked on a very different kind of area with eight missions of one week each, spread over 17 weeks from January to the end of May. Some centres were nearly 200 miles apart in mountainous country. She had never been in such precipitous terrain before: the highest point in Denmark is only 600 feet above sea level! After 22 years in China she was no longer young, and somewhat heavily built. When she developed heart trouble she began to use a sedan chair, but one team of porters abandoned her in the wilds. Another group used extra men to carry her and "gave her the most frightening journey of her life".

James Fraser, the famous evangelist to the Lisu people, his wife, Roxy, and their pre-school daughter travelled with her, by mule or sedan chair, sleeping on straw in local inns.[52] Everywhere Anna went, she reached the hearts of the people. Roxy commented:

> [Fraser] had seen great blessing come to the Chinese churches in west Yunnan following the visit of Miss Anna Christensen from Denmark, when deep conviction of sin and fear of judgement came upon them all, and he saw the desperate need of widespread revival among all the churches.[53]

There was still a sense of the power of God at work, and her teaching led to a deepening of spiritual life and commitment which stood the test of time, and prepared the believers for the persecution lying ahead.[54] This was followed by summer meetings with missionaries at a mountain resort, away from the summer heat on the plains, and then another autumn campaign in Sichuan.[55]

The years 1939–40 found Anna ministering in the northwest provinces of Gansu and Shaanxi.[56] Travel now involved perching for hours on top of goods piled high on the back of a lorry, and she was nearly 50 years of age. She was inside the cab when her truck was in a head-on collision with a heavy oil lorry on a sharp bend on a mountain road, but she escaped with only minor injuries. She had already been involved in several mishaps on the journey north from Sichuan and her leg had almost been broken; she was a day late arriving at the conference where she was expected. There were false reports that summer that her health had broken down, but in fact she was just very tired. She had worked steadily for nine months with very little rest. Her engagements for the autumn of 1939 again followed the familiar pattern: thirteen six-day missions in mission centres in Shaanxi and eastern Gansu. It was a demanding schedule and she did not spare herself.

## Was it revival?

There had already been some discussion about the nature of the changes in the church in China. An editorial comment, probably from the hand of Leslie Lyall, had prefaced an article by Theodore Benson in the CIM Annual Report for 1937. Lyall suggested that the word "revival" had been used too loosely for any kind of evangelism, or gatherings for deeper spiritual life, almost regardless of the results. In fact, China had never seen anything in the nature of the "great religious awakenings, like the Welsh Revival" when whole churches were affected. Benson quoted Bishop Frank Houghton as saying that, while people were converted, and others found assurance of salvation and a deeper spiritual life, it was not a mass movement.[57]

In part this discussion reflected a difference in American and British usage of the word "revival". In British usage, "revival" usually referred to renewed spiritual life in the church, by the supernatural intervention of the Lord himself, rather than to evangelism. Moreover, the contrast drawn between the Welsh and Chinese churches was not entirely valid. The Welsh churches had become lukewarm after centuries of Christian teaching, whereas the younger churches in China, with no Christian background, were still battling to escape from the entanglements of Buddhist and animistic religion which surrounded them. Of the 18 centres in eastern Sichuan, only nine had existed 40 years earlier. Benson also said "it was only individuals", but the sins that lay on their consciences revealed how much repentance and new life was needed. He went on:

From the awful confessions that were made in private talks, it is possible to imagine in part, what lies behind the lives of those who, having seen the Way, have not yet dared to walk therein.[58] Among the leaders there are as yet too many unclean hands and impure hearts to make it easy for a landslide of blessing to sweep into the church at large. Let us therefore continue in prayer: "Wilt Thou not revive us again: that Thy people may rejoice in Thee?"[59]

That was not the end of the story: the following year two more articles appeared in the annual report. The first also had a preface by an unnamed editor, who described Anna Christensen as one of God's "skilled workmen (*sic*)... commissioned with a special message of radical repentance, living faith and entire consecration". Western Sichuan was described as one of the most difficult fields she had visited, and a fellow-worker endorsed this description of the area, commenting that, for him and his fellow missionaries, "the temptation all along was to make difficulty the excuse for lack of blessing". The missionaries in particular had appreciated her messages the previous year, and were later convicted of their own lack of faith to believe God could work in a special way in their area. In consequence, they began to pray with more faith, preach with more power and hope, and see more results.[60]

The second article was written by Bishop Houghton about eastern Sichuan. The flight of refugees from the east had brought some eminent Chinese leaders to the simple churches of Sichuan, and one of these was Marcus Cheng, who would later become a bishop. His messages brought a wave of blessing to the churches in 1938 and Houghton summed it up:

Miss Christensen in 1937 and Marcus Cheng in 1938 – the church in Sichuan needed them both. One found the ground so hard that the time was spent mainly in ploughing, and it needed the other to sow and to reap... In view of the condition of the church, it was inevitable that Miss Christensen roused the questionings in the minds of many – "Am I truly born again? Have I been deceiving myself?" – and Marcus Cheng answered them, so that the Gospel which men and women had previously heard "in word only" now came "in power, and in the Holy Ghost, and in much assurance."[61]

## Tensions in interdenominational missions

Leonard Street commented that the revival that took place in north and central China did not affect Gansu.[62] In November 1939, Anna visited four of the cities in eastern Gansu occupied by the Scandinavian Alliance Mission (CIM associates). Apparently, Anna had written to the superintendent of the CIM area in Gansu offering to take meetings when she was in the province. When E. J. Mann, the superintendent, declined her offer because she was a woman, she had asked, "Are you all [Plymouth] Brethren up there?" to which he had replied, "No, but we try to be scriptural." [63]

This gives a rare glimpse of the underlying tensions in an interdenominational mission. Hundreds of missionaries from many different evangelical church streams had united to focus on the central Christian truths on which they were agreed, and to put on one side the lesser matters on which they disagreed. In the past, the ministry of missionary women had been essential for the evangelisation of Chinese women shut away in their homes. This ministry had revealed their remarkable gifts of evangelism and teaching, their ability to work alongside Chinese church leaders, and their physical stamina under conditions that could be extremely harsh at times. When necessary, while still working with women, they had also been able to encourage and guide emerging national church leaders without threatening or supplanting them.

Now, as the "women's world" began to disappear, the gifts of teaching and evangelism found in people like Anna Christensen and Marie Monsen were being more widely recognised as they ministered to the whole church – though some people still found it hard to understand why God had apparently chosen to send revival through women.[64] When the number of women missionaries expanded rapidly in China in the 1890s, the issue of their ministry had been debated in the *Chinese Recorder*.[65] In the light of the spiritual needs of women in China, and the spiritual gifts manifestly given to women, Hudson Taylor had insisted from the start that their ministry was essential. Nevertheless, the accepted interpretation of certain biblical passages led him and most other evangelicals of that period to believe that Christian leadership must remain in male hands. Most missionary women accepted this, but it left them in an ambiguous position. By the very nature of their work and calling they were in effect leaders, and they had much to contribute in terms of helping the young pastors. Because they were women, they could do this quietly and discreetly. They proved an effective method of encouraging and guiding local leaders, provided that the issue of authority did not rear its ugly head. Surprisingly, in such a male-dominated culture, Chinese men had been eager to listen to foreign women as well as men; perhaps even more surprisingly for the traditionalists, God had used the women's ministry to bring blessing to the men, too.[66]

There must have been a spectrum of personal views within the CIM on where the lines should be drawn, but in an interdenominational mission a distinction had to be made between personal views on matters that were considered "secondary", and the fundamental call in which all had united to proclaim the gospel and build up the church. For this reason controversial views were not usually debated or recorded, with the exception of the cryptic ruling in the 1925 *Book of Arrangements*, drawn up and approved by the CIM China Executive after consultation with the superintendents. This stated that "in the absence of a man on a station, there were certain things a woman could not do". Leslie Lyall, a CIM historian who reached China in 1929, was unaware of this ruling or any restrictions on their ministry, beyond the fact that women could not be mission directors or superintendents of the provinces.[67] Still, China was a big country and the application of rules would depend to some extent on the individual leaders concerned. Some women may well have set their own boundaries more widely or narrowly, depending upon what they were happy to do.[68] Most, when asked, commented on the large degree of freedom they had, especially when compared with women in the churches at home.

We do not know whether the Gansu CIM superintendent consulted his advisory Provincial Council when he declined to accept Anna's offer, or whether he acted alone, which he was free to do. His interpretation of scripture was a matter for his own personal conscience, but his decision could have repercussions for his Chinese and missionary colleagues. Gansu was a remote frontier province bordered on two sides by Tibet and Mongolia, with a mixed population of Tibetan, Chinese and Central Asian nomadic groups. For the new believers and the scattered missionaries confronting Buddhism and Islam, life was hard, and results slow. They might well have been blessed and encouraged through Anna's ministry as others had been elsewhere, but Mann's conscience did not allow it, and this explains Leonard Street's comment that "the revival did not affect Gansu". Perhaps it reflects the dangers and limitations of hierarchy. Authority can so easily be misused to the detriment of those who must live under it. In later years CIM/OMF superintendents and Directors were not expected to act without consultation with their elected advisory Field Councils.

## The Second World War

After four years of teaching and evangelism across the mission stations of China's four western provinces, Anna returned to Shanghai in time for a Keswick-type conference for Chinese Christians held at the Kiangwan Theological Seminary in January 1941. As a result she was invited to Anhwei province.

While she had been away, the Japanese had occupied Hankow in central China in 1938, and the following year, they set up Wang Chin-mei as a puppet emperor in Nanjing. In 1940 Japan joined the Rome–Berlin axis, and invaded Indo-China. Chiang Kai-shek and the Chinese Nationalist troops, based in the western city of Chongqing in Sichuan province, had all access to the outside world cut off except for the Burma road.[69] There was huge disruption as universities, schools and thousands of people fled west from the Japanese. Foreigners were still politically neutral, but China was divided and travel between the two areas was difficult and dangerous.

At this time Anhwei province was occupied by the Japanese, and while resident missionaries were allowed to continue their work, it was difficult to obtain permission to move around the country. Anna was able to get the requisite papers, and commented, as she and Marie Monsen had done in the past, that the work she came to do "had been prepared" ahead of her and she just followed step by step. In the first city 800 people gathered every day during a ten-day conference. At the final meeting there were testimonies from 200 people in two hours: most of them managed to be concise and keep to their allotted half-minute. The people paid their own expenses and gave Anna $360 towards hers. This was followed by missions in two large schools which included girls as well as boys: the response in both places was good. She moved on to Tianjin (Tientsin) Holiness Bible College for eight days, and went on to visit churches and Bible colleges in the north, returning to Yantai (Chefoo) for the summer. Fourteen years earlier, in Yantai (Chefoo), she had prayed for revival with Marie Monsen and others: how much had happened since those days of small beginnings! Now several pastors were increasingly confident that if missionaries had to leave, the churches would be able to continue without them.

She described these hot summer weeks as a time "for rest and refreshment, and for 'mending my nets' in preparation for further service if He tarry". She could look back with joy and thanksgiving for all that God had done.

"There failed not aught of any good thing which the Lord had spoken – all came to pass." In other words, it is the Faithfulness of our blessed Lord, the surety of His Promises, and His continued Presence that make the soul rejoice. Oh what peace, what joy, what safety there is in being in His will.[70]

Those words were the last recorded from her in *China's Millions*. How often did she have to reaffirm those words in the years ahead? Nothing is known. Just four months later, in December 1941, the Japanese bombed Pearl Harbor. When other missionaries were sent to prison camps, Anna – a Danish citizen, and therefore neutral – was not interned. She spent the next four years in the Beijing area, and was repatriated in the spring of 1946.

## Closing doors

Undaunted by her wartime experiences, Anna was back in China in 1947. She spent several months travelling in the province of Jiangxi, ministering to churches that had suffered particularly under the Japanese occupation.[71] In 1948, Beijing fell to the Communist forces; in 1949, Arnold Lea reported that at long last there were signs of a new awakening in the three western provinces of Yunnan, Guizhou and Sichuan, with their combined population of 74 million people. There were more missionaries operating in the area, and also more Chinese Preaching Bands visiting the churches. There was new interest, and the door was still open with new opportunities. Anna spent the spring taking meetings in Yunnan again, and planned to go on to the other two provinces in the autumn of 1949, but the Nationalist army was crumbling before the Communists: Shanghai fell in May, Canton (Guangzhou) in October and Chongqing (Chungking) in November.

It was to be Anna's last year in China: she returned to Denmark in December, just as the People's Democratic Republic of China was proclaimed in Tian An Men Square in

Beijing.[72] She had spent 35 years in China, 23 of these as an itinerant teacher and evangelist.[73] There can be very few men or women who have sustained such a far-reaching ministry for so long over such a wide area.

How can her work be assessed? To my knowledge, no complete account of it has been written in English, but her letters were regularly published in *China's Millions*, along with frequent reports from missionaries in the places which she visited. Others described the long-term influence of her teaching on people's lives and relationships in both family and community. Arnold Lea (who guided the CIM/OMF into new areas in South-east Asia as Overseas Director in 1951) acknowledged his personal debt to her. He probably met her in Sichuan in 1937; later he told new recruits that he would never have survived his first term as a missionary if it had not been for Anna Christensen's ministry. That ministry was not only in evangelism but also in steady teaching, which must have strengthened the church. As the Communist forces gained power in the 1930s and restricted the activities of missionaries in the post-war years, the Chinese churches were able to move forward to take over evangelism and teaching, even shouldering responsibility for distant Xinjiang. Her work also prepared the believers for the traumatic times of testing and persecution in the years ahead.

Many other Christians, both Chinese and Western, were involved in leading the churches into a deeper spiritual life in the 1920s to 1930s, but Leslie Lyall saw Anna as the one who picked up the torch from them. She continued the ministry across China through all the trauma of the Sino-Japanese War and then the political struggle between the Communist and Nationalist forces which followed in the post-war years. She had the gift of enabling people to face themselves and their circumstances, and to find that God was with them in the midst of the darkness, if they repented and turned to him.

## Notes to Chapter Nine

1 Monsen, *Awakening*, p. 22.
2 Ibid., pp. 23–24.
3 Ibid., p. 25.
4 Ibid., pp. 24–27.
5 Ibid., pp. 30–32.
6 His first visit to Korea was in 1907 and marked the beginning of his outstanding revival ministry. Goforth, *Goforth*, p. 182.
7 C. Y. Cheng, "Problems and Needs of the Church", in *China Christian Year Book 1926–38* (Shanghai: CLS, 1931) pp. 92–102.
8 Ibid., p. 36. Women communicants in CIM outnumbered men for the first time in 1939. *China and the Gospel* (1940) p. 86.
9 Ibid., pp. 44–49.
10 Monsen, *Awakening*, pp. 44–49.
11 Ibid., pp. 37–44.
12 Nine-tenths of the 8,300 Protestant missionaries complied, and of these, 4,000 left on leave, half of whom never returned to China again. The rest retreated to the three coastal cities of Chefoo, Tientsin and Shanghai. Broomhall, vol. 7, p. 547. *China's Millions* (June 1927) p. 175. A total of 130 women remained at their stations by choice. Some were in distant, but safe areas. Miss A. M. Johannsen chose to remain on the mission premises in Yüshan, Jiangxi with the local Christians. Together they risked their lives to try to protect the church and school premises from the depredations of hundreds of soldiers who passed through: desks, windows and door frames could provide essential firewood. *China's Millions* (August 1927) p. 128.
13 Ibid., pp. 53–55.
14 Sofie Romcke, "Signs of Spiritual Revival", *China's Millions* (December 1928) pp. 182–83.
15 Sofie Romcke, "Times of Refreshing in Shanxi", *China's Millions* (May 1929) p. 75.
16 *Monthly Notes* vol. 34. 1 (January 1929), 2; Monsen, *Awakening*, pp. 98–99.
17 She recorded the extraordinary story in "In Perils in the Sea", in Strauss *et al.*, *Escaped*, pp. 105–33.
18 Monsen, *Awakening*, pp. 77–80.
19 Crawford, *Shantung*; Carlberg, *China* pp. 67–83; Culpepper, *Revival*.
20 Crawford, *Shantung*, pp. 1f.
21 Ibid., p. 127.
22 Ibid., pp. 81–83.
23 The Ping-tu area of Shandong saw 3,000 people converted in 1932.

This was the area where the well-known American single missionary Lottie Moon had worked so effectively in the nineteenth century. Crawford, *Shantung*, p. 25.

24 Bebbington, *Evangelicalism*, pp. 151f.

25 R. W. Frame, "From the Front Line: Henan", *China's Millions* (May 1933) p. 93.

26 Paul R. Abbott, "Revival Movements", in *China Christian Year Book 1932–33*, pp. 175–92.

27 Ibid., pp. 176–77.

28 Monsen, *Awakening*, pp. 113–14.

29 Paul R. Abbott, "Revival Movements", in *China Christian Year Book 1932–33*, pp. 176–77.

30 Monsen, *Awakenings*, pp. 78, 107–109, 115–16.

31 Daniel H. Bays, "Monsen, Marie", in Anderson, *Dictionary*.

32 Crawford, *Shantung*, p. 8.

33 Monsen, *Awakening*, p. 97.

34 Ibid., p. 99.

35 Leslie T. Lyall, "Historical Prelude", in Monsen, *Awakening*, pp. 20–21.

36 Ibid., pp. 21, 105–107.

37 Anna Christensen, "Hunger Satisfied", *China's Millions* (January–February 1942) p. 7.

38 Some years later a colleague commented that "Miss Christensen, being Danish, was not kept back from the interior after the evacuation in 1927 as long as some of other nationalities. Being alone amongst the mountains of Shanxi, it was her privilege to conduct services and know that there was a special manifestation of the presence and power of the Holy Spirit." J. Gardiner, "The Day of God's Visitation", *China's Millions* (May 1933) p. 85.

39 Sofie Romcke, "Times of Refreshing in Shanxi", *China's Millions* (May 1929) p. 75.

40 Anna Christensen, "Blessing in Shanxi", *China's Millions* (November 1929) p. 172.

41 Ibid.

42 Torjesen Malcolm, Kari, *Signed*, pp. 47, 52. After furlough in 1928, the Torjesens and their three pre-school children returned to Hequ. The final stage from Taiyuan by mule took ten days.

43 Anna Christensen, "More Stories of Blessing in Shanxi", *China's Millions* (May 1930) p. 71.

44 H. S. Cliff, "Revival Blessing", *China's Millions* (March 1933) pp. 50–51.

45 Leslie Lyall refers to John Sung, Wang Ming-dao, Dr Chia Yu-ming,

Andrew Gih and the Bethel Bands. "Historical Prelude", in Monsen, *Awakening.*

46 One road carried a notice for the children that it was not a public playground. "The middle of the road was like a tiger's mouth – carefully to be avoided", *Monthly Notes* (February 1929) p. 3.

47 *Monthly Notes* vol. 38. 2 (February 1933) p. 3.

48 James Stark, "Our Shanghai Letter, 27 April", *China's Millions* (July 1933) p. 133; (August 1933) p. 150.

49 Geraldine Howard Taylor, *Triumph*; Watson, *Bosshardt.*

50 Lyall, *Passion*, pp. 119–21.

51 T. E. Benson, "A Campaign in Retrospect", *China's Millions* (December 1937) pp. 228–29. See also (March 1937) p. 52; (July 1937) p. 127; (September 1937) p. 177; (October 1937) p. 196.

52 Geraldine Howard Taylor, *Ranges.*

53 Fraser, *Prayer*, p. 20.

54 Crossman, *Mountain Rain*, pp. 168–71.

55 Anna Christensen, "A Campaign in Retrospect", *China's Millions* (May 1939) pp. 72–73.

56 *China's Millions* (August 1939) p. 121; (November 1939) pp. 169, 171, 180; (March 1940) p. 40; (July–August 1940) pp. 101–102.

57 Lyall, *Passion*, p. 55.

58 "The Way" was used from New Testament times to describe the Christian faith, and this was already a familiar picture in Chinese culture where the Dao also referred to a religious pathway. cf. John 14:6, Acts 9:2.

59 Lyall, *Clouds*, pp. 56–57.

60 L. G. Vinden, "Miss Anna Christensen in Western Szechwan", in *Through Fire: The Story of 1938* (London: CIM, 1939) pp. 45–48.

61 F. Houghton, "Marcus Cheng in Eastern Szechwan", in *Through Fire: The Story of 1938* (London: CIM, 1939) pp. 49–50.

62 Private conversation with the author, Vancouver 1992.

63 Ibid.

64 The teaching ministry of women had always been controversial in evangelical circles, and in 1877 Adele Field had caused a stir when she stood up and spoke spontaneously in a discussion period at the Shanghai Conference. A. H. Smith, "How mission work looked when I first came to China", *Chinese Recorder* (February 1924) p. 92.

65 *Chinese Recorder*, 27 (June 1896) pp. 261–66; (October 1896) pp. 467–75; 28 (February 1897) pp. 56–66.

66 The place of women in revival movements is receiving increasing attention. See Tucker, *Daughters*, chapters 7, 10; Hassey, *Silence*, pp.7–10; Nixson, *Liberating*, pp. 196–97; Olive Anderson, "Women

Preachers in Mid-Victorian Britain: Some Reflections on Feminism, Popular Religion and Social Change", *The Historical Journal*, XII 3 (1969) pp. 467–84; Mimi Hadad, "Women and Revival Work: Acts 2: 17–21 – Revival's Magna Carta", *Priscilla Papers*, vol. 8, no 3 (Summer 1994) pp. 10–12. Revival movements often overflowed the traditional structures of the church and involved all members regardless of gender. In consequence women were set free from tradition to use the gifts they had received. As time passed, churches tended to re-establish formal structures and women were once again marginalised.

67  Personal telephone conversation with the author, March 1995; CIM Conference Report 1922, p. 78.

68  Ruth Adeney described how a deacon told her she was expected to preach on her first visit to an outstation. She declined on the grounds of youth and being a woman, but this was interpreted as humility! She subsequently felt she had been given a message for the people, but said nothing. When the deacon led the service, he simply announced that she would preach, so she did. Personal letter to the author, 1993.

69  *China's Millions* (July–August 1941) p. 57.

70  *China's Millions* (January–February 1942) pp. 6–7.

71  *China's Millions* (November–December 1947) p. 70.

72  *China's Millions* (March 1950) p. 36.

73  Monsen, *Awakening*, p. 110.

*Chapter Ten*    # The Gift of Writing

Looking back on her youth, Phyllis Thompson remembered being "indescribably weary of dancing, of card-playing, of the pleasures that never satisfied". A teenage friend of hers remembered the sophisticated Phyllis as being "very wicked", and hoped she could be like her when she grew up! Phyllis came from a solid middle-class home, and her only vocational training was a short course in journalism and some office experience. In the 1930s she was a modern girl with bobbed hair, and she and her mother and brother filled their spare hours with a social round of bridge parties, tennis and dancing. There were young men to whom she was attracted, and others who found her attractive, but her first real relationship developed with her employer, who was already married. Being involved in a divorce case would have brought both shame and embarrassment to her family; she escaped by changing her job.

Both her parents had had Christian connections when they were younger, but these had faded. However, in mid-life her father returned to a deep Christian commitment, both in the Anglican Church and also in preaching for the Methodists. This change of heart led to divisions within the family, for his Sundays were now very different from theirs.

One Sunday a clergyman friend of her father's came to visit. In the middle of the conversation Phyllis suddenly blurted out, "I'm not saved, but I'm trying to be!" The clergyman replied gently, "Oh, don't try! It's all been done for you... Jesus Christ died on the cross to give you everlasting life and all you have to do is accept it." She must have heard the Christian message countless times before, but it had never touched her. Now, suddenly, she understood it. She knew that becoming a Christian would mean changes, not only in her faith, but in her lifestyle. That night, she gave her life to Christ, and indeed, things began to change at once. She had a deep desire to know more about her new Lord, and eagerly drank in the teaching of various well-known Bible speakers. She met a group of Christians who took their faith into the market square of Andover and held open-air meetings, with texts displayed on long poles: she admired their courage in doing something of which she was incapable. Some 65 years later she described her next experience as a milestone in her life.

> An evangelistic tent campaign was being held in my home town about the time of my conversion, and I went every night to the meetings. One evening, the speaker spoke on the words "We came to Kadesh Barnea", referring of course, to the Children of Israel coming out of Egypt to the border of the Promised Land, when the Lord told them to go forward and possess the land and they were afraid and held back – with the result that they had to spend 40 years in the wilderness. I had been impressed by three Brethren members who carried banners with Scripture verses on them in the market place every Saturday and felt I should do something of the sort. As a result of that sermon on Kadesh Barnea, I went and borrowed one of the banners on a pole and walked up and down the High Street carrying it! It was the most difficult thing I ever did, but I knew I had to do it – or I'd be 40 years in a spiritual wilderness. I remember working out that it would bring me up to 66 years of age! I feel everything hinged on my obedience to go forward at that time.[1]

One day a friend lent her a new book about north-west China called *Something Happened*, by Mildred Cable and Francesca French. It was this book that aroused Phyllis's interest in China: she wondered if the Lord was asking her to serve him there. At first her mother could not accept the idea, and as an unmarried woman living with her parents, Phyllis could not imagine going against her mother's wishes. However, in time, her mother's attitude softened, and Phyllis applied to the China Inland Mission.

She entered the women's training home in 1935. The senior student remembered her arrival in a very fashionable coat, and wondered how she would get on. She need not have worried: Phyllis loved the six months she spent there. The regime was strict: a combination of domestic chores, lectures and practical service in the churches. Phyllis already loved writing, but she treated this gift with caution. She was anxious to put her previous life behind her, and she wanted to focus her energies entirely on evangelism in China. She would write letters home to her friends encouraging them to pray for China, but there would be no time for anything else.

She was finally accepted by the CIM, although she was regarded as anaemic and highly strung, and it was thought that she might not be able to complete the first seven-year term. Most of her fellow students had little income and were trusting God to provide for them financially through various means, but Phyllis was supported financially by her father. Rather surprisingly, her acceptance was apparently made conditional on her father's continued support – fortunately he was happy about this. She never knew why this was, as financial considerations were never the main criteria in the China Inland Mission. No mention is made in the records of such a condition, so her father may have volunteered to support her himself, and this may have led to a wrong inference on Phyllis's part. At that time parents often felt responsible for providing for their unmarried daughters – or perhaps this was her father's way of sharing in her calling overseas. Her parents were saying goodbye to their only daughter for seven years – and because of the Second World War, this actually stretched to eight.

## China in the 1930s

The 1930s were years of great instability in China. Chiang Kai-shek and the Nationalist government were supposedly in control of the country. However, after the Bolshevik Revolution in Russia in 1917, the Communists were committed to world domination and began moving south into the province of Xinjiang in the far north-west of China. By 1933, the Communists were encouraging the Muslim ethnic groups in Central Asia to rise against China. That same year, the Japanese army invaded Manchuria in the north-east and also threatened Shanghai from the sea. The Nationalists managed to make a truce with Japan while they turned their attention to the Communists and pushed them back from central China in 1933, but these three forces continued a three-cornered fight for control of China for the next fifteen years.[2] Missionaries, as guests in the country, tried to remain neutral, avoiding involvement in politics lest it threaten the evangelism which was their main purpose.

Phyllis arrived in China in 1936, aged 30. After a few days in Shanghai, the new group of single women left by train for the women's language school in the port of Yangzhou (Yangchow) where they spent the next six months studying Chinese. Phyllis wrote home about the daily life of China as it reached her on her balcony: the grey tiled roofs and high walls; the birds singing in the garden; the shouts of the coolies; the women water-carriers stooped under bamboo poles with heavy, swinging buckets; the friendly smiles; and the Chinese Bible woman who described her work in the villages and ended "There are still so many who have never heard his name."

In November 1936, Phyllis's senior missionary, J. W. Tomkinson from Australia, escorted her on the three-day journey from Yangzhou to Hweiyang, in Henan province, her home for the next stage of her training.

There were 30 million people in the province of Henan, which covers the vast central rice plain of China; Hweiyang was an important educational centre. In her letters home, Phyllis described the endless crowds of people everywhere she went. They jostled their way through the narrow streets of the city, and filled the roads outside the city walls with wheelbarrows, baggage, rickshaws, bullock wagons and mule carts. The main street was bordered by small shops which overflowed on to the street. Dogs, pigs and goats wandered past, and churned the road into mud when it rained. She noted that foot-binding still lingered on in the villages. Even though the more enlightened Chinese were giving up the custom, many women suffered all their lives from the damage done in childhood. Life in Hweiyang was hard: two years of famine had driven many people to the edge of starvation. Preoccupation with the difficulties of daily life meant that they were scarcely aware of the renewed Japanese invasion into north China, and the storm of war that was about to break again.

The editor of the CIM monthly magazine, *China's Millions*, spotted Phyllis's gift for writing from the beginning, and over the next fifteen years excerpts from her letters home were published regularly. From those small contributions her first books emerged.

Language study was still Phyllis's priority, but now she was living alongside the Tomkinsons with Irene Steele, who was younger than Phyllis but had already been in China for two years. It was their task to introduce her to life in the province, and help her to identify with the local church there. It was part of the long process of being born again into another culture. In some ways, living inside the church compound with its walls and gates separated them from their neighbours, but between the mission and the street there was a large room for guests – it was very simple, with some rough benches and posters on the wall – and people would wander in during the day to talk. Beyond that was a courtyard, a couple of rooms used by the Sunday school, a two-storey house for the Tomkinsons and a three-roomed bungalow for Phyllis and Irene. Phyllis's bedroom was basic, with a bed, a washstand, a table and chair: she remembered the room provided by the Shunammite woman, and Elisha seemed less remote! Isolated from the people around her by lack of language, she drew closer to people she met in the Bible. It was a far cry from her parents' home in Andover, but she was quite content with the simplicity.

Here men and women lived separate lives. She had to learn not to look Chinese men in the eye, but to address her remarks to their second button! The missionaries wore long trousers like the local women, but instead of jackets, wore the longer gowns of Chinese teachers. This avoided the distraction of Western clothes, but nothing could disguise their European features and larger build. The universal colour of gowns was dark blue, and they covered the whole body to the neck, without any decoration or jewellery.

The local Christians rallied to the help of the new missionary, and the pastor's wife took her visiting. Phyllis asked questions using what phrases she knew, but she could not understand the answers; when the women were chatting, she tried to look intelligent, but understood nothing. So little seemed to have been achieved by her months of hard work, and trying to speak Chinese could be discouraging and humiliating. It was also hard for shy Chinese women to be seen with a foreigner: only a few decades earlier no Chinese woman would have appeared on the street at all.. The crowds gathered to stare at her, and ask about her sex, age, parents, marital state, food, and why she was in China – questions which the Christians had to answer for her. Gradually the more extrovert missionaries found they could use these occasions as opportunities to explain the Christian message to those who asked questions.

It was important for Phyllis to practise her Chinese, so she used to sit near the guest room, and women and children came in from the street to chat to her. The children began coming in regularly, and even with her limited language skills she could teach them hymns and choruses. One ten-year-old boy from the church was her special helper. "Eastern

Light" organised the children, helped to clarify what Phyllis was trying to say, and gathered his friends to hear her. As her fluency improved, she was able to tell Bible stories, and she took over the church Sunday school, held twice on Sundays.

Another church member who helped her in these early days was Mrs Fan, the mother of five children. She was unusual because she had had some education, and her feet had never been bound, so walking was not a problem for her. Hesitantly, Phyllis asked Mrs Fan if she would help her to visit women in their homes, since they could not be contacted on the street or in coffee shops, as men could. Mrs Fan replied that she had recently prayed that she would be able to serve God in some way, and she felt this was the answer to her prayer.

This put their relationship on a new footing, and they became fellow-workers. Mrs Fan helped Phyllis put a simple message together, using a Christian poster. She arranged to take her to the house of another Christian who had gathered non-Christian neighbours to hear the foreigner, and then she steered Phyllis through the message, clarifying what she said when necessary. Hundreds of Chinese Bible women and missionaries followed this pattern, brought together in a mutual desire to share their faith with other women. The Bible women were usually older, sometimes widowed and with minimal education. They helped the missionaries to communicate within the Chinese culture, and the missionaries helped them to understand and explain the gospel. Each of them facilitated and complemented the other.

One day, on a visit to a village, Phyllis took a group of children out of the church and encouraged them to sing a song they had learned. They were surrounded at once by a crowd of curious men and women. One old lady asked a question that Phyllis was unable to answer; she tried to explain that she hadn't been in China long, and then in short, simple sentences, began to give her testimony. When she paused and asked if they understood, they said that they did. For Phyllis, it was a major landmark and she remembered the promise; "If...God so commands, you will be able" (Exodus 18:23, NIV).

Confidence in speaking Chinese made it easier for her to visit the villages with others. They piled their bedding and food into mule carts and then climbed on top to travel fifteen or 20 miles across the rice paddies. They stayed in the mud-brick homes. Most of the women who gathered to hear their teaching were elderly and illiterate; they found it difficult to concentrate and remember, and yet they had believed in the gospel, and treasured this rare opportunity of learning more. In one village half a dozen of the "grannies" had become Christians in the previous two years, and every Sunday, in spite of the good-humoured banter in their village, they had regularly walked three or four miles to the nearest worship service.

## Behind the Japanese lines

Phyllis was beginning to feel settled after 18 months in Hweiyang, when she was abruptly uprooted. In 1938 she was asked to replace someone due to go on leave from Taikang, 25 miles away behind the thinly occupied Japanese lines. She travelled by rickshaw, with her luggage piled in the traditional wheelbarrow. There was a tense moment crossing the Japanese lines, but three off-duty soldiers just stared as she and the mission superintendent passed by. Westerners were still neutral. The army was so thinly spread that the soldiers were keeping a low profile and daily life continued as usual.

Eva Wallis was the senior missionary in Taikang. Her Chinese gown failed to disguise the fact that she was a very English, middle-aged woman in her fifties. Phyllis described her "moving with the calm assurance of one whose undisputed position was that of mistress of the household"! No matter what crises occurred, Eva maintained a quiet composure and a great sense of humour. Their home, with its verandas and balconies, was on a large walled compound which included the church among other buildings. Outside the gate was the Chinese town with its thatched roofs, gravel roads, shops and alleys, and beyond that, the huge, agricultural plain of central China where the great Huanghe (Yellow River) wound its way to the Yellow Sea.

When the Japanese withdrew for a while, the town was occupied by Chinese guerrillas – the locals feared them even more than they feared the Japanese. They waged a campaign of terror, abducting young girls and extracting whatever they wanted by torture. Eva Wallis steadfastly insisted on maintaining neutrality, but did all she could to protect the girls by allowing them to take refuge in the compound.

Two events were indelibly etched on Phyllis's memory from the eleven months that she spent there. The first was the arrival from the villages of an elderly refugee called Mrs Peng, who turned up at the church regularly. Her money was exhausted, and she was grateful for a place in the town workhouse where she had shelter and two meals a day. For anything else, she had to beg. She had learned to accept her situation, and expected nothing. She thanked God for the shelter he had given her, and urged the other people there to believe in him too.

Phyllis saw more of Mrs Peng when her arm became infected and she came to the mission for medical help. It became clear that she owned no blankets or warm clothes, and, as winter approached, the cold kept her awake at night. She said that when she couldn't sleep, she prayed, and gave thanks for the roof over her head. Then she fell ill and failed to appear at the mission for a few days. During that time the Christian women had made her a padded winter quilt, and warm clothes for herself and her grandson, and two of them visited and gave them to her as a gift from God in answer to her prayers. Mrs Peng was adamant that she had never asked God for anything for herself. When she was too cold to sleep, she had prayed for "the foreign teachers and the church and the Christian sisters and brothers", and since she always prayed aloud, she could call on the other occupants to verify this!

Phyllis was deeply humbled by the selflessness and faith of this poor, illiterate woman: reduced to begging as a refugee, too cold and ill to sleep, she had prayed for Phyllis as she slept in warmth and comfort. This was a woman whose knowledge of the Christian faith was probably minimal, but whose daily walk with God was very real. Phyllis was vividly reminded that those who are among the last in this world's ranking will find themselves among the first in the kingdom of heaven. She recorded the story in her quarterly prayer letter, and again it was spotted by the editor and printed in the monthly CIM magazine, *China's Millions*.[3]

The second event took place as the Japanese were about to retake Taikang. Once again the mission compound had filled up with girls seeking protection from the soldiers, and Phyllis had reluctantly begun a weekly Bible study for them – reluctantly, because speaking in Chinese was still an ordeal for her. She took the opportunity to teach some of them to read the phonetic script, and occupied their time by encouraging them to make clothes for the poor. Every week she devoted Monday to preparing her message, taking a verse from the Bible and explaining it. Usually she focused on Jesus, but on one occasion a rather unlikely verse was imprinted on her mind: "The angel of the Lord encamps around those who fear him, and delivers them" (Psalm 34:7). She believed in angels, but did not want to embark on a discussion about them with a group of girls who needed to know about Jesus. Yet the verse would not go away, so she prepared a message on the subject and delivered it.

The following day, at breakfast, what they thought at first was the sound of fire crackers turned out to be guns, as the Japanese reoccupied the city. The noise of guns was followed by the sound of running feet as over 500 men, women and children took refuge in the compound. By the end of the day there were several hundred more, filling the courtyards with their hastily collected bedding and food. Eva had been through invasion before: there was nothing she could do about it, so she calmly went off to her desk to prepare for the day's programme. For Phyllis it was different. She had once seen a Zeppelin drop bombs on London during the First World War, but that was all. She wondered what to do.

With the help of two Christian girls, she began to explain the gospel to several groups of people, and finally found herself heading for the open gateway of the compound. Outside, she could see soldiers with guns alighting from armoured cars a couple of hundred yards away. Those inside the compound were urging the gatekeeper to shut the gates and keep the soldiers out, but people were still arriving for shelter. The verse she had preached on the previous day came back. "The angel of the Lord encamps around those who fear him and he delivers them." Phyllis decided that because she was a neutral foreigner, her presence at the gate might discourage soldiers from entering. So she stood there for hours, unafraid, her mind turning over all the Bible references about angels that she could think of. She saw no angels, but felt their presence; no Japanese came along the street all day.

Two or three years later, in another town 70 miles away, she met some refugees from Taikang. One woman was delighted when Phyllis said she had been in Taikang at the time of the occupation. "You're Teacher Dong! I heard about you," she said. Then she added, "People said they saw Teacher Dong standing at the compound gate, and two men with wings standing beside her."

This time the Japanese stayed, and tensions increased. The compound, as a neutral area, was officially out of bounds to the soldiers, but occasionally they wandered in looking for girls, or just wanting to practise their English. One soldier posted a letter home for Phyllis when it was difficult to do so from Taikang. The missionaries did what they could to protect the girls, and tried to share the gospel with the soldiers. One soldier used to sit quietly in services, and finally said in broken Chinese, "We have Jesus Christ in Japan too." Then he drew the Chinese character for "disciple": it would be pronounced differently in Japanese, but the meaning was the same in both written languages. Here was a believer far from his own country.

People flocked into services in the Taikang mission compound; there were so many that it was impossible to talk personally to them all. Yet a steady stream of people said they had become Christians, and, on being questioned, simply said they had heard the messages and they believed. Months later, two girls were found reading the Bible and singing hymns together. When questioned, they said they had come to faith in the literacy classes Phyllis held with the refugees in the compound.

By 1938, the Japanese had spread across the northern provinces and moved down to central China, taking the major cities until they could control the central gorges of the Yangtze River. They focused on the cities but lacked the manpower to control the countryside. With the eastern ports closed, supplies could only reach Free China via the hazardous Burma Road or by air. Yet, in spite of all the turmoil, 10,000 baptisms were registered in 1939 in the CIM churches across China.

By the summer of 1939, political tension was rising in Europe, and anti-British demonstrations were taking place in China. The Pacific war had not yet started, but Japan sympathised with Germany. One of the advantages of operating an international mission in China in those days was that if missionaries of one nationality became unacceptable, they could be replaced by another. In June 1939, the mission decided to evacuate Eva and Phyllis back to Hweiyang, and replace them with politically neutral Swiss missionaries. The Japanese continued to move south, trying to cut off the Chinese army from the Russian and Communist forces in the north-west who were currently allied with the Nationalists against Japan. Hweiyang was soon occupied, and the Japanese asked the missionaries to leave. They were allowed to load one hastily packed trunk each; books, ornaments, clothes and crockery were abandoned. It was so sudden that they had gone before many of the local people knew what was happening. Their destination this time was Shanghai, over 450 miles away by river.

# No man's land

Phyllis was a city girl, born in London. After three years in the isolation of inland China, returning to the cosmopolitan port of Shanghai was like finding an oasis in the desert. She loved Shanghai. The two six-storey blocks of headquarters were the hub of the mission, and in the French concession section of Shanghai there was little sign of the Japanese. Missionaries came from all over China to go on leave, and others passed through on their way back from their home countries. There were plenty of other Westerners, so she was no longer conspicuous on the streets. There were pavements, avenues, shops, and a wide choice of churches and activities. Phyllis was in her element, but she knew that this was only a temporary change of scene while her future was decided.

While various mission opportunities were considered and rejected – including the possibility of a rescue mission to prostitutes – another issue arose. An attraction had developed between herself and a single man staying in the mission home at the same time. As she faced the possibility of once more leaving the Shanghai she loved for the loneliness and privations of inland China, the possibility of companionship in marriage was very attractive. However, it was notoriously difficult to get to know someone of the opposite sex while operating within the constraints of Chinese culture. A decision had to be made about her future before the relationship could develop further, so she faced the closing of two doors in her life: Shanghai and marriage. It was one of her darkest moments.

The directors had asked her to join her old colleague, Irene Steele, in another small city in Henan province; the nearest missionaries would be 20 miles away, and there were no telephones. It was some weeks before arrangements were completed for the two women to settle in Xiangcheng, and they were weeks of depression for Phyllis. She felt as if she was "stepping into her coffin" with "a featureless wilderness" stretching ahead. As she sorted through her luggage and prepared to leave, the frail wife of the retired General Director of the mission gave her an eight-page booklet. It included a reference to John the Baptist, in prison, sending two disciples to ask Jesus whether he was the Messiah or not. Jesus reminded him to look at the signs, but gave him no word of hope for his own situation. Only after John's disciples had left did Jesus commend John to the crowds as "the Elijah who was to come", but John never heard those words. He had to walk his own pathway through prison and finally death, without losing faith. The words from the Bible spoke to Phyllis in her situation. She described it as "the challenge of going forward to obtain the blessing for those who do not fall away".

Xiangcheng would be home to her for the next five years. She and Irene Steele cycled the 20 miles on gravel roads and found, not the Western-style mission homes they had known before, but a Chinese home with traditional courtyards and outbuildings. There was a barn where the church met, a field for the goats (for milk) and a home for the Bible woman, all on a narrow piece of ground hemmed in by the usual high walls on either side. It had little outward appeal and yet, as she entered, she felt her depression lifting and being replaced with a deep sense that she was where God wanted her to be.

Soon afterwards she received a letter from the London CIM office, asking if she could submit the stories of a number of local Christians to be published as a book. The result of this was a collection of ten stories published under the title *They Seek a City* in 1940. Her prayer letters had developed into her first book; the gift of writing which she had surrendered in going overseas had been given back to her. Looking back nearly 50 years later, she wrote:

> I felt as though waters that had been dammed up had suddenly been released to start flowing; or as though I had emerged from a tunnel out into the sunlight. A stream of satisfying activity was opened up that day that has continued right up to the present time.

The town really was isolated. It lay on the border between two provinces, in the "no man's land" between the advancing Japanese 20 miles away in one direction, and the Chinese Nationalist army 20 miles away in the other. The missionaries were hardly aware of the Second World War raging elsewhere, and Pearl Harbor still lay ahead. If the Japanese made forays into the area, news spread by word of mouth and the people evacuated. With no radio or telephones, an erratic mail service (overland from war-torn Europe), shortages of supplies and reduced finances, their lives were not very different from those among whom they lived.

The small group of Christians had no church building of their own, and met in the barn on the property rented by the mission; several smaller groups of Christians met in the surrounding villages. There was a widowed Bible woman and her daughter, but no pastor, so a group of deacons cared for the members as best they could. Most of the problems that arose with the families, marriages, and daily concerns of the believers could be handled much better by the deacons than by any foreigner. The mission's indigenous church policy meant that leadership in the church was in the hands of the Chinese, and Irene and Phyllis had to be careful not to interfere in any way. Their task lay with the women, in literacy, evangelism, teaching and training. They also worked with the children, and visited in the villages and preached there when necessary. Everything possible had to be done to ensure that the churches became self-governing, self-supporting and self-propagating. This left missionary women walking a knife-edge, but it meant that many single women had a significant role in encouraging the emerging national leaders. Such leaders might have felt compelled to defer to missionary men if they had been present. In Xiangcheng the deacons did well.

In their first year there, Irene organised a women's preaching band. This included a deacon's wife, an official's wife, and a widow. They were appointed by the deacons to help Irene and Phyllis visit the village Christians once or twice a year, in pairs. Sometimes others joined them. Each night they stayed in village homes, removing their outer garments and spreading out their padded quilts on the floor with the rest of the family. They used picture rolls to tell Bible stories, and were usually received with interest and curiosity, because the stories were entirely new to the audiences. Phyllis said the country folk were particularly touched by the story of the cross. They were very familiar with death.

Mrs Han, the Bible woman, regularly accompanied Phyllis to the local women's prison. On one occasion, after Phyllis had given a message, the prisoners asked if God would get them out of prison if they prayed to him. To Phyllis's dismay, Mrs Han assured them that he would. Phyllis believed he *could*, but wasn't at all sure he *would* choose to release a group of convicted criminals into society. She attempted to add something about the need for repentance and obedience to God. On the way home she talked to Mrs Han, explaining that justice honoured God, and that some of the women there had done great evil, even murder. Mrs Han listened, and agreed. But on the next visit, she reassured them again that if they prayed, God could and would get them all out.

Soon after this incident, the Japanese moved back to Xiangcheng and the city emptied; Phyllis and Irene left on their bicycles. When the army retreated again a few days later, they all headed back. The whole episode seemed rather pointless. When Phyllis suggested another visit to the prison, Mrs Han said there was no need: "There's no one there." Phyllis was puzzled. How could 16 prisoners disappear? Mrs Han explained that when the Japanese advanced, everyone fled, including the guards, so they sent the prisoners home. Phyllis pondered this for a moment. "So God answered their prayers. He got them out of the place…" Smiling confidently, Mrs Han replied "Yes. He answered their prayers." She hadn't even bothered to tell Phyllis![4]

# Famine, festival and flight

As the years passed, it wasn't easy to maintain momentum. In no man's land, there was nowhere to escape to for a break. Books had been abandoned long ago in the Hweiyang evacuation. There were no annual holidays, no hope of leave in Britain after six years away, no friends passing through, and little to break the monotony of small-town life.

In 1942 the local crops failed, and in spite of bumper harvests elsewhere, little help was available in Xiangcheng. There was nowhere to flee to. Starving people dragged themselves through the streets or died quietly at home. When the church received some relief money, they decided to give it to the most needy to keep them alive, whether they were Christian or not. The believers were drawn together as they worked daily to distribute help.

When 1943 dawned, with little sign of an early end to the war, a letter arrived from the emergency headquarters of the mission in Chongqing. It called the missionaries to re-examine the principles underlying their work. It was all too easy for leadership in national churches to revert back to the missionaries. In Xiangcheng, Phyllis had gladly left the church affairs to the deacons, so she could focus on the women, and the deacons had simply maintained the status quo and made no progress. For one thing, they were still content to use mission property for their meeting place. The letter galvanised Phyllis into action. She met with a committee to discuss the need for the church members to take responsibility for all evangelism, to get their own building, and to build closer links with other churches in the province. They were enthusiastic.

A suitable building was found and renovated, and the great day finally arrived when they held their first services in their own building. People came in from the villages to celebrate and special meetings were organised. The festivities were in full swing when a telegram was handed to Phyllis, advising her and her junior worker to evacuate within 36 hours: the Japanese were advancing. She said nothing to the church members until the celebrations were over. At least, when they vacated the mission premises, the church would be able to function in its own building.

Phyllis later recorded the events of that final day in a small book, which described the leading church members as they rallied to help, supplying food and selling unwanted missionary possessions in the market to raise money for the women's long journey ahead. There was the sorting, the discarding, the packing of a minimum of baggage, the farewells. They were all used to fleeing, but this departure was different. One of the deacons surveyed the scene and commented, "It looks as though you hope you won't return." Phyllis replied, "It's not that I *hope* I won't return – I *fear* I won't return." The following morning at dawn, the baggage was loaded onto the traditional wheelbarrows, while Phyllis and her co-worker got on their bikes and left for their destination 40 miles away.[5]

It was only the beginning of a long and dangerous journey. As 1943 was drawing to a close, the Second World War had spread across the globe. Phyllis joined thousands of others fleeing west across north China, before turning south to Chongqing in western Free China, where both the Chinese National Government and the CIM had set up emergency headquarters. As she went through Xi'an in the north she met Gladys Aylward for the first time, and heard of her flight with 100 children over the mountains to the safety of Xi'an as the Japanese army advanced.[6]

In Chongqing Phyllis discussed her future with the CIM directors and mentioned her special concern for Tibet and north-west China, wondering if that door might open. They advised her to return to Britain on leave first: she had not been home for eight years. She worked in the offices for a few months until it was possible to fly across Burma to India to get a boat back to Britain. It was the only route left out of China.

In 1944 the Japanese pressed further into south-west

China to Guiyang and the notorious Burma Road, and there were more evacuations of women and children to the homelands, until missionaries remained only in the three western provinces of Gansu, Sichuan and Yunnan. Calcutta was crowded as people arrived by plane from China in groups of 70 or 80 and then had to wait for the few berths available on ships. The CIM set up a mission home and office to deal with their own members as they arrived.[7] By that stage of the war not even home was safe: when Phyllis's troopship finally arrived in the Clyde, it had to wait for three days in the dangerous approaches until it was able to berth. She had arrived home in time to follow the closing events of the war in Europe.

Phyllis spent the next few years in the CIM editorial office at Newington Green. The CIM had already published two of her books, which gave rare glimpses into the lives of ordinary Chinese Christians. Now she was asked to produce a biography of D. E. Hoste, Hudson Taylor's successor as General Director of the China Inland Mission from 1903 to 1935, who died in 1946. This was a major undertaking, and it launched her into a ministry that would become increasingly important for her, the mission, and the evangelical world in Britain and beyond.

With the end of the Pacific war, after decades of political turmoil, many China missionaries were looking forward to a time of greater stability, with increasing opportunities for evangelism and consolidation in the churches in the post-war period. The Japanese had gone, but now the Communists had settled in north China and occupied the province of Henan where Phyllis had spent her first eight years. When she sailed back to China with 60 other missionaries in 1947, she was 41 years old. The mission directors wanted her to spend more time writing for the CIM, and were happy for her to head west, where pioneer work was still being done: if Phyllis could make it better known, people at home could support and pray for it with better understanding.

## Western China and Tibet

Phyllis was hoping to get to Lanzhou in the far north-west, the area which had first challenged her with the needs of the mission field when she read Mildred Cable's book over ten years earlier. However, she was asked to go first to Kangting, on the borders of Tibet, to gather material for writing. Five years earlier, there had been one elderly CIM woman in the city; now, in post-war China, several groups were using it as a base for reaching Tibetans.

Supplies for the area had been delayed in Shanghai for several months; they included drugs for three hospitals, and three and a half tons of Bibles. Travel was very difficult: the railway lines were blocked and air haulage prices were prohibitive. Finally, an American missionary and his wife decided to buy trucks and drive the goods across southern China by a different route. It was a mammoth undertaking: 1,800 miles west to Chongqing, and then 1,100 miles north to Xi'an in the north-west. They assembled two jeeps with trailers, two Dodge trucks and a saloon car. The team consisted of three Americans, one Swede, two English and one Chinese. Phyllis was to go as far as Chongqing.

She described the first half of this epic journey in a small booklet, *Bible Convoy*.[8] Their route took them through Zhejiang Province, over the hills and down the Guangxin River, an area devastated first in the 1930s by civil war, and then in the 1940s by the Japanese occupation (see Chapter Four). It was a gruelling journey where bridges were still down, and ferries were unaccustomed to big vehicles, even in 1948. Sometimes there were two or three rivers to cross in a day, and often everything had to be unloaded from vehicle to boat, and then reloaded on the other side. For security, the men slept in the cabs, and the two women slept in local inns if there was no mission station nearby. In Zhejiang they found a welcome in the "Jesus Halls" which seemed to be established in most places of any size, but as they moved west, Christian presence was much less common. There were endless delays caused by breakdowns, flooded rivers and bridges being repaired – on one occasion the Bible truck fell off the ramp into the river, and they had to spend several days drying Bibles before they could continue. (Even a dried-out Bible was precious in places where people had none.)

It took a month to cover the first 1,800 miles to Chongqing. Phyllis's account of the journey captures a vivid picture of post-war southern China: the landscape, the people, and the Christian story in different places. They arrived in Chongqing only to hear that Xi'an, their ultimate destination, had been occupied by Communist troops. The others all decided to press on, hoping that by some means they could deliver the needed supplies safely.

From Chongqing, Phyllis flew to Chengdu, and then took a day's bus trip before leaving conventional transport behind and spending five days being carried in a mountain chair over the Erlang Pass to Kangting, a town on the road to Lhasa, the Tibetan capital. Kangting lay at 8,500 feet with a population of 10,000 Tibetans and Chinese. The journey from Shanghai had taken nine weeks. In the event the political situation became so delicate that it was unwise to publish much about the area beyond the occasional, general article in *China's Millions*. Phyllis joined in the daily work of the mission station, learned about the different ethnic groups, and got to know local Christians.[9]

It was here that she had an opportunity that she treasured for the rest of her life. She met two young Chinese women who visited the *caravanserais*, the roadside inns where travellers could stay with their camels and packhorses. On one unforgettable occasion, she spent the night with them in the tent of a Tibetan family. In the evening, they sat round the charcoal fire with the couple and their three daughters on one side, and Phyllis, Miss Liu and three baby yaks on the other. As Phyllis told them the story of the prodigal son in Chinese, Miss Liu translated it into Tibetan.

After leaving Kangting, she spent four months near Chongqing, finishing her fourth book, *Beaten Gold*. She could not write much about western China as the Communists closed in and the political clouds began to gather, so instead she went back to the war-time story of Mrs Yen. She wanted it "to be representative of the great rural population of the whole of China... The city... is a very small city... in many ways not so very different from a market town or country village" at a time when lawlessness was not uncommon, but it had a small community of Christians. Mrs Yen was a baker's wife. She sold bread on the street, and had been a church member for 20 years, while resisting all encouragement to learn to read.

The area was then under the control of guerrillas, who skirmished in no man's land between the Chinese Nationalist army on the one side and Japanese soldiers on the other. Far from fighting for their country, these Chinese were exploiting the local population. People were kidnapped, money extorted and girls abducted at will. Mrs Yen frustrated the intentions of one guerrilla officer, protecting the girl he wanted by arranging her marriage to a local lad. The officer was furious and had her arrested, even though Phyllis and Mrs Han, the Bible woman, tried to protest.

Under torture, Mrs Yen offered her own daughter as a substitute, and the next day the officer took her into the country to finalise the arrangements. Out of the town, he could do what he liked and force her to sign away her daughter. Phyllis felt helpless and unable to pray. There was no one to turn to. The police could do nothing against the guerrillas. Phyllis opened her Bible at random at Jeremiah chapter 33, where God spoke to Jeremiah in prison. The story seemed a long way from her situation and she was ready to turn to another passage when her eyes fell on a particular verse:

> Call unto me and I will answer thee, and show thee great and mighty things which thou knowest not (Jeremiah 33:3).

So she called to God, and slept.

Two days later, to Phyllis's astonishment, Mrs Yen turned

up at church. When the officer had taken her into the country, he was unaware that he was taking her back to her clan and home territory. Though she herself was an insignificant peasant, her clan leader commanded respect, even from the guerrillas. When word of her situation reached him, he called at the inn to see the officer, and asked to take Mrs Yen home for the night to see her relatives. The officer was reluctant, but hours passed and, in the normal cycle of Chinese courtesies to avoid loss of face, pressure was gently applied and eventually the officer released her to her extended family. Sometimes God does "mighty things" for ordinary people in desperate situations through the ordinary processes of daily life.[10]

## North-west China

Fifteen months later, Phyllis was writing from Lanzhou on the Silk Road 1,000 miles to the north. Again her letter was full of description. Leaving Chongqing with a car and trailer, they had wound their way over the hills and then crossed a beautiful, fertile plain for 200 miles to reach Chengdu. As they continued north, the mountain ranges grew higher, and the cultivated land was dotted with small farms.

Across these mountains they came to the city of Baoji where the North-west Bible Institute was based, with 50 students led by Pastor Ma. Known as the "Back to Jerusalem Band", Pastor Ma and a small group of Chinese had a vision of taking the Christian message westwards back across central Asia to Jerusalem.[11] Phyllis had taken a deep interest in their work ever since she travelled from Shanghai to Chongqing perched on their lorries, carrying Bibles to the north-west. Now she was able to share with them the needs of the Tibetans as she had seen them in Kangting, and challenge them to pray for that situation. Missionary work was not just about missionaries preaching the gospel, but concerned with encouraging national Christians to take up their responsibilities as well. In this post-war period at least five Chinese groups were independently responding to a call to witness in the neglected area of north-west China as the doors closed for foreign missionaries.[12]

From Baoji she joined the ancient Silk Road and travelled 90 miles north-west into Gansu province as the Trio had done 26 years earlier. The capital, Lanzhou, was squeezed into a narrow valley along the banks of the great Huanghe (Yellow River) – the bridge was the last to cross the river before it reached the sea a thousand miles away. North of the city, CIM missionaries ran the Borden Memorial Hospital and an adjacent leprosarium; others worked with school and university students, and also with the Spiritual Training Institute for the "Back to Jerusalem Band".

In the summer of 1949, the Communist Army of Liberation was approaching Lanzhou. It was Phyllis who recorded the story of the local Spiritual Training Institute: they had been collecting building materials in order to extend their premises, but feared total destruction in the path of the advance. The pastor and students had nowhere to go, and could only trust in "the Living and True God" and stay put. They needed to hide their precious building materials from army requisitioning, so overnight the students buried the wooden beams, and the pile of bricks suddenly emerged as a new wall. In the battle that followed, the buildings were undamaged, and the students were able to build their extension eight months later. When they found themselves inadvertently in debt with no money to pay the creditor, they received an unexpected gift of money sent from London for their use, which arrived just on the day it was needed, and they saw it as a gift from the living God who knew their needs and did not fail them.[13] The Christians learnt to trust God in very direct ways in those days.

Few people anticipated the removal of all missionaries within the next two years, but such experiences were already preparing the Chinese for the time when they must trust in God alone. George Hunter had been the last missionary in the province of Xinjiang, and he had been imprisoned in 1940 and subsequently deported to Lanzhou in 1941.[14] Now the Chinese were sensing a call to take responsibility for the areas from which missionaries had been ejected. Phyllis prayed earnestly for the young Chinese students, both men and women, who were leaving Bible school and setting off in pairs to the distant borders of China and beyond, taking the gospel to cultures and languages as alien to them as to any Westerner.[15]

As the Liberation Army threatened Lanzhou, Phyllis left the city for the northern province of Ningxia, which is today included in Inner Mongolia as part of China. She and Mary Welander, a fellow-worker from the Lanzhou hospital, got a lift with six local people on top of the mail-bags in a post office truck. The road wound past scattered mud-brick villages in desert landscapes, occasional fertile valleys with farms and apple trees, and then further desert. After a night in a local inn, they reached the missionaries in Chungwei the following day. The four CIM stations, led by three couples and three single women, were strung along the Huanghe river valley for some 200 miles. The great ranges of the Alashan Mountains formed the northern border of the province, separating it from the deserts of Mongolia. The inhabitants were mainly Muslim, though some small churches were emerging. However, political change was hanging over the whole of China, and reaching even to these remote corners. Phyllis joined Dorothy Jupp in the city of Ningxia, but she could write little of what she learned, apart from describing the towns and people of the river valley and plain, because of the sensitive political situation.

Phyllis was still in Ningxia when the Communist forces finally arrived to "liberate" them all: it was a peaceful time of celebration and street entertainment which everyone enjoyed, and the Christians' visiting and teaching was allowed to continue. The worst aspects of Communist rule – the accusation meetings and people's courts – still lay in the future. For the moment, the churches had freedom of belief, and could continue in evangelism and teaching. Missionaries withdrew from administrative positions and became "guests" who went on teaching. Adjustments were made as the maturing Chinese churches took complete control over their own affairs, but otherwise life continued almost as usual in Ningxia. It was so pleasant that, when ordered to evacuate, the missionaries were reluctant to leave!

In the adjacent province of Gansu, and elsewhere in China, it was very different. Gradually the pressures on foreigners increased; the government wanted them to leave, but was extraordinarily reluctant to let them go without appearances, accusations and fines in the people's courts. Some missionaries were kept under house arrest for up to two years.[16] Many were able to leave the country only if Chinese stood as their guarantors, and they owed a great deal to these faithful Christians. For nearly 30 years nothing was written about the withdrawal of CIM missionaries from China, lest it endanger those who had helped them. When it was finally deemed safe, in 1979, to tell the story of God's provision for those 617 CIM men and women and 200 children, it was Phyllis who wrote it.[17]

Phyllis flew home from Hong Kong to London in 1951 on an empty cargo plane returning from Korea, chartered by the CIM. With limited money, and hundreds of people to evacuate, it was a providential opportunity to transport the missionaries cheaply, but flights were tedious, with frequent stops for refuelling. Some 45 years later, one young woman from another mission recalled:

> As we touched down at several places and spent time waiting in airport lounges, I well remember seeing Phyllis tapping away on her typewriter at every opportunity. Not a moment was wasted! She was pointed out to me as Phyllis Thompson the author, and it was with great awe that I observed this missionary author at work.[18]

## New directions

Back in London, the mission was praying and heart-searching. It had been called into being 86 years earlier, specifically to take the gospel to inland China. Now the door had closed: did this mean that the mission should close down? Some people thought so, but when they enquired further, it became clear that there were millions of Chinese who had emigrated to other countries in South-east Asia in search of markets for trading. The mission might have left China, but its commission to evangelise the Chinese had not ended. The decision was taken to move into these new countries to reach the "overseas" Chinese there. Compared with China, little evangelism had been done in some places, and those already working there urged the CIM to join them. Some missionaries moved directly to the new areas when they left China; others went home on leave.

Phyllis had no guidance that she should remain in the East; she was appointed instead to the home staff in Britain, to serve in the editorial department again. She was responsible both for *China's Millions* and for the monthly summary of prayer needs from overseas. From its foundation, the mission had always recognised the significance of communication with the churches at home, whether it was through magazines, books, or information for prayer. Once again, her gift for writing was called into service, and this became her main task for the next thirteen years.

In addition to the daily editorial work, she also began writing more books for the CIM. *Climbing on Track* recorded the life of the British Home Director of the CIM, Fred Mitchell, who died in the Comet disaster over India in 1953 as he returned from a crucial mission conference on the newly-developing work in South-east Asia. Three years later *Proving God* told the story of how God had faithfully supplied the financial needs of the mission over a period of 90 years, without the need to go into debt or make any public appeal for funds.

However, by 1964 Phyllis found herself frustrated and struggling. Life in Britain had unexpectedly proved harder than the political chaos, deprivation and isolation in China. As a woman in China she had been freed from the cultural constraints of evangelical Britain; she had experienced great freedom in ministry, working alongside local pastors, preaching, and teaching ordinary women. Back in London she exchanged her "women's world" for one where leadership was all in male hands; although her workload was heavy, and carried great responsibility, she lacked the authority needed to fulfil it. She did not feel she could make suggestions, or be "heard": she was even excluded from discussions and policy-making in the work for which she was responsible. Finally, sitting at her desk one day, she concluded "I'm not in God's place for me – I must get out!" She did, and experienced "a tremendous sense of relief". The Home Director was overseas at the time, and when he returned he could not persuade her to change her mind.[19]

After 28 years in a mission where most people stayed until retirement, it was a brave decision to make at the age of 58. Phyllis never regretted the step she took, but rarely referred to this crisis in her life. She had no desire at all to criticise the mission. She simply stressed her conviction that God had led her out and blessed her in her new sphere. She remained on good terms with the mission, and continued to write for it.

Meanwhile, she had discovered the growing world-wide interest in learning English, so she developed a Bible-based self-study course for complete beginners who wanted to learn English. The first book was based on parables and stories from the Gospels, teaching simple grammar and vocabulary. People could work on the course at home, have their written answers corrected, and take exams. There were twelve lessons in the first book, and later she added two more books on the first three chapters of Genesis, and the narrative parts of John's Gospel. These proved very popular, and as they spread around the world, people came to faith as they studied. In

1988, a Chinese friend, Gwek Khor, revised the three early courses and added nine more, which were published by Good News Publications. The same company also produced 18 cassettes and two booklets of translations to go with the course, which is now distributed free in over 40 countries.[20] Phyllis was thrilled with these developments. She felt that the course, which reached young people around the world, sometimes in countries that were closed to other Christian witness, may have been her greatest contribution to world evangelism. She once commented to Gwek Khor, "These little books mean more to me than all the other books I've ever written."[21]

In the 1970s Phyllis found herself at the local hospital in Hackney with a broken arm, and to her surprise found nurses from Singapore and Hong Kong around her. She had left China 20 years earlier, and was unaware of the growing numbers of Chinese studying in Britain. This opened up a new world of friendships with Chinese in London, and contact with some of the Chinese churches too. Her circles of friendship were always expanding, and many international students found a welcome in her home. In her eighties, her concern for the women in Hackney took her across London to workshops on evangelism for women, as she searched for new ways to reach out. She had a real zest for living, without losing sight of God. He was always at the centre.

She maintained contact with a wide circle of friends, and faithfully prayed with them for many areas that God laid on her heart. One person spoke of her "hunger for information". Her interests and concerns expanded with the passing years. China and Tibet were always there, but Russia and Siberia were added, and writing took her to India, Nepal, Taiwan and the USA. In total, she completed over 40 books, including the histories of well-known evangelical institutions such as London City Mission, Scripture Gift Mission, the Gideons, and Mildmay Mission Hospital. She wrote about work in China, India, Mozambique, and Latin America. Her biographies ranged from Madame Guyon and Gladys Aylward to Minka and Margaret, two OMF leprosy nurses who were abducted and shot in South Thailand. The one story she had no intention of writing was her own – Phyllis could be strong-minded! When Edward England, the publisher, pressed her to do this, she capitulated only on condition that he let her write the book on Madame Guyon that she really wanted to do. Her own story emerged over a period of two years in letter-form to Edward, relying very much on her memory. The diaries and papers had vanished long ago in the upheavals of moving round the world.[22] She was 88 when she published her last book, *Six Dots for Asia*, on work among the blind in India.[23]

She always felt that missionary work itself was more important than books written about it, but saw the books as a means of encouraging prayer support and publicising the work. In her autobiography, she claimed that she was "not a creative writer" and "inspiration comes to me through other people, not from within myself".[24] The "other people" who inspired her to write in China were the Chinese themselves, and her earliest writing left a rare record of the daily lives and faith of ordinary people in local churches during fifteen terrible years of war and turmoil. These books are the more significant because Chinese women had limited education and left few records of their own. They form part of the history of the Chinese church.

When Phyllis sailed for China, she expected to spend her life there. In fact, as world politics ran their course, she stayed for only fifteen years, but those years laid the foundation for the rest of her life. The gift of writing that she had surrendered to God was given back, and she used it to the full in serving him wherever she was.

At the age of 80, she moved from Hackney to join her friend Flora Sarpy in Wandsworth. When Flora died five years later, Phyllis moved into sheltered housing at Wimborne House, and while there, organised a weekly meeting for the residents. Three years later, at 88, she moved into a new flat in Tooting, south London. In December 1996, her many friends gathered to celebrate her ninetieth birthday and presented her with a red album, "This Is Your Life". Up to the age of 92 she still lived alone, with a stream of friends dropping in, and a large map of China filling the wall in her living room. In her ninety-third year she was making a daily early-morning phone call (cheap rate!) to pray with a friend for Tibet. Her friend commented, "BT never thought of advertising 'It's good to pray!'"

In 1999, Phyllis joined some of her colleagues from China days at Cornford House, the CIM retirement home near Tunbridge Wells. The following year she was very ill as her heart grew weaker, and she expected to die. When a friend asked her afterwards what it was like as she faced that moment of moving on to meet her Lord, she said, "It was awesome." She rallied for some weeks, and finally came to that "awesome" moment on 1 November 2000, just before her ninety-fourth birthday.

The gift of writing, which she was willing to give up in 1935, became her greatest contribution to the Christian world. The people she wrote about became much better known than she was, but she was the channel through which their lives touched many others.

## Notes to Chapter Ten

1   Unpublished note to the author, 3 March 1999.
2   Broomhall, vol. 7, pp. 549–50. Or see 2000 edition, *The Shaping of Modern China* (OMF/Paternoster/William Carey Library).
3   P. Thompson, "The Father Seeketh Such to Worship Him", *China's Millions* (July 1939) p. 110.
4   P. Thompson, "The Lord Looseth the Prisoners", *China's Millions* (July–August 1941) p. 54.
5   Thompson, *Day*.
6   She later wrote a book on the life of Gladys Aylward which included her time in Taiwan after leaving China. Thompson, *Sparrow*.
7   P. Thompson, "The CIM in India and Kalimpong", *China's Millions* (March–April 1945) pp. 12–13.
8   Thompson, *Convoy*.
9   *China's Millions* (May–June 1948) pp. 29–30. Unpublished personal prayer letters (7 January 1948); (12 May 1948); (3 March 1949).

10  Thompson, *Gold*; Thompson, *Pilgrim*, pp. 171–90.

11  Neill, *Missions*, pp. 94–96, 120. See also *Steppe by Step* by Hugh Kemp (London: Monarch/OMF/Interserve, 2000) for an overview of Mongolian Christian history.

12  P. Thompson, prayer letter (21 May 1949).

13  *China's Millions* (September 1950) pp. 94–95.

14  Cable and French, *Hunter*.

15  *China's Millions* (April 1951) p. 47.

16  Phyllis records the story of Rupert Clarke, one of the last two CIM missionaries to leave China in July 1953, in her book *No Way Back*. Isobel Kuhn described the plight of the Matthews family and Arthur's final release in *Green Leaf in Drought*.

17  Thompson, *Exodus*.

18  Effie Berry (BCMS), "This is Your Life" 1996, when Phyllis was 90.

19  From an unpublished questionnaire sent to some CIM/OMF missionary women and retirees in 1992. Because senior leadership could only be held by men, there were no mission appointments available for the more gifted women once the "women's world" was lost. For example, Mildred Cable took an administrative post with the Bible Society organising women's support groups across Britain. Although the CIM had pioneered the extensive use of women in a wide range of ministries overseas from the nineteenth century, their structures regrettably did not allow them to benefit from the potential of their most gifted women at that time.

In 2001, OMF International decided that in future all appointments would be based on call and gifting, and there would be no restrictions on the grounds of gender.

20  Nine years later the Chinese Broadcasting Centre in New York took over the material, and planned to put it on the Internet.

21  Gwek Khor, "This is your Life", 1996, when Phyllis was 90.

22  Thompson, *Pilgrim*.

23  She said this was to be her last book, but she also helped in the editing of *Killing Fields, Living Fields* by Don Cormack, published in 1997.

24  Thompson, *Pilgrim*, p. 8.

*Chapter Eleven*     # Building the Chinese Church

When Hudson Taylor freely welcomed a wide spectrum of men and women to serve together in the China Inland Mission in 1865, he challenged the common secular and religious assumptions which defined and restricted their roles. He was not suggesting that men and women were identical, but rather that the gifts of both were equally needed if the command to take the gospel to all nations were to be fulfilled. The Society for Promoting Female Education in the East (SPFEE) had encouraged schools as the gateway for women to reach mothers as well as their children; Sophia Cooke in Singapore had organised a boarding school for girls, held Bible classes for their mothers, and also taken her girls to the local Malay-speaking congregation; but Taylor went much further than that.

His primary goal was evangelism and the planting of national churches, and in consequence the single women he sent out worked closely with the missionary wives to reach women and integrate them into the emerging churches. In this context, by 1870 the primary purpose of the small schools was to educate the children from Christian families for the future development of the church. Boys' schools came first, but girls' schools were soon added since Christian women were equally necessary as teachers and evangelists for the women, and also as wives and mothers for the future.[1] Too many Chinese church leaders were struggling with their own unbelieving and even hostile wives, because the women were shut in their homes.

So, while a few women supervised small schools, most of the early CIM women were also involved in evangelism, systematically going from home to home telling women about Jesus. The examples of Maria Dyer, her older sister, Burella, and the early missionary wives in China had convinced Taylor that women were essential in taking the message of Jesus to Chinese women, and were just as significant as men in establishing an indigenous church. When foreign women appeared in the walled courtyards of the extensive Chinese families, curiosity could draw several generations of women at a time out of their houses to stare at the first white people they had ever seen. Geraldine Guinness (Mrs Howard Taylor), just out of language school, spent an afternoon with three other women visiting 16 extended family homes: afterwards she estimated that at least 500 women had heard the story of Jesus for the first time that day and received tracts and Gospels.[2]

## The CIM married women

The CIM was a lay movement in which Taylor was eager to facilitate the spiritual gifts that all members received, be they male or female, and these took precedence not only over gender, but also over educational qualifications. In this policy he departed from the concept that missionaries must be ordained men with a calling from God. He was not the first to hold this view. As early as 1811, in a letter to her friend, Ann Hasseltine Judson searched her heart for its motives, weighing up the loss of friends and family against the persuasive charm of the young Adoniram, her future husband, and still claimed that God himself had called her as a woman to serve him overseas.

> Nor were my determinations formed in consequence of an attachment to an earthly object; but with a sense of my obligations to God, and with a full conviction of its being a call in providence, and consequently my duty.[3]

In the Protestant churches of her time such a calling to work in a local church was not possible for women, but going overseas was different. At their commissioning service the Judsons' pastor specifically charged the wives to take the gospel to women:

> Teach these women to whom your husbands will have but little or no access. Go then, and do all in your power to enlighten their minds, and bring them to the knowledge of the truth... Teach them to realise that they are not an inferior race of creatures; but stand upon a par with men.[4]

These were fighting words in 1811, but traditions die hard, and 50 years later, Taylor's policy of mobilising women in evangelism and church-planting still seemed radical, and in many places it was still not implemented. Where denominational missions were concerned, practice overseas usually reflected church structures at home.

Taylor's policy also challenged traditional approaches to marriage, where a wife's role revolved around her husband and children. Women did not go overseas simply to care for their husbands, if they had them. They were the only ones who could undertake the evangelism and teaching of Chinese women. They were expected to learn the language and take part in reaching out to Chinese women as their family responsibilities permitted.

The role of married women in particular has always been a matter of debate in missionary societies. Even in recent times, some societies interviewed the husband alone, without meeting the wife at all. In the early days some people felt that family demands in the tropics were more than enough for most women, and they should not be expected to shoulder other responsibilities outside the home. However, others felt that as the only Christian women in many situations, they could not neglect their responsibility as Christian witnesses to those among whom they were living. If emphasis were placed on the spiritual gifts and calling that each individual

Christian received, the wife had her own gifts and calling, and the CIM accepted couples only on this basis.

For the China Inland Mission, the full commitment of women, both married and single, was vital, and the mission would not accept couples unless each of them had a clear call to serve overseas. Whatever money the mission received was distributed equally between all the members, regardless of responsibility, sex, age or length of service. As the mission grew and more organisation became necessary, Taylor wanted all members, whether male or female, to have as much freedom as possible to work in their own way, and he insisted that "the sisters be recognised as equals".[5] He was anxious not to do anything that might hinder the contribution that he believed God intended women to make. He was not afraid to be radical and challenge church and even state when it came to his use of women, in spite of criticism he received from those in high positions.

However, he still accepted the common interpretation of the Bible at that time, that final authority and leadership must be restricted to men. This led to ambiguities for decades afterwards. Some of the men who came from a working-class background had minimal education. Some of the women came from middle-class homes and were well educated. At one point Taylor commented that "our men are not equal to our women" as far as their ability was concerned.[6] His willingness to accept a wider spectrum of people than other missions, based primarily on their calling and gifts, led to some major problems with the early members and he had to recognise that other skills were needed as well – not least that of being able to live and work happily together with a variety of people.

Authority and leadership come from various sources. They may be bestowed or usurped. They may depend on training, gifts, experience or age. Initially, Taylor and his 32-year-old wife Maria were the only ones with language skills and experience of China – and Maria had more than her husband! As leader, Taylor insisted on the absolute loyalty and support of the team, and when he was away travelling, he left Maria in charge of urgent mission affairs. On the basis of her language ability and experience, he expected the new recruits to give her the same respect and loyalty that they gave to him, even though she was a woman. As novices, new recruits were expected to give way to those with more experience. In their early days in China their lives and the lives of others might depend on it.

People found Maria quiet and almost retiring, but she was wise and highly respected. She cared for the children, guests and younger mission members, and stood by her husband in all he was trying to do. She was also able to relieve her husband of some of the enormous burdens he carried by taking decisions in his absence, handling correspondence with the London base, and defending mission policy when criticism rained down upon them. In daily life Maria's gifts were widely used, and Taylor could not have survived without her. At times this arrangement could clash with the generally held principle of male leadership. Taylor once summarised his views in a letter to his son, Ernest:

> I think women may do what God has gifted them to do if they do it in a biblical way, and that what Paul wanted was order in the churches and not talking, also that the husband must be the head.[7]

Did headship belong just to the husband in the home, or to any man in the church, or to the CIM director? Taylor never seems to have gone into a detailed biblical defence of his position; CIM women were probably more directly involved in church work and evangelism than women in most other missions, but at the same time they were left walking a knife-edge between being what they were and conforming to what people thought they should be. In spite of his courage in defying so many conventions, Taylor never openly took the final logical step of considering the members truly equal. "Equal but..." was not really equal.

## The CIM single women

The single women proved themselves effective in two particular areas. First, since they could meet women only in their
homes, they actually gained a far more intimate knowledge of
Chinese family life than men did. (Men met and talked in the
coffee shops.) As the women itinerated round the villages,
frequently accompanied by Chinese Bible women, they stayed
in inns, with Chinese evangelists and their families, or in
local Christian homes, and so developed a deep understanding of the women's lives, which enabled them to make the
Christian message relevant to them in their own culture.

Secondly, they were able to work closely and effectively
with the pastors and evangelists as co-workers in the separate
worlds of men and women. At the end of the nineteenth century the majority of Chinese Christians were older men, and
the churches were led by men – though these leaders were
themselves first-generation Christians with only the minimum of training and experience. If Western men were
involved with the church, the Chinese would defer to them,
and the opportunity for the development of indigenous leadership would be lost. As it was, the missionary women presented no threat to male Chinese authority, but were on hand
to encourage the evangelists, help with Bible teaching and
give advice when it was requested. The presence of the single
women not only encouraged Chinese workers to take leadership in the churches, but also provided a source of wisdom
and guidance if necessary.

It was not the hierarchical structure which so often con-
trols many church relationships, but rather one of mutual
respect. At a later stage some missionaries were slow to hand
over responsibility to nationals when they should have done so
– but the women's focus on the world of women made a collegiate relationship with the pastors easier. Their letters and
writing always referred to national workers with respect. There
were comparatively few fully ordained pastors, which meant
that evangelists and lay members carried a lot of responsibility.[8]

It is also significant that in spite of the tedium of daily routines, walking for miles and spending their time with simple country women, many missionary women still saw beyond the immediate needs and crises to a greater vision for the future. Nellie Marchbank kept her team plodding on with evangelism until eleven more churches emerged in the villages around Guixi, but she also developed schools, almshouses and a major church centre. Jessie Gregg ended up holding meetings for country women in province after province across China. Susie Garland, isolated in the far north-west, produced resources for the whole Chinese church. Margaret King was concerned for the first educated Christian girls to have tertiary Bible training so that they too could become teachers and lecturers, training future leaders among the women. Marie Monsen and Anna Christensen and their colleagues were used to bring new life to men and women in the churches across China in the revival. The Trio made the gospel known across the trade routes of Central Asia by distributing literature in the desert oases scattered for 1,000 miles along the Silk Road.

These extraordinary achievements did not come about in a year or two. These women devoted their whole lives to fulfilling their calling. Initial language study takes at least two years, even today. It was an act of faith when the first young wives travelled across China to the distant west and north-west provinces, and two of the four laid down their lives within a couple of years. But as she was dying, Fanny Clarke whispered, "Others will come after us", and they did. Most of the women discussed in this book spent 30 to 40 years of their lives in China, and the extraordinary opportunities which opened up for them in later life were rooted in the fifteen to 20 years they had first spent in the villages and towns, mastering the language and adapting to Chinese culture until they were able to speak to the hearts of the local women. It was a long apprenticeship, but in mid-life these women were used by God throughout China, far beyond the CIM boundaries.

## In leadership – almost

In the CIM, women served alongside men from the beginning. The separate worlds of Chinese women and men functioned in parallel, and all the believers were brought together in the churches. When the mission redoubled its efforts to hand over established work to nationals in the 1930s, far from making women missionaries redundant, it redeployed them to the front line, because church-planting had always been the basis of the whole mission. When diabetes brought Jessie Gregg's itinerating to an abrupt end, or the Trio saw their senior school sacrificed to the growth of secular provincial schools, or Susie Garland completed her work of launching the phonetic Bible, these women did not return to Britain or Australia. They simply went back to evangelism and church work alongside local Bible women, pioneering in new towns, doing as much as their age and strength allowed. As for the Trio – in mid-life they launched out into one of the great pioneer evangelistic ventures of the twentieth century![9]

Although the women missionaries still focused on the "women's world", that world was rapidly disappearing as the years passed and China was ravaged by war. That did not mean that their work was over: the single missionaries had always been integrated into local churches, and they were able to continue. From the beginning, Hudson Taylor had been astonished at the way Chinese men, in a patriarchal society, were nevertheless willing to listen to young women. (At first curiosity must have played a large part, but they *listened*!) One advantage for the missionary woman was that, as a foreigner, she stood outside local culture, and traditional norms for male and female were dropped. In that respect missionary women had more freedom than Chinese women, whose Christian lives had to conform to Chinese cultural expectations.

As time went on, the CIM women continued working within the mission, making up two-thirds of the membership. Where the women's world still existed, they served it. If wider opportunities arose, they took them. If the call of God came to women in Britain, it had to be lived out in a Western culture cluttered with centuries of history and traditions that sometimes had little to do with the Christian faith, but constrained them as Christian women. In China, away from all that, they were set free to take up opportunities of service unknown in most of their home churches then, and still not recognised in many churches today. They may have been fearful of stepping out of their traditional role, but they believed the Lord had called them to China to make him known, and there were so few of them that in the end they did whatever had to be done, according to the gifts and calling they received. When they were set free in this way, they saw God's blessing on their work and new churches emerged across China.

In 1922, concern was expressed that the extensive work undertaken by the women was not represented at the top administrative levels in the mission. The CIM directors and superintendents proposed to invite some of the leading women to join the China Council (which advised the General Director) and mentioned several names of suitable people, though these were not recorded. However, most of the women members lacked higher education of any kind, and the members could not envisage women working in executive positions. Moreover, two of the CIM Councils in the home countries had not faced up to what women were actually doing overseas, and were equally restricted in their views of women's roles. The proposal was turned down. It would take another 60 years before women were enabled to take a full part in the administration and policy-making of the CIM, and by then the mission would no longer be working in China. Meanwhile the work among women probably suffered. Except for the 1922 conference, there was no forum for sharing, discussing and targeting the work among women, which involved two-thirds of the missionary force and half the population of China.

Ultimately both the women's boards and the CIM came

up against the same barrier. As long as women were working with women, they had great freedom, but when the "women's world" began to disappear, they should have been able to work alongside men as co-workers and equals. At the Fall, humanity's relationship with God, with each other and with creation was broken;[10] Christ's death and resurrection brought healing to that disunity,[11] and the Holy Spirit was poured out on men and women together.[12] That renewal is an ongoing process. Helen Montgomery was right when she feared that men and women were not yet ready to function side by side as they were meant to do – but that is no reason for nurturing and promoting the divisions caused by sin.[13]

## Impact on the Chinese women's world

The Western women were not the only ones to find themselves set free from their own culture to serve God. Chinese women were also set free from centuries of tradition. In the nineteenth century they still spent most of their adult lives inside their walled courtyards, the life in the street outside barely visible except through small, high windows. Unable to read or write, and too many scarcely able to walk, their lives were incredibly confined. It was not surprising that the arrival of Western women had such an impact. At first, as rumours spread of the kidnapping of children, cannibalism and witchcraft, fear also spread like wildfire; but as the Western women visited their homes, wore their clothes and spoke their language, fear subsided, and curiosity took over. These foreign women were doing things they thought were impossible for women. Their unbound feet gave them liberty to walk from village to village. Their single state left them free to leave their families half a world away. They could read and write – even in Chinese. Such a life for a woman had never been heard of before. Their very presence was a state-ment about a new freedom and a new way of living, and it was not long before the first simple Bible women also began to live out this freedom alongside the missionary women. The absence of hierarchical church structures in the women's world made it easier for all of them to identify more closely as sisters in the church.

The Hong Kong theologian and historian Kwok Pui-lan points out that little is known about the early response from Chinese women.[14] Most were illiterate until the 1920s, and their stories come to us only through the foreign eyes of missionary women. Writers such as Phyllis Thompson have given valuable glimpses into the lives of country folk, and scattered through missionary literature are the stories of many Bible women who taught the foreigners how to communicate with local women. Some spent many years of their lives working alongside the missionaries, visiting the villages with them, sharing the Bible story and living out before their neighbours the transforming power of the Christian gospel.

In the process, the Bible women themselves became effective evangelists. When young girls had to remain at home, and young mothers were fully occupied with their families, it was the elderly and the widowed who braved public criticism. It took courage to face the amusement of neighbours, hobble painfully through the streets to church services, and learn to read the romanised alphabet and later the phonetic script. It could take even more courage to accompany these foreign women with their man-sized feet, large noses and poor language skills, explaining their presence to the local women and helping the missionaries to build bridges. As one Bible woman introduced yet another new arrival from overseas: "This one cannot speak. She can only smile!" The influence of these humble, ground-breaking women cannot be overestimated.

## A new community

Gradually new communities of Christian believers emerged, where people no longer smothered their baby girls or bound their daughters' feet. They also found that their daughters could learn as well as their sons. Disastrous marriages were no longer arranged between infants; men had only one wife, and when the revival came, husbands apologised to their wives for the way they had treated them. In the face-saving patriarchal culture of China such apologies were unheard of. Opium was abandoned, so that whole families were rescued from abject poverty and destitution. Neighbours watched with amazement as stolen goods were returned to their owners by the barrowload! Belonging to the church broadened their horizons as they met people outside their own families and visited churches in other towns. The early Christians may have seemed strange to their neighbours, but people could see that the lives of Christians were being changed.

The early training of Bible women was very basic, even under people like Eva French. Literacy did not become widespread in the churches until after 1920 and the small Christian community was soon well ahead of the rest of the population. Meanwhile they could learn by rote, and in spite of their lack of education the Chinese Christians demonstrated an extraordinary ability to learn chapters and even whole books of the Bible by heart. Gradually, as education for girls developed, Bible training was also upgraded until it reached college standards in Margaret King's time. A new generation of young Chinese Christian women emerged who worked alongside missionaries as teachers, speakers and evangelists.

In her study on Chinese women and Christianity, Kwok Pui-lan referred to "the potential of Christianity to liberate women from the underside of history". She concluded that no history of Chinese women in the twentieth century could ignore the impact of the Christian message on them, however small the church was in comparison with the huge population of China.[15] The lives of Christian women were radically changed; they were set free from centuries of tradition, and the work and example of the Western women played no small part in this. They were not always right, and not everything Western was good by any means: mistakes were often made. Still, the Chinese received the Bible as the Word of God and they had the Holy Spirit to guide them; they were able to filter out some of the Western culture that came with the gospel, and work out for themselves what it meant to live out their faith in their own culture.

We have traced the stories of some of the first women called to take the good news of Jesus to the Chinese: Maria Newell from Malacca, the first Protestant single woman to go east of India for the gospel; Mary Ann Aldersey from Ningbo, the first Western single woman to set foot in China and open the first school for girls; Sophia Cooke from Singapore, the first to send her pupils back to China as missionaries to their own people; the orphaned Dyer girls in their teens, heading for Ningbo to follow the call their parents had been unable to fulfil. There were so few of them, and they went in great weakness and sometimes great sorrow, but they began to sow the seed that has sprung to life in the Chinese church today, and thousands of others followed them.

> All of these died in faith without having received the promises, but from a distance they saw and greeted them. They confessed that they were strangers and foreigners on the earth... If they had been thinking of the land that they had left behind, they would have had opportunity to return. But as it is, they desire a better country, that is, a heavenly one. Therefore God is not ashamed to be called their God; indeed, he has prepared a city for them (Hebrews 11:13–16).

Immersed in the vast population of China, a few hundred missionaries were only a drop in the ocean. When the Boxers murdered 188 missionaries and children in 1901, journalists hailed it as the death knell of the churches. When political unrest forced the evacuation of 3,000 missionaries to the coast in 1927, the same forecast was made. In 1949 when Communism took over and all missionaries were ordered to leave within two years, the churches suffered severe persecution, and again it looked like the end.

Yet the Protestant Church, which numbered 1.2 million members in 1949, numbered 17 million in registered churches in the year 2000. The unregistered churches added an estimated 45 million more, in spite of the fact that it was still forbidden to hold public meetings outside registered church buildings, or teach young people under 18 years of age. In the same period the Roman Catholic Church grew to 12 million. The growth rate of the Chinese church since 1977 is unparalleled in history. For five decades the leadership of the church has been entirely Chinese, and they have been cut off from the rest of the world. Throughout those difficult years, Christian women have played a particularly significant role.[16] In times of severe persecution, they travelled quietly from place to place encouraging the believers, because women were less conspicuous than men. Today, when life in the unregistered churches is still hazardous, many of the house churches are led by women and the membership in some areas is around 80% female. The Chinese church has endured terrible suffering in the last hundred years, but it has weathered the storms with great courage to become a vibrant witness to Jesus Christ throughout the world today.

## Notes to Chapter Eleven

1  In the early days there was little danger of people professing belief in order to get their children educated. Society was hostile to the new religion, and educating girls was regarded as impossible and a waste of money.

2  Guinness, *Web*, p. 76.

3  James Knowles, *Memoir of Mrs Judson 1829*, quoted in James, *Heart*, p. 39.

4  R. Pierce Beaver, *Pioneers in Mission*, quoted in Pierce Beaver, *Loves*, pp. 51–52.

5  Broomhall, vol. 6, p. 382.

6  J. H. Taylor to W.B. Sloan, 16 October 1899. Personal papers, CIM Archive, SOAS Library, London. Quoted in Peter Williams, *The Recruitment and Training of Missionary Candidates, 1850–1900* unpublished M. Lit. Thesis 1976, p. 332.

7  Letter to his son Ernest, 1895, quoted in Dr and Mrs Howard Taylor, *Growth*, p. 397.

8  In 1938, there were only 66 Chinese pastors for the 1,348 CIM

churches (in addition to the 1,000 CIM missionaries). This could be interpreted as a missionary-organised church with little control given to the Chinese, but this was not so. The stress was on lay leadership and many churches were led by evangelists or local elders. Most missionaries by this stage were either training pastors or pioneering new churches. The CIM or the churches also supported 1,100 Chinese men and 400 Chinese women for church work and evangelism.

9   In 1986, Virago, the secular women's press, republished *The Gobi Desert* and included the Trio among the great women travellers of the twentieth century.

10   Genesis 1:26–31; 3:16–24.

11   Galatians 3:27–28; Acts 15:8–11. As the image of God is renewed within us, the barriers are obliterated. Colossians 3:10–11; Ephesians 2:14–19.

12   Acts 2:17–18.

13   Montgomery, *Western*, p. 269.

14   Kwok, *Chinese Women*, pp. 1–5.

15   Ibid., pp. 191–92.

16   Johnson and Mandryk, *Operation World*, p. 161. Johnson wrote that the majority of evangelists and church planters have been women.

# The American Women's Missionary Societies

In 1834, the first women's missionary society was established in London for supporting and encouraging single women called to serve God as teachers overseas. In nineteenth-century British culture, when single women remained with their parents or relatives unless they married, it was a radical step to take. David Abeel, passing through London on his way home to America from China, knew there were millions of women in the East who were confined to their homes and would never hear the Christian message unless women took it to them. Women in London caught his vision, and set up the Society for Promoting Female Education in the East.

Abeel returned to Boston, Massachusetts, and made a similar appeal to the women there. Sarah Doremus and others responded and were about to set up a similar society when the influential American missiologist Rufus Anderson wrote to them begging them not to do so. He felt that single women could not survive without the protection of their families. The Boston women were divided, but finally bowed to his authority. As a result (since the existing societies would not normally accept single women) there was no clear channel through which single women could serve overseas for a further 26 years.[1]

In 1860, Mrs Mason returned to America on leave from Burma. She was a controversial figure: her pleas for women to go overseas, though rejected by her own Baptist mission, reached Sarah Doremus, who had never lost her vision over the years. Rufus Anderson was retiring and informed his successor that he still did not approve of single women going overseas, but he thought it was probably inevitable! Sarah Doremus and her friends organised the interdenominational Women's Union Missionary Society (WUMS) in 1861, and the first woman left for Burma that same year.

Where they led, other women soon followed. Some focused on prayer and financial support as auxiliaries within the denominational missions, but many others set up independent societies, supported by women, sending other women overseas to reach women there. Starting from their homes, they developed organisations and structures, and appointed directors, secretaries, treasurers, etc. They discovered they had gifts and abilities they did not know they possessed. Some travelled the country on deputation, talking to women's groups in the churches. Helen Montgomery and Lucy Peabody emerged as gifted leaders (Lucy had served on the mission field herself). Helen claimed they were the first group to make women use their brains! They certainly challenged the church women's meetings, where people preferred to chat and knit.

They celebrated their jubilee in 1910 with meetings across the United States. By that time there were no fewer than 44 women's societies co-operating together, backed by 2 million women meeting in small groups in the churches throughout the nation. Few of the women worked outside the home, and few were wealthy, but they took very seriously the responsibility to pray for and support the 1,900 women they had sent out. The work had expanded enormously in those 50 years. If everyone gave just five cents a week, that was two dollars fifty cents a year per person; their annual income was 4 million dollars, a huge amount in those days.

There are 800 teachers, 140 doctors, 380 evangelists, 79 trained nurses, 5,783 Bible women and other native helpers. There are 2,100 schools, including 260 boarding schools and high schools, 78 hospitals and 76 dispensaries. In addition to carrying out these large tasks, the women's organisations have built col-

leges, hospitals, dispensaries, orphanages, leper asylums, training schools and industrial plants.[2]

An annual study book was published from 1900 to 1910. For
the first book they could produce only $50 towards its publi-
cation and only one publisher would accept that; he refused
to print more than 5,000 copies on the first run. These were
sold out in six weeks, and the books went on to sell 50,000
copies annually for the next ten years.

The women who had been excluded by the main societies
for so long were finally able to respond to the call of God.
Those who were sent abroad were single or widowed, but
married women were active at the home end, and as the different women's missions expanded, they faced consternation
and criticism. These supposedly frail, gentle creatures, who
could not survive without the care, protection and authority
of men, were casting the stereotypes to the winds. Some
accused them of using a Christian cover-up for women's
rights and liberation, but nothing could be further from the
truth. These women were not fighting for their rights, but
laying down their lives in Christian service.

In the early years of the twentieth century an interdenominational committee organised a triennial conference
which kept the different women's foreign missions in touch
with each other; they worked together to run summer schools
and produce a wide range of literature for prayer and information which they could all use. They were also in touch with
women's missionary organisations internationally, including
the British Society for Promoting Female Education in the
East. One of their enduring achievements is the Women's
World Day of Prayer, still celebrated throughout the world
across a wide spectrum of churches. The women demonstrated an ability to co-operate rather than build hierarchies.

By 1910, the World Conference for Mission in Edinburgh
was urging men and women to work more closely together.
Most societies were now accepting single women and it was
not helpful for church growth for a denomination to have its

couples in one area and its single women in another. Many delegates praised women for their special gifts for praying and collecting money, but felt they should hand the money over to wiser male leadership to spend! Others accused them of deflecting money from the main societies.

The women stoutly defended themselves. They had never set out to compete with anyone. When all the doors were closed to them, they had carved out a niche working with women and children in hospitals, schools and orphanages. While the larger missions debated the pros and cons of focusing on evangelism or social needs in medicine and education, the women's societies had a more holistic approach: they evangelised as they dealt with the social needs around them. If they amalgamated with the larger missions, they were afraid these "lesser areas" would be buried under major issues. They were quite happy to leave the major work and decisions to men, and keep to their "women's world", but they had also discovered they were able to achieve things they could not have imagined, and they cherished these new avenues of service which they felt God had given them. They were fearful that the knowledge and gifts they had acquired would count for nothing if the men's and women's societies amalgamated. They believed that as women they had their own special contribution to make, and this could easily be obliterated in larger mission situations. Even if women were included on the amalgamated mission boards, could they continue the same work with the same freedom? Helen Montgomery asked,

> Are men ready for it? Are they emancipated from the caste of sex so that they can work easily with a woman, unless they be head and woman clearly subordinate? Certainly facts seem to indicate that in spite of the rapid strides undoubtedly made in this direction we have still a long stretch of unexplored country to be traversed before the perfect democracy of Jesus is reached.[3]

They also feared that if they united with the main societies, the women in the churches would lose their personal sense of responsibility towards the women who had gone overseas. Personal contact was vital.

In the midst of these tensions, the women leaders pioneered to bring missionary societies together in Britain and North America. The aim was to co-operate in funding Christian tertiary education and theological training for women in China, Japan and India, when no alternative was available. These Union Colleges became very significant for the early women students. In China, Ginling Women's College and the North China Union Women's College led the way. By the early 1920s the first women graduates in China were moving out to take their place in society.[4]

Over the next 20 years, most of the women's societies were amalgamated with their denominational societies; some were taken over against their will. As this happened, many of the missions began to transfer women representatives to their main boards. The women had, after all, developed the executive and managerial skills needed for running the women's work in their own societies. However, no further women were gaining the administrative and executive experience such a position required, and when the original appointees retired, they were replaced by men. That generation had proved that they were perfectly able to do such work. They had carved out their own niche and their structures had been more collegiate than the men's. Now the large number of women serving overseas (67% of the missionary force in 1929) was once more left unrepresented at board level.[5] Social change also played its part. After the First World War, more church women began to work outside the home, women's groups declined, and the personal link with women overseas was lost. The wide support network disappeared, as they had feared, and with it the praying, giving and learning.

The amalgamations took place at a point when social concerns were replacing evangelism in many of the denominational societies. These societies faced a further problem because they were usually expected to build churches over-seas that reflected the history and traditions of the home churches, and these often restricted women's roles. The women had found remarkable freedom serving overseas in the women's societies. The more recent interdenominational faith missions were less tied to church history and traditions, and were emerging with renewed stress on the primacy of the Bible, evangelism and church planting. While few people may have consciously thought this through, many women may have moved towards these faith missions, sensing an oppor-tunity for greater freedom in service. The extraordinary era of the women's missionary societies was forgotten until unearthed by researchers 50 years later.

## Notes to Appendix

1   Tucker, *Daughters*, pp. 300–304. *Guardians*, pp. 99–111.
2   Montgomery, *Western*, p. 211.
3   Ibid., p. 269.
4   R. Pierce Beaver, *Loves*, pp. 164–75.
5   Ibid., p. 109.

# Select Bibliography

Aldersey White, E. *A Woman Pioneer in China: The Life of Mary Ann Aldersey*. London: Livingstone Press, 1932

Anderson, Gerald H. (ed.) *Biographical Dictionary of Christian Missions*. New York: Macmillan, 1998

Bebbington, D. W. *Evangelicalism in Modern Britain: A History from the 1730s to the 1980s*. London: Unwin, 1989

Broomhall, A. J. *Hudson Taylor and China's Open Century*, vol. 1, *Barbarians at the Gates*. Sevenoaks: Hodder & Stoughton, 1981

Broomhall, A. J. *Hudson Taylor and China's Open Century*, vol. 2, *Over the Treaty Wall*. Sevenoaks: Hodder & Stoughton, 1982

Broomhall, A. J. *Hudson Taylor and China's Open Century*, vol. 3, *If I Had a Thousand Lives*. Sevenoaks: Hodder & Stoughton, 1982

Broomhall, A. J. *Hudson Taylor and China's Open Century*, vol. 4, *Survivors' Pact*. Sevenoaks: Hodder & Stoughton, 1984

Broomhall, A. J. *Hudson Taylor and China's Open Century*, vol. 5, *Refiner's Fire*. Sevenoaks: Hodder & Stoughton, 1985

Broomhall, A. J. *Hudson Taylor and China's Open Century*, vol. 6, *Assault on the Nine*. Sevenoaks: Hodder & Stoughton, 1988

Broomhall, A. J. *Hudson Taylor and China's Open Century*, vol. 7, *It Is Not Death to Die!* Sevenoaks: Hodder & Stoughton, 1989

Broomhall, Marshall. *Martyred Missionaries of the China Inland Mission*. London: China Inland Mission, 1901

Broomhall, Marshall. *The Bible in China*. London: British and Foreign Bible Society, 1934

Burton, Margaret. *The Education of Women in China*. New York: Revell, 1911

Cable, Mildred & French, Francesca. *A Desert Journal*. London: Constable & Co. Ltd, 1934

Cable, Mildred & French, Francesca. *A Woman Who Laughed*. Basingstoke: (London: CIM, 1934) 1984

Cable, Mildred & French, Francesca. *George Hunter*. London: CIM, 1948

Cable, Mildred & French, Francesca. *Something Happened*. London: Hodder & Stoughton, 1933

Cable, Mildred & French, Francesca. *The Gobi Desert*. London: Hodder & Stoughton, 1942

Cable, Mildred & French, Francesca. *The Making of a Pioneer*. London: Hodder & Stoughton, 1935

Cable, Mildred & French, Francesca. *Through Jade Gate to Central Asia*. London: Constable & Co. Ltd, 1927

Cable, Mildred. *The Fulfilment of a Dream*. London: CIM, 1917

Carlberg, Gustav. *China in Revival*. Rock Island, Illinois: Augustana Book Concern, 1936

*China and the Gospel*. London, CIM

*China Mission Yearbook*. Shanghai: Christian Literature Society in China, 1910–1925

Clarke, Agnes. *A Daughter of Lausanne*. Unpublished MS, CIM Archive, SOAS

Crawford, Mary K. *The Shantung Revival*. Shanghai: China Baptist Publication Society, 1933

Crossman, Eileen. *Mountain Rain*. Sevenoaks: OMF, 1982

Culpepper, C. L. *The Shantung Revival*. Dallas: Baptist General Convention of Texas, 1968

Daggett, L.H. *Historical Sketches of Woman's Missionary Societies In America and England*. Boston: Daggett, 1899

Davies, Evan. *Memoirs of the Rev. Samuel Dyer*. London: John Snow, 1846

Ellis, H.W. *Our Eastern Sisters*. London: Religious Tract Society, c. 1884

Fraser, Roxanne. *Fraser and Prayer*. London: CIM, 1963

French, Francesca. *Luckchild*. London: Marshall, Morgan & Scott, 1954

Goforth, Rosalind. *Goforth of China*. Grand Rapids: Zondervan, 1937

Guinness, Geraldine. *The Story of the China Inland Mission*, vols I, II. London: Morgan & Scott, 1893

Guinness, Joy. *Mrs Howard Taylor – Her Web of Time*. London: CIM, 1949

Hassey, Janette. *No Time for Silence*. Grand Rapids: Zondervan, 1986

Houghton, Frank. *The Two Hundred*. London: CIM, 1932

Howard Taylor, Dr & Mrs. *Hudson Taylor and the China Inland Mission: The Growth of a Soul*. London: CIM, 1912

Howard Taylor, Dr & Mrs. *Hudson Taylor: The Growth of a Work of God*. London: CIM, 1918

Howard Taylor, Geraldine. *Behind the Ranges*. London: Lutterworth, 1944

Howard Taylor, Geraldine. *Margaret King's Vision*. Philadelphia: CIM, 1934

Howard Taylor, Geraldine. *The Call of China's Great North West*. London: CIM, 1923

Howard Taylor, Geraldine. *The Triumph of John and Betty Stam*. London: CIM, 1935

Hunter, Jane. *The Gospel of Gentility*. New Haven: Yale University, 1989

James, Sharon. *My Heart in His Hands*. Durham: Evangelical Press, 1998

Johnstone, Patrick & Mandryk, Jason. *Operation World*. Carlisle: Paternoster, 2001

Kuhn, Isobel. *Green Leaf in Drought*. Singapore: OMF, 1948

Kwok, Pui-lan. *Chinese Women and Christianity 1860–1927*. Atlanta, Georgia: Scholars Press, 1992

Lewis, Donald (ed.). (Blackwell) *Dictionary of Evangelical Biography 1730–1860*. Oxford: Blackwell, 1995

Loane, Marcus L. *The Story of the China Inland Mission in Australia and New Zealand 1890–1964*. Sydney: CIM/OMF, 1965

Lyall, Leslie T. (ed.) *The Clouds His Chariot: The Story of 1937*. London: CIM, 1937

Lyall, Leslie T. *A Passion for the Impossible*. London: Hodder & Stoughton, 1965

Monsen, Marie. *The Awakening*. London: CIM, 1961

Montgomery, Helen. *Western Women in Eastern Lands*. New York: Macmillan 1910

Morgan, Jill. *A Man of the Word*. London: Pickering & Inglis, 1951

Morrison, E. *Memoirs of the Life of Robert Morrison, D.D.* vol. II. London: Longman, 1839

Neill, Stephen. *A History of Christian Missions*. Harmondsworth: Pelican, 1964

Nixson, Rosie. *Liberating Women for the Gospel*. London: Hodder & Stoughton, 1997

Pierce Beaver, R. *All Loves Excelling: American Protestant Women in World Mission*. Grand Rapids: Eerdmans, 1968

Pierce Beaver, R. *American Protestant Women in World Mission*. Grand Rapids: Eerdmans, 1980

Piggin, Stuart. *Evangelical Christianity in Australia*. Melbourne: OUP, 1996

Platt, W. J. *Three Women*. London: Hodder & Stoughton, 1964

Rouse, Ruth & Neill, Stephen (eds). *A History of the Ecumenical Movement 1517–1948*, 2nd edition. London: SPCK, 1967

Sng, Bobby E. K. *I Must Sow the Seed. Liang Afa: China's First Preacher*. Singapore: Trinity Theological College, 1998

Sng, Bobby E. K. *In His Good Time*. Singapore: Graduates' Christian Fellowship, 1980

Stock, E. *History of the Church Missionary Society*. vols II, III. London: CMS, 1899

Strauss, F., Weller, E., Hayward, A. & Monsen, M. *We are Escaped*. London: CIM, 1931

Suter, Edward. *History of the Society for Promoting Female Education in the East*. London: Edward Suter, 1847

Thompson, P. *A London Sparrow.* London: Word Books, 1971

Thompson, P. *Beaten Gold.* London: CIM 1950

Thompson, P. *Bible Convoy.* London: CIM, 1950

Thompson, P. *No Way Back.* Crowborough: Highland Books, 1992

Thompson, P. *Pilgrim in China.* Crowborough: Highland Books, 1988

Thompson, P. *Reluctant Exodus.* Sevenoaks: Hodder & Stoughton, 1979

Thompson, P. *There Came a Day.* London: CIM, 1945

Thompson, P. *Each to Her Post.* London: Hodder & Stoughton, 1982

Torjesen Malcolm, Kari. *We Signed Away Our Lives.* Downers Grove: IVP, 1990

Tucker, Ruth. *Daughters of the Church.* Grand Rapids: Zondervan, 1987

Tucker, Ruth. *Guardians of the Great Commission.* Grand Rapids: Zondervan, 1988

Walker, E. A. *Sophia Cooke.* London: Elliott Stock Esq., 1899

Watson, Jean. *Bosshardt.* Sevenoaks: Monarch, 1995

Wood, Frances. *No Dogs and Not Many Chinese.* London: John Murray, 1998

Young, Florence S. H. *Pearls from the Pacific.* London: Marshall Brothers, 1925

# Index

## Periodicals

## Places mentioned in Text

### (a) **Chinese provinces**

# English-speaking OMF Centres

**AUSTRALIA:** PO Box 849, Epping, NSW 2121
   Freecall 1800 227 154   email: omf-australia@omf.net
   *www.au.omf.org*

**CANADA:** 5155 Spectrum Way, Building 21, Mississauga, ON
   L4W 5A1
   Toll free 1-888-657-8010   email: omfcanada@omf.ca
   *www.ca.omf.org*

**HONG KONG:** P O Box 70505, Kowloon Central Post Office,
   Hong Kong
   email: hk@omf.net   *www.omf.org.hk*

**MALAYSIA:** 3A Jalan Nipah, off Jalan Ampang, 55000, Kuala
   Lumpur
   email: my@omf.net   *www.my.omf.org*

**NEW ZEALAND:** P O Box 10159, Dominion Road, Auckland
   1030.
   Tel 9-630 5778   email: omfnz@omf.net   *www.nz.omf.org*

**PHILIPPINES:** 900 Commonwealth Avenue, Diliman, 1101
   Quezon City
   email: ph-hc@omf.net   *www.omf.org*

**SINGAPORE:** 2 Cluny Road, Singapore 259570
   email: sno@omf.net   *www.sg.omf.org*

**SOUTHERN AFRICA:** P O Box 3080, Pinegowrie, 2123
email: za@omf.net   *www.za.omf.org*

**UK:** Station Approach, Borough Green, Sevenoaks, Kent,
TN15 8BG
Tel 01732 887299   email: omf@omf.org.uk
*www.omf.org.uk*

**USA:** 10 West Dry Creek Circle, Littleton, CO 80120-4413
Toll Free 1-800-422-5330   email: omf@omf.org
*www.us.omf.org*

> *OMF International Headquarters:*
> *2 Cluny Road, Singapore 259570*